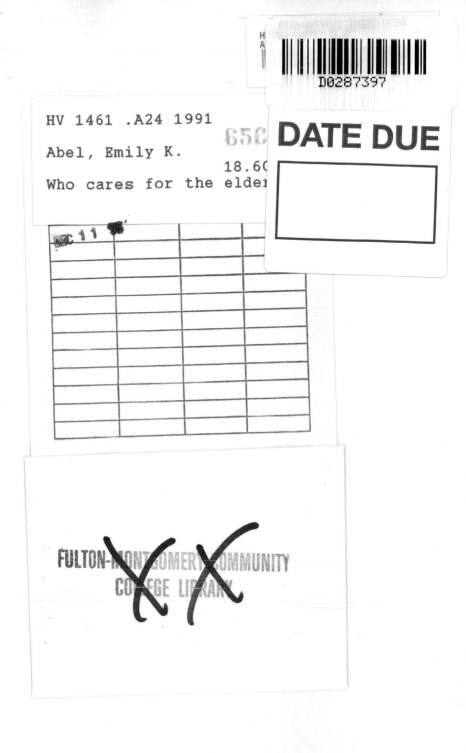

In the series Women in the Political Economy,
Edited by Ronnie J. Steinberg

Who Cares
for the
Elderly?

Public Policy
and the Experiences
of Adult Daughters

Emily K. Abel

Temple University Press
Philadelphia

Temple University Press, Philadelphia 19122
Copyright © 1991 by Temple University. All rights reserved
Published 1991
Printed in the United States of America

The paper used in this publication meets the minimum
requirements of American National Standard for Information
Sciences—Permanence of Paper for Printed Library Materials,
ANSI Z39.48-1984 ⊗

Library of Congress Cataloging-in-Publication Data
Abel, Emily K.
Who cares for the elderly? : public policy and the experiences of
adult daughters / Emily K. Abel.
p.   cm. — (Women in the political economy)
Includes bibliographical references and index.
ISBN 0-87722-814-0
1. Parents, Aged—Home care—United States.   2. Caregivers—
United States.   3. Adult children—United States.   4. Daughters—
United States.   5. Aged—Government policy—United States.
I. Title.   II. Series.
HV1461.A24   1991
362.6—dc20   90-11244

Contents

Acknowledgments

During the six years in which I have been studying family care for the elderly, numerous people have helped me in various ways. I owe a particular debt of gratitude to my sister, Margaret K. Nelson, with whom I coedited a previous volume on caring and held many discussions about the issues addressed in this one. I also draw heavily on the insights of Edna Bonacich, Carole H. Browner, Timothy Diamond, Hanna Haavind, Joel Handler, Mary Rothschild, Karen Sacks, Andrea Sankar, and Julia Wrigley. My husband, Richard L. Abel, was, as always, an excellent critic and a wonderful source of support. Other people who have offered valuable critiques of sections of this book include Donna Myers Ambrogi, Karen Anderson, Nancy Blum, E. Richard Brown, Robert Emerson, Carroll L. Estes, Jaber F. Gubrium, Sybil Houlding, James Lubben, Baila Miller, Regina Morantz-Sanchez, Robyn Stone, Phyllis Vine, and Deborah Ward.

I presented portions of this book at the UCLA Center for the Study of Women; the Academic Geriatric Resource Center at the University of California, Irvine; the Women's Research Center of the University of Lancaster, England; the Center for Inter-Cultural Studies and Education at Josai University, Tokyo; Ewha Woman's University, Seoul, Korea; the Center for Public Representation at the University of Wisconsin, Madison; and annual meetings of the American Educators' Research Association, the American Sociological Association, and the Gerontological Society of America. I wish to thank the many people who commented on these presentations.

I received financial support from both the UCLA Center for the Study of Women and the Alzheimer's Disease and Related Disorders Association, Inc., for which I am very grateful.

Portions of Chapters 4, 6, 9, and 10 were originally published in slightly altered form as the following: "Informal Care for the Disabled Elderly: A Critique of Recent Literature," *Research on Aging* 12(2): 139–57, copyright © 1990 by Emily Abel, used by permission of Sage Publications, Inc.; "The Ambiguities of Social Support: Adult Daughters Caring for Frail Elderly Parents," *Journal of Aging Studies* 3(3): 211–30, copyright © 1989, used by permission of JAI Press, Inc.; "Daughters Caring for Elderly Parents," in *The Home Care Experience: Ethnography and Policy,* ed. Jaber F. Gubrium and Andrea Sankar, pp. 189–298, copyright © 1991 by Emily Abel, used by permission of Sage Publications, Inc.; chapters 4 and 6 of *Love Is Not Enough: Family Care of the Frail Elderly,* copyright © 1987 by the American Public Health Association, used with permission. I am grateful for permission to use this material.

Who Cares
for the
Elderly?

1

Introduction

Each day, more than 4 million family members care for disabled elderly people at home (Stone and Kemper, 1989). They help them in and out of bed, administer their medications, cook their meals, drive them to doctors, manage their finances, mow their lawns, and replace their broken windows. Although these "informal caregivers" typically are absent from analyses of long-term care, they render the great bulk of services the elderly receive.

Most people 65 and over can care for themselves and their households without assistance, but approximately one-quarter require at least occasional help (Liu, Manton, and Liu, 1985). Moreover, the prevalence of disability rises steeply with age. Sixteen percent of people 65 to 74 living in the community need some type of practical assistance, compared to 47 percent of those 85 and over (Special Committee on Aging, 1989:236). Despite the widespread belief that Americans rely extensively on nursing homes, just 1.4 million disabled people 65 and over reside in such facilities (Liu, Manton, and Liu, 1985). Almost four times as many live at home (Macken, 1986).

Researchers have exploded the myth that families abandon their elderly relatives. From her classic study conducted in 1975, Ethel Shanas concluded that elderly people do remain in close contact with surviving kin. Over half of the older persons in her survey who had living children had seen at least one child either the day of the interview or the day before; 75 percent had seen a child within the previous week. Approximately 40 percent of those who had not seen a child during the preceding week had seen another relative. Elderly persons without children tended to interact more closely with siblings and other relatives (Shanas, 1979a).

Frequency of contact translates into assistance during times of crisis. Researchers consistently find that families deliver 70 to 80

3

percent of long-term care (Community Council of Greater New York, 1978; Comptroller General of the United States, 1977; Stone, Cafferata, and Sangl, 1987). Three quarters of unpaid caregivers to the noninstitutionalized disabled elderly live with the care recipient, and the majority render care every day of the week, devoting an average of four hours a day to caregiving activities (Stone, Cafferata, and Sangl, 1987). Although the frequency and level of care vary dramatically, a study conducted in 1976 found that two-fifths of the people who care for elderly parents in their own homes perform the equivalent of full-time jobs (Newman, 1976). Caregiving can last a long time. Approximately 44 percent of caregivers have been furnishing assistance for one to five years, a fifth for five years or more (Stone, Cafferata and Sangl, 1987).

The burdens of care typically fall disproportionately on a single individual. Although friends and neighbors constitute an essential source of support, family members deliver most care. Because married elderly people turn first to their spouses in times of need, husbands and wives are the most common caregivers. They are more likely than other caregivers to live with the person they tend and to take responsibility for such intimate aspects of caregiving as bathing, dressing, and feeding (Stone, Cafferata, and Sangl, 1987). Although they frequently care for very impaired people, they receive little assistance from either paid providers or other family members. Because many spouses are disabled themselves, caregiving often imposes extreme burdens (Hess and Soldo, 1985, Horowitz, 1985a; Johnson, 1983).

Adult children constitute 37 percent of all caregivers. Although they provide a smaller proportion of the total care and receive more help than spouses, they are more likely to hold paid employment and face competing demands from other family members (Stone, Cafferata, and Sangl, 1987). Caregiving also appears to be especially difficult for them emotionally (Johnson and Catalano, 1983; Ungerson, 1987).

Like other forms of domestic labor, care for the elderly continues to be allocated on the basis of gender. Women represent 72 percent of all caregivers and 77 percent of the children providing care. Almost one-third (29 percent) of all caregivers to frail elderly persons are adult daughters (Stone, Cafferata, and Sangl, 1987).

Daughters are more likely than sons to live with dependent parents (Wolf and Soldo, 1986) and to serve as the primary caregivers (Stone, Cafferata, and Sangl, 1987). Sons and daughters also assume responsibility for very different chores. Sarah Fenstermaker Berk (1988:295) writes, "Husbands are more likely to undertake those household tasks that have clear and identifiable boundaries (such as mowing the lawn) [and] tasks that have greater discretion in both how and when to complete them (such as minor household repairs)." Sons and daughters divide caregiving responsibilities along similar lines. Sons are more likely to assist parents with routine household maintenance and repairs, while daughters are far more likely to help with indoor household chores and personal health care (Coward and Rathbone-McCuan, 1985; Stephens and Christianson, 1986; see Stoller, 1990). This gender division of labor may help to explain why caregiving has different consequences for sons and daughters. Sons take responsibility for tasks they can perform whenever they choose. Daughters, however, often assume responsibilities that keep them on call twenty-four hours a day.

Nevertheless, daughters who provide care are less likely than sons to receive assistance (Stone, Cafferata, and Sangl, 1987). Sons caring for elderly parents obtain more help from their wives than daughters can expect from their husbands (Horowitz, 1985b.) Some evidence suggests that formal services also are distributed inequitably. Men caring for elderly spouses or parents seem to obtain more in-home services than their female counterparts (Evandrou et al., 1986; Hooyman and Ryan, 1985; Wright, 1983).

Daughters and sons choose different solutions to the conflict between waged work and informal caregiving. Daughters are more likely than sons to curtail labor force participation, while sons are more likely than daughters to reduce caregiving responsibilities. According to data from a 1982 government survey, the proportion of caregiving daughters who relinquished paid employment was more than twice that of sons (11.6 and 5.0 percent). Of those who worked at some point during the caregiving experience, higher proportions of daughters than sons reduced their working hours as a result of caregiving obligations (22.8 versus 15 percent), rearranged their schedules (34.9 versus 27.7 percent), and took time off without pay (24.8 versus 14.1 percent) (Stone, Cafferata, and Sangl, 1987). Conversely, a 1983 study found that sons who held paid employment reduced the number of hours they helped their parents but that labor force participation had no significant impact on care by daughters (Stoller, 1983).

Not surprisingly, daughters are more likely than sons to perceive caregiving as stressful. The proportion of sons who reported in a recent study that caregiving presented "no problems" was more than three times that of daughters (34 versus 11 percent); the proportion of daughters who believed that caregiving had negatively affected their health was nearly twice that of sons (59 versus 31 percent) (Horowitz, 1985b).

Although caregiving is predominantly women's work, care for the elderly is largely absent from the feminist agenda in the United States. Feminist scholars lavish attention on motherhood, but they continue to slight other forms of caregiving. Numerous observers note, however, that child rearing occupies a much smaller place in women's lives today than in the past. Colonial women devoted most of their adult years to bearing and raising children. But today the typical mother has preschool children for slightly longer than a decade and can expect to live well into her seventies (Gerson, Alpert, and Richardson, 1984). Rather than reducing the period of caregiving, however, the demographic revolution may have shifted it to other parts of the life course. Some women devote more years to caring for aging parents than to raising children (Subcommittee on Human Services, 1987).

The shape of women's caregiving responsibilities may change even more dramatically in the future. The elderly were just 4 percent of the population in 1900 (Feldblum, 1985), but they increased to 8 percent in 1950 and 12 percent in 1984. It is projected that those 65 and over will constitute approximately 17 percent of the population by 2020 (Siegel and Taeuber, 1986). The rate of increase of the very old, who are most at risk of illness and disability, is even greater (Manton and Soldo, 1985). The number of those 85 and over rose 165 percent between 1960 and 1980 and is expected to increase a startling 500 percent by 2050 (Day, 1985). The "old old" constitute the fastest growing segment of the population (Siegel and Taeuber, 1986). Analysts project that the number of elderly people who require help at home with some of their daily activities will increase from 2.5 million in 1984 to 6.5 million in 2025 (Kovar, Hendershot, and Mathis, 1989:779).

The analytic framework that feminists have developed to understand mothering also can illuminate informal care for the elderly. Gerontologists frequently remind us that care of elderly persons differs in fundamental ways from care of small children. Nevertheless, feminist scholarship on motherhood can help guide the study of family care for aged people.

For example, the concept of choice is an important focus of feminist writing. Because child-care services and paid maternity leaves frequently are unavailable, many women have little choice about the amount and type of care they render. Inadequate access to family planning and abortion services even deprives some women of the ability to decide whether to become mothers. There also are more subtle pressures on women to bear and rear children. When women are denied opportunities for achievement in the public arena, they tend to look to mothering as the sole source of pride and self esteem (Gerson, 1985; Glenn, 1986; Johnson, 1988).

In addition, feminists have called attention to the ways in which external conditions shape the experiences of mothers. Ever since productive activity left the home in the nineteenth century, most women have tended children in isolated settings; as a result, they receive little support from other adults.* Some critics charge that isolation encourages women to become too involved with their children and thus distorts the mother-child relationship (Arcana, 1979; Chodorow, 1978; Chodorow and Contratto, 1982; Dinnerstein, 1976; Flax, 1978; Glenn, 1986; Jaggar, 1983; Johnson, 1988; Rich, 1976; Trebilcot, 1983). If feminists focus on the context of mothering, however, they also emphasize the need to illuminate women's lived experience as mothers. Feminist scholars have examined the powerful, if ambivalent, feelings evoked by mothering, noting the ways this activity can gratify as well as frustrate and burden (Boulton, 1983; Rich, 1976).

Feminists also have highlighted the connection between women's responsibilities for children and their disadvantaged position in the labor market. Although the majority of women now work for pay during their child-rearing years, some mothers still delay entry into the labor force, accept only part-time positions, or quit their jobs. The belief that all women are intermittent workers serves as a rationalization for relegating them to jobs with depressed wages, limited fringe benefits, few routes for advancement, and high turnover rates (see England and McCreary, 1987; see Sokoloff, 1981).

Finally, feminists have criticized the social devaluation of mothers. Although mothers are widely romanticized in our society, their growing impoverishment, the absence of adequate day care, and the failure of many men to share their responsibilities both create and reveal the low status accorded to care of young children (Glenn, 1987).

Each of these themes is relevant to family care of the frail elderly. The paucity of long-term care services, like the dearth of publicly funded day care, narrows women's freedom of choice. Obligations for elder care can have the same impact on labor force participation as

---

*Some observers argue that in many African-American communities, mothering is not such an isolating experience (see Stack, 1974).

responsibilities for child rearing. Just as mothering often imposes isolation, so care for disabled elderly family members confines many women to the home. Informal care for aged people, like child rearing, frequently provokes a range of intense but contradictory emotions. And cultural attitudes toward family members caring for elderly people resemble those toward mothers. Caregivers, like mothers, are simultaneously sentimentalized and devalued.

These themes inform this book, which explores family care for disabled elderly people in several ways. Chapter 2 examines how public policies affect the nature of caregiving at home. It argues that the amount of care women deliver to elderly relatives is determined not only by inexorable demographic trends but also by the inadequacies of the long-term care system in the United States. These deficiencies have the greatest impact on low-income people and members of racial and ethnic minority groups.

Chapter 3 traces the history of family caregiving in the United States since 1800. It challenges the persistent belief that the nineteenth century offers a superior model of care for sick and disabled persons. It also demonstrates that many features of caregiving we accept as immutable actually are conditioned by specific social and historical forces. Although caregivers deal with biological universals—pain, illness, and death—the content and meaning of their work has changed dramatically over time.

Chapter 4 criticizes the current research agenda on caregiving, which has focused almost exclusively on the issue of stress. In part, this emphasis represents a response to recent governmental policies seeking to shift responsibility for care from the state to the family. By demonstrating that caregiving poses severe strains, researchers have been able to argue that families cannot absorb additional obligations and that the government must devote adequate resources to support them. But this preoccupation with stress has denied us a full understanding of the experience of caregivers. Furthermore, studies that view caregivers as objects without consciousness foster policies that treat caregivers in an instrumental manner. This chapter argues that we need to understand women's actual experience rather than manipulate their actions to suit government demands for efficiency and cost containment.

Chapters 5 through 9 present my study of women caring for disabled elderly parents. Although their experiences do not provide simple answers to the problems policymakers encounter, an understanding of women's perspectives can help broaden the policy debate.

The concluding chapter (Chapter 10) returns to the policy issues with which I began. It asks how the accounts of the women I interviewed can guide policy analysis and how we can frame an agenda for change that responds to their needs.

The study on which this book is based involved in-depth, open-ended interviews with fifty-one women. Thirty-seven (73 percent) were caring exclusively for mothers, seven (14 percent) for fathers, and seven (14 percent) for both. Thirty-eight (75 percent) stated that at least one parent suffered from Alzheimer's disease or a related dementia. Some researchers report substantial differences between the experience of caring for elderly persons with dementia and those without cognitive impairments (Silliman and Sternberg, 1988), but other researchers find similarities between these two types of experiences (Liptzin, Grob, and Eisen, 1988; Montgomery, Kosloski, and Borgatta, 1988–89). I identify the distinctive aspects of caring for parents with dementia whenever appropriate.

Additional demographic information may help to introduce the women in this study. Approximately two-thirds were married, and over three-fourths were between the ages of 45 and 64. The great majority were white (two were African-American, and one was Asian-American). Just two had children under the age of 18 at home. Three-fourths lived apart from their parents. Over half were working for pay.

Caregiving was not a short-term event for these women. At the time of the interviews, three (6 percent) had rendered care for less than one year, twenty-five (49 percent) for one to four years, and twenty (39 percent) for longer. (The father of one woman had died one month prior to the interview; two women had placed their mothers in nursing homes during the year preceding the interviews.)

The women I interviewed and the parents they cared for were disproportionately middle class. Many had adequate resources to live apart and to purchase some formal services. Most of the daughters who worked full time held middle-class positions: seven were professionals, five were managers, and nine held administrative support positions. The caregivers also were relatively well educated. Just five had no schooling beyond high school, fifteen had one to three years of college, thirteen had graduated from college, and eighteen had some form of advanced education.

Although most of these women enjoyed considerable advantages, five delivered care under very difficult conditions. The latter all were unmarried and lived alone with severely impaired parents. None was working for pay; four had left the work force, largely in order to care for their parents (the fifth had quit her job several years earlier when her husband was dying). These women also experienced more economic insecurity than most of the women I interviewed; as a result, none was able to purchase services privately. Comparisons between the members of this group and the other caregivers in the study reveal some of the ways in which financial resources affect the experience of delivering care.

(Further information about the sample and the research methods is included in the Appendix.)

2

The Policy Framework of Caregiving

Although family caregiving involves an intensely personal relationship between individuals, it cannot be examined apart from the public policies surrounding it. A major argument of feminist analysts of the welfare state is that our system of social provision rests on the assumption that women deliver a broad array of unpaid services for dependent groups at home (Balbo, 1982; Land, 1978; Land and Rose, 1985; Pateman, 1988; Wilson, 1977). Just as the United States provides very limited public support for day care, so it funds only a narrow assortment of long-term care services. In place of comprehensive and universally accessible public services, we have a patchwork of limited programs for specific constituencies. As a result, when elderly people need help, many families have no option but to provide it themselves.

Governmental treatment of the frail elderly clashes sharply with old-age policies in general. It is only with regard to the elderly that the United States has developed a program of social services resembling that of Western European welfare states (Skocpol, 1988). In contrast to the means-tested programs directed toward the poor, Social Security and Medicare are federally administered, social insurance programs with uniform eligibility standards and relatively generous benefits. But the protections of social insurance programs end when elderly persons become disabled. Medicare is based on an acute-care model and thus provides minimal assistance for care of chronic diseases. Elderly persons who need long-term care either pay privately (out of pocket or through private insurance) or turn to Medicaid, a means-tested welfare program. This section thus examines the inadequacies of the long-term care system and their relationship to family caregiving.

Gaps in Services

Nursing homes dominate long-term care in the United States, absorbing the great bulk of government funds. They also provide the clearest alternative to informal caregiving. Although family members often remain involved in the care of nursing home residents (Bowers, 1990; Soldo, Agree, and Wolf, 1989), institutions replace family care more thoroughly than do community and home-based services. Nursing homes, however, are not universally accessible. The ratio of nursing home beds to population varies widely throughout the nation, but most facilities have lengthy waiting lists (Harrington and Swan, 1985). The cost of a nursing home stay is prohibitive to all but the very wealthy. The median annual charge is approximately $25,000, a sum which exceeds the median family income of elderly persons by $5,000 (Special Committee on Aging, 1987b:27). Medicaid foots 42 percent of the nursing-home bill (Special Committee on Aging, 1987b:30), but residents must exhaust their resources before they can qualify. Widely publicized exposés of the conditions within institutions also may deter many families from considering nursing home placement. A report prepared by the Institute of Medicine in 1986 confirmed the worst fears of many family members, concluding that a high proportion of nursing-home residents receive "shockingly deficient care" (Committee on Nursing Home Regulation, 1986:2).

Although Medicaid picks up the tab for nursing home residents who have exhausted their resources, public funding of any kind for community and home-based care is negligible in most states. Medicare emphasizes medically oriented home health care, not the social services many elderly persons need to live independently in the community. And the home health benefit under Medicare is extremely restrictive; recipients must be homebound, require skilled nursing care, and need services on an intermittent, rather than continuous, basis. In 1987, home health care consumed just 3.3 percent of total Medicare expenditures (Special Committee on Aging, 1988:4).

Medicaid regulations do not require home and community-based care under this program to hew so closely to a medical model; nevertheless, the individual states are responsible for determining eligibility and coverage, and they differ dramatically in the extent to which they fund noninstitutional services. New York alone absorbs over 75 percent of all federal Medicaid spending for home care (Rabin and Stockton, 1987:183). Section 2176 of the Omnibus Budget Reconciliation Act of 1981 allowed states to apply for waivers to include non–medically oriented home and community-based services under Medicaid. Because the Health Care Financing Administration fears that this program may greatly increase the cost of long-term care, it has granted such waivers very sparingly. The Special Committee on Aging of the U.S. Senate estimates that recipients of Medicaid waiver programs constitute just 3 percent of the population at risk (Special Committee on Aging, 1987b:45).*

The two major programs that fund social services for elderly persons living in the community are the Social Services Block Grant (formerly Title XX of the Social Services Act) and Title III of the Older Americans Act. The former provides coverage for homemaker and chore services, including meal preparation, house cleaning, and home repairs. The latter covers information and referral services, meals programs, transportation, homemaker services, and adult day care. These are the services that permit elderly persons to remain at home without relying on relatives and alleviate the burdens on family members who do provide care. The level of resources devoted to both programs, however, is meager. Also, the Omnibus Budget Reconciliation Act of 1981, which replaced the Title XX program with the new Social Services Block Grant, sharply reduced federal funds and removed both state matching funds and state reporting requirements (see Bertghold, 1987).

Because government funding for noninstitutional care is sparse, most disabled elderly people living at home fail to receive assistance from formal providers. A study conducted in 1982 found that just 25 percent of frail elderly people in the community used any home care services (Rivlin and Wiener, 1988:190). Elderly persons who do obtain help tend to finance it themselves. Sixty-six percent of the elderly who use formal services pay at least part of the cost themselves, and 41 percent pay the entire cost (Soldo and Manton, 1985).

Cost Containment

Although it has become almost commonplace to bemoan these deficiencies of the long term care system, several factors suggest that they will not soon be remedied. The past decade has been a time of increased anxiety about changing family relationships and especially about the growing independence of women. Some policymakers may view reliance on family care for the elderly as a way to foster social stability by giving women more work at home and strengthening intergenerational ties. Concerns about the rising cost of health and welfare services also have heightened. Since 1980, the federal government has instituted a variety of measures designed to shrink public

*The Omnibus Budget Reconciliation Act of 1987 established a new waiver program under which states can provide community and home-based services for the elderly. Some observers believe that this new program has the potential to substantially expand noninstitutional services under Medicaid (Special Committee on Aging, 1989:268–69).

social spending. In addition, a growing number of people recently have argued that the elderly have received more than their share of resources and that we should shift our attention to other worthy groups, including children (see Preston, 1984).

Although persons 65 and over represent approximately 11 percent of the total population, they absorb one-third of all federal budget outlays and over half of all government spending on social services (Minkler, 1987:49). Social Security constitutes the major portion of federal spending on the elderly, but health care and related supportive services consume a significant share. The high cost of nursing home care attracts particular attention. Medicaid funding for nursing homes jumped from $9.8 billion in 1980 to $17.3 billion in 1987 (Special Committee on Aging, 1987b:30). The rate of increase of expenditures on nursing homes outstrips that of the health-care industry as a whole (Lave, 1985). In 1983, nursing homes consumed 44 percent of all Medicaid spending (Rabin and Stockton, 1987).

A central preoccupation of policymakers thus is to keep people out of nursing homes as long as possible. Several states have attempted to use certificate-of-need programs to limit the supply of nursing home beds and have instituted preadmission screening programs to control utilization of those that exist. Federally funded "channeling" demonstration projects have sought to divert the disabled elderly from nursing homes (Kane and Kane, 1987).

Policymakers also seek to contain public funding for noninstitutional services. Most endorse community and home-based services only insofar as they can serve as cost-effective alternatives to nursing home care. Thus they want to ensure that home care substitutes for nursing home placement and that the cost of providing home care for clients is less than the cost of supporting them in institutions. A guiding principle of many government officials is that publicly funded home and community-based care not substitute for the services provided by family and friends.*

The Impact of Funding Cutbacks on the Poor

Efforts to control the cost of long-term care affect low-income people disproportionately. It is important to note that there is ex-

---

*Although this chapter focuses on measures to reduce public spending on long-term care, recent attempts to save money on acute health care also affect informal caregiving. Chapter 3 discusses the impact on family caregivers of the prospective payment system for hospitals.

tensive overlap between public and private long-term care services. Rather than delivering services directly, the government purchases care through contracts with private nonprofit and proprietary organizations. As a result, a single agency frequently serves both persons paying privately and recipients of public funds. But these two groups of clients tend to be treated very differently.

The Distribution of Nursing Home Care

Studies repeatedly find that nursing homes discriminate against people attempting to enter as publicly funded patients. In an attempt to curb Medicaid expenditures, states seek to keep the nursing home reimbursement rate low. In most states, the Medicaid rate is substantially beneath the amount nursing homes charge their private-pay residents. Institutions thus look for clients who can pay their own way, at least initially (Committee on Nursing Home Regulation, 1986). The majority of nursing homes are proprietary, and an increasing proportion are controlled by major corporations; as a result, profit-making considerations frequently govern admissions criteria.

Medicaid recipients who require intensive care are especially disadvantaged. A variety of studies reports that Medicaid recipients requiring "heavy care"* have a difficult time finding facilities willing to accept them (Committee on Nursing Home Regulation, 1986:92; Cotterill, 1983; Feder and Scanlon, 1980; Lewin and Associates, 1987; Scanlon, 1980). Hospital discharge planners in California estimate that it is over four times harder to obtain a nursing home bed for a patient on Medi-Cal** requiring light care than for a private pay patient needing light care and that it is over seven times more difficult to place a "heavy care" Medi-Cal recipient than a private pay patient requiring the same level of care (Lewin and Associates, 1987:31–32). Some "heavy care" Medi-Cal patients are unable to find any nursing homes that will accept them (Lewin and Associates, 1987:42). In short, Medicaid recipients who have the greatest need for nursing home care are least likely to receive it.***

Medicaid beneficiaries who do gain admission to nursing homes tend to be relegated to institutions that, according to some measures,

---

*This term refers to patients who need at least two and one-half hours a day of personal and nursing care (Committee on Nursing Home Regulation, 1986:9).
**The Medicaid program in California.
***Some states have attempted to overcome this problem by instituting "case-mix reimbursement," paying nursing homes more for patients who require greater care (Kane and Kane, 1987:275–77).

offer the poorest quality care (Rivlin and Wiener, 1988:8–9). In California, a third of Medi-Cal beneficiaries reside in facilities in which over 80 percent of the patients receive Medi-Cal, and another third are in institutions where 60 to 79 percent of the residents are Medi-Cal funded (Lewin and Associates, 1987:35). Nursing homes with high concentrations of Medi-Cal recipients spend substantially less than others on items related to patient care. Institutions in which more than 75 percent of the patient days are Medi-Cal funded spend an average of $26.68 a day on nursing, dietary, and social services; institutions in which fewer than 25 percent of the patient days are reimbursed by Medi-Cal spend an average of $41.85 (Lewin and Associates, 1987:36–37). If family members in general view nursing homes with alarm, the relatives of Medicaid beneficiaries have reason to be especially suspicious of these facilities.

The Allocation of Community and Home-based Services

Income level also affects the distribution of noninstitutional services. Because most people who receive community and home-based care pay privately, utilization varies directly with income. Not surprisingly, persons with higher incomes spend far more than others on care (Liu, Manton, and Liu, 1985). Moreover, self-pay clients receive more hours of home health care than those who rely on public funds (Kane, 1989:27).

Recent developments have accentuated the class bias of noninstitutional care. Mirroring changes throughout the rest of the health-care industry, home health agencies have undergone a major transformation. First, the type of ownership has changed from voluntary and governmental organizations to private. The number of Visiting Nurses Associations (VNAs) and other voluntary and government home health agencies—the entities that traditionally have been responsible for serving the poor—has remained stable. The number of private nonprofit and for-profit agencies, however, has risen. In 1960, voluntary and public sector agencies constituted 92 percent of all home health agencies; by 1983, their share of the market had declined to 43 percent (Lindeman and Wood, 1985:14). The growth of the for-profit sector has been particularly striking. Legislation passed in 1980 gave a major boost to profit-making organizations by allowing them to be certified as home health agencies under Medicare. By 1986, the number of proprietary agencies had tripled (Rabin and Stockton, 1987:183). Second, as large corporate organizations capture an increasing share of the home health market, the number of free-standing agencies declines. Large multihospital systems looking for a relatively inexpensive way to expand have been particularly eager to acquire home health care (Lindeman and Wood, 1985:21).

The growing dominance of for-profit, corporate enterprises has had a profound impact on the distribution of home health services. Organizations committed primarily to maximizing profits tend to have little interest in serving a low income clientele (see Salmon, 1990). Moreover, because the home care environment is becoming increasingly competitive, private nonprofit agencies also have found themselves under pressure to generate revenue by focusing on the most remunerative patients (Lindeman and Wood, 1985:14). Although agencies certified under Medicare are automatically eligible for Medicaid certification, nonprofit as well as for-profit agencies increasingly spurn Medicaid beneficiaries (Rabin and Stockton, 1987:162).

Patients relying on Medicare also have increasing difficulty finding agencies willing to serve them. Although home health agencies expanded in the early 1980s to capture the Medicare market, changes in the second half of the decade encouraged agencies to reduce the size of their Medicare clientele. In 1985, the Health Care Financing Administration (HCFA) attempted to scale back funding for the home health benefit by reducing both the ceilings on allowable costs per visit and the number and frequency of visits by home health aides. In addition, because HCFA instructed fiscal intermediaries to define "medical necessity" more strictly, the rate of Medicare home health denials rose (Kane, 1989). According to a report of the Special Committee on Aging of the U.S. Senate, over two hundred home health agencies dropped their Medicare certification in 1986–87 (Special Committee on Aging, 1988:13). Over half of the 2,100 agencies surveyed by the National Association for Home Care (NAHC) in 1986 reported that they were trying to decrease their reliance on Medicare funding. NAHC concluded that the agencies were seeking to "raise revenues through the care of individuals who would pay privately" (quoted in Kane, 1989:29). Because the number of VNAs and public-sector agencies has not grown, these organizations cannot accommodate the publicly funded clients whom private agencies abandon.

Recent changes also have reinforced the tilt toward medically oriented home care services. As noted, the Omnibus Budget Reconciliation Act of 1981 replaced Title XX of the Social Security Act with the Social Services Block Grant and reduced government funding for the new program. Many community agencies, which relied heavily on Title XX, sought to recoup their losses by reorienting their programs toward the medical services Medicare reimburses (Wood et al., 1986:35). The programs most likely to be dropped or reduced were homemaker and chore services and personal care services, which both enable frail elderly persons to live independently without relying on friends and relatives and lighten the burden on family members who do provide care (Bertghold, 1987:15). At the same time, however, some nonprofit agencies have created for-profit subsidiaries, offering social support services to a predominantly self-pay clientele (Lindeman and Wood, 1985:50).

In short, the access of low-income people to any type of noninstitutional care appears to have dwindled. As the elderly population expands and hospitals discharge older patients earlier, an increasing number of people require care at home. But the for-profit entities that control a growing segment of the home care industry give priority to patients who can afford to finance their own care. Social, as opposed to medical, services are especially difficult to obtain. Researchers at the University of California, San Francisco, have coined the term "the no-care zone" to highlight the problems of low-income, disabled elderly people searching in vain for community and home-based services (Estes and Wood, 1985:18).

How can we account for the enormous inequities that exist in the distribution of noninstitutional services to the frail elderly? One obvious explanation is that, as noted, the need for community and home-based services is rising just when cost containment in health care has become a preeminent government concern. Many policy-makers argue that we cannot afford to equalize access by expanding services for low-income people.

An equally compelling explanation may lie in the fact that, unlike acute health care, long-term care involves a combination of social and medical services. Americans traditionally have viewed the allocation of social and medical services in very different lights. If we occasionally waver in our commitment to regarding health care as a right, surveys repeatedly demonstrate that we believe that market principles alone should not govern the allocation of medical care (Bayer, 1986–87). Publicity about the denial of critical health services provokes widespread concern. But we never have had a strong tradition of providing social support services to dependent populations. Perhaps as a result, we find it difficult to distinguish between care for the needy and the personal services elite members of society routinely command (see Waerness, 1984). One congressman explained his opposition to expanded in-home care this way: "I'd like someone to come fix my roof or do my shopping for me too, but why should taxpayers have to provide me with that?" (cited in Vladeck, 1980:217). As long as we view personal care services as a luxury to which the wealthy alone are entitled, we will continue to withhold essential care from the bulk of disabled people.

The reluctance of some policymakers to expand noninstitutional services also is grounded in the fact that they lack natural gatekeepers. Although fee-for-service reimbursement schemes encourage some physicians to overutilize health services, these providers do help to guard the portals of the health-care system. Moreover, home care services do not have built-in limitations on consumption. Stephen Crystal (1982:92) notes: "Just as people usually subject themselves to surgery only when convinced it is needed, hardly anyone goes into a nursing home if he feels there is an acceptable alternative. There is no disincentive for home care. In fact, help with household maintenance is a key part, in some cases all, of home care, and almost anyone, disabled or not, would appreciate having this."

But one person's "latent demand" is another's "unmet need" (see Feldblum, 1985). Those who fear that the expansion of home and community-based services will open the floodgates implicitly acknowledge that the elderly are drastically underserved. And, although the potential pool of clients of home care programs is vast, some evidence suggests that the demand for services is not as great as policymakers fear (Montgomery and Borgatta, 1989). As Alan Sager (1983:15) comments: "The notion of a horde of greedy old people and lazy family members anxious to soak up new public benefits appears to be more a projection by a few wealthy legislators accustomed to domestic and hotel and restaurant service than it is a realistic image of our nation's elderly citizens."

Barriers to access affect caregivers as well as clients. Relatives caring for low-income elderly persons typically can rely on few, if any, supportive services to alleviate the burdens. Family members who seek services for people who can pay privately tend to receive very different treatment from family members whose relatives rely on public funds. Agencies serving private pay clients increase business by relieving family members of caregiving responsibilities. They thus encourage relatives to shed the chores they find physically onerous or emotionally taxing. Programs relying on public funding typically operate under very strict spending caps. The more relatives of the clients dependent on such programs relinquish their responsibilities, the more agencies risk exceeding their funding limits. Rather than urging family members to reduce their care, such agencies promote increased family involvement. Some agencies seek to locate relatives who have refrained from rendering care and solicit their participation. The home care programs operated by New York City's Human Resources Administration deliver services only when family members can justify their inability to help (Caro and Blank, 1987:48). Agencies also train family members to provide care to elderly persons so that they can discontinue visits when eligibility for public funding ends (Lindeman and Wood, 1985:40).

But the greatest class differences may lie in the area of services provided outside the bounds of established organizations. Although private organizations sell many of the services required by frail elderly people, they tend to avoid substitutes for the personal care services rendered by family members; these services are labor intensive and thus are especially expensive to provide. People with resources to purchase such care often do so through ad hoc, informal arrangements. Some studies suggest that caregivers rely disproportionately on aides, attendants, and companions whom they recruit independently (Brody and Schoonover, 1986; Noelker and Townsend, 1987:75). The help provided by such workers typically is not included in government statistics; however, it constitutes a major source of assistance to the affluent that is not available to others.

Private Sector Initiatives

The two-class system in long-term care may become even more apparent if private sector initiatives win increased support. Such initiatives take two forms. Some, such as home equity conversions and individual medical accounts, seek to promote private saving, which can then be used to finance long-term care. Others attempt to bring individuals together to pool the risks of paying for long-term care; these mechanisms include private long-term care insurance, continuing-care retirement communities, and social/health maintenance organizations (see Rivlin and Wiener, 1988).

Advocates of such programs argue that the growing segment of the elderly population that is sufficiently well off to be able to pay for long-term care should not rely on limited government funds (Ricardo-Campbell, 1988; Task Force on Long-Term Health Care Policies, 1987). Critics charge that the expansion of the private sector would sharpen the divide between rich and poor. Most programs are far beyond the reach of low-income elderly people. A high-option, long-term care insurance policy, for example, costs approximately $1,500 a year for persons 79 to 80 (Rivlin and Wiener, 1988:60). Entry fees for continuing-care retirement communities range from $50,000 to $100,000 (Leutz, 1986:136). Because substantial numbers of low-income elderly people are homeowners, some potentially could take advantage of home equity conversion schemes; but many do not have enough equity in their homes to pay for adequate levels of long-term care (Leutz, 1986:136). Critics also note that increased private financing may well dissolve whatever popular support public programs currently enjoy. Walter Leutz (1986:139) writes: "The Medicaid budget could be cut not only because private policies keep some people from spending down, but also to encourage or stimulate the private market. . . . This could clearly lead to a two-class system of care, which would be rationalized by arguments that blame elderly victims for not insuring. It would not be uncommon to hear the argument that those who don't plan for the future don't deserve such a generous program, and so on into the all-too-familiar pattern."

Ethnic and Racial Minorities

Members of ethnic and racial minorities also encounter formidable problems when they seek long-term care. Elderly persons who are members of minority groups are most likely to suffer from functional disabilities (Markides and Mindel, 1987), but ethnic and racial minorities are underrepresented among the nursing home population. For example, among the population 65 and over, 2.9 percent of African-American women and 1.9 percent of African-American men are residents of nursing homes, as opposed to 5.1 percent of white women and 2.9 percent of white men (Eustis et al., 1984). This discrepancy has been attributed variously to the concentration of minority populations in geographic areas that are underserved by nursing homes, to the greater reluctance of certain ethnic and racial groups to institutionalize family members, and especially to discriminatory admissions policies (Eustis et al., 1984; Markson, 1980; Vladeck, 1980). Whatever the explanation, members of ethnic and racial minorities remain in the community with higher levels of functional impairments than do whites (Crystal, 1982). We can assume that a high proportion of noninstitutionalized minority elderly persons receive care from relatives.

Community and home-based services also are sparse in minority communities. Those that are accessible to members of ethnic and racial minorities frequently lack sensitivity to individuals from diverse cultures (Markides and Mindel, 1987).

Conclusion

Laura Balbo (1982:263) argues: "Because of services provided by women either free or at low cost, an enormous amount of needs, although recognized as legitimate in a welfare state or service society system, in fact do not compete for scarce available resources and therefore do not become a political demand capable of developing into pressures, strains, and conflict." Other observers note that the reverse also is true: gaps in social welfare compel women to provide a wide array of unremunerated services for their families (Graham, 1985; Land, 1978). The intense emotional involvement of many women in caring work suggests that they are not simply responding to external pressures. Nevertheless, long-term care policies create the framework within which the experience of caregiving unfolds. The decisions women make about care are not solely private choices. Because publicly funded services are not universally accessible, many women lack the power to determine when they will begin to care for elderly parents, the power to control the intrusions of caregiving in their lives, and the power to hand over responsibilities that have become overwhelming.

3

Family Care in the United States since 1800

As fears about the cost of supporting the frail elderly escalate, it becomes fashionable to plead for a return to the nineteenth-century world of caregiving. Numerous policy analysts contend that family members used to take better care of elderly relatives than formal organizations do today and that, in the interests of both humanity and cost effectiveness, government policies should encourage increased family assistance. But they assume that the nature of caring has remained constant over time and ignore the complex social forces that have fundamentally transformed this activity (see Daniels, 1988:21–28).

This chapter investigates the content and cultural meaning of family care in the nineteenth century in order to illuminate distinctive aspects of contemporary caregiving. It focuses on women because they constituted the overwhelming majority of family caregivers. Because the historic record on care for aging relatives is very thin, it is important to expand the scope of the inquiry to informal care for a wide variety of relatives.

Women and Care

"Every woman is a nurse," Florence Nightingale proclaimed in the opening paragraph of her book, *Notes on Nursing*, published in England in 1860 (Nightingale, 1860). Her statement captured an important feature of women's lives. In the United States, as in England, most women could expect to spend lengthy periods of time caring for the sick and the dying. Despite the stereotype of the delicate Victorian woman, most nineteenth-century women were intimately familiar with pain, illness, and death. They dressed wounds, changed bandages, held basins for vomiting patients, and emptied chamber pots, "the most disagreeable item in domestic labor," according to one influential writer of household treatises (Catharine Beecher quoted in Strasser, 1982:95). Because they cared for patients of both sexes, women were not shielded from exposure to male bodies. Girls as well as mature women assisted the sick, watched the dying, and laid out the dead. As a 15-year-old, Lucy Sprague Mitchell (later a prominent educator) became the primary caregiver for her mother, who suffered from depression, and for her father and an older cousin, both victims of tuberculosis. In her autobiography, she described her morning ritual (Mitchell, 1953:105): "I began to empty the cuspidors. Every room except mine had at least one cuspidor partly filled with water. . . . I knew cleaning the cuspidors was dangerous work, for no maid was ever allowed to touch one. . . . I half resented this job, but who else was there? I thought. It was an unpleasant job, too, and I often sent my breakfast down the toilet as a finish." Women's journals and letters revealed their intimate acquaintance with illness and death. If they scrupulously avoided any mention of sex, they portrayed the sick and the dying in vivid detail (Douglas, 1988; Hampsten, 1982).

Nursing care dominated women's lives for many reasons. One was the high incidence of disease and disability. Although improved nutrition had decreased susceptibility to many infectious diseases by the late eighteenth century, poor sanitary conditions made growing urban areas breeding grounds for disease. Epidemics of yellow fever, cholera, and smallpox occasionally swept through the major industrial cities along the East Coast. Even more common killers in the nineteenth century included pneumonia, typhus, typhoid fever, diphtheria, scarlet fever, measles, whooping cough, dysentery, and tuberculosis (Leavitt and Numbers, 1985).

The reigning ideology assigned the work of caring exclusively to women. Various accounts of life in the early New England colonies suggest that caregiving responsibilities fell primarily on women as early as the seventeenth century (see, e.g., Cowan, 1987; Ulrich, 1987, 1990). But men worked nearby and were available to help when needed. After 1820, the connection between women and caring grew closer. Men increasingly worked in the new factories, abandoning domestic responsibilities to the women who stayed behind. In addition, between 1820 and 1865, popular writers expounded a new doctrine exalting women's special sphere. This cult of domesticity was in part a response to the phenomenal social change wrought by industrialization. Proponents of the domestic code idealized the home as a bulwark against the social turmoil threatening the world they had known. The rise of the inexpensive printing industry enabled the cult to spread widely. Mass-produced books and magazines addressed to women rapidly propagated the new ideology throughout the country (Ryan, 1975:75).

At the heart of the domestic code lay the belief that women were innately different from men. They were calmer, purer, more loving, and more sensitive. The traits that are central to caregiving—responsiveness to the needs of others, patience, and an ability to adapt to individual change—became part of a new cultural definition of womanhood. Some feminist scholars recently have argued that caregiving involves a series of skills that men as well as women can acquire (Rose, 1986; see Abel and Nelson, 1990). But the domestic manuals, religious tracts, etiquette guides, and women's magazines flooding the market in the mid–nineteenth century defined the ability to render care as a natural attribute of women. In addition, prescriptive literature exhorted women to serve and strive to please others, while subordinating their own needs. Caregiving thus became imbued with self-sacrifice and selflessness even as it was identified more closely with women.

Symbolic representations of the home reinforced the link between caregiving and women. The new domestic literature described the home as a place of regeneration, restoration, and salvation. At the same time, writers expressed their anxieties about the values of the business world by employing the language of disease and contagion. Thus Nancy Sprout, a housewife who published her own domestic writings, stated that "the air of the world is poisonous. You must carry an antidote with you, or the infection will prove fatal." Sarah Josepha Hale, the editor of influential women's magazines, counseled her readers: "Our men are sufficiently money-making. Let us keep our women and children from the contagion as long as possible" (quoted in Cott, 1983:68). Writings such as these suggested that the home served to rehabilitate those compelled to venture into the outside world.

Many historians have pointed out that proponents of the cult of domesticity venerated women's role as mothers and regarded child care as the province of women alone (e.g., Cott, 1983; Ryan, 1982). They note less frequently that women also had a special obligation to safeguard the health of their families (see Motz, 1983; Verbrugge,

1979). Advice about health promotion and care for the sick filled domestic manuals. In the words of Catharine Beecher, a preeminent author of such treatises, a woman was "the responsible guardian of the health of a whole family" (Beecher, 1977:47). Many health reformers addressed their messages primarily to women in their capacity as wives and mothers (Cayleff, 1987; Morantz, 1984; Verbrugge, 1979).

Although it is impossible to determine the extent to which women followed the advice to devote themselves to others, women frequently explained their motivations in terms of the duty to care. In her autobiography, Lucy Sprague Mitchell (1953:110) recalled that she had not questioned her family's expectation that she care for her parents and cousin: "As a dutiful daughter, I simply did my job. . . . I accepted the standards of the times that daughters belonged to their families." In some cases, women identified so closely with the needs of others that they effaced their own sense of self. One woman who nursed her dying mother later wrote: "The end came very quietly and I felt that my life, too, was all done; that the only reason for which I had come into the world was to comfort and care for my mother in her loneliness; that there was no more need on earth for me. I was thirty-one and very tired" (Eddy, 1981:157). Women who resented caregiving obligations occasionally tried to conform their emotions to the prevailing ideology. Judith Breault notes that, after Emily Howland began caring for her father, her letters to friends were replete with phrases such as " 'I try to do right,' 'I must,' 'I should,' . . . 'I should feel,' 'I strain with all my might' " (Breault, 1976:121).

Material as well as ideological factors compelled women to render care. In the nineteenth century, as in the twentieth, caregiving responsibilities were intertwined with economic dependence; women furnished care in exchange for a variety of goods and other services. Because few women worked for pay and welfare services were virtually nonexistent, women relied on a broad network of kin. Single women boarded with relatives, earning their keep by engaging in a range of household tasks. Autobiographical accounts of growing up in nineteenth-century households frequently describe the ambiguous place of the "maiden aunt"; although a figure of pity, she provided critical services in times of need. Married women also relied on extended kinship ties. As Marilyn Ferris Motz (1983:82) writes, "By the aid she gave to other family members, a woman could hope to ensure future assistance for herself and her children." Although divorce was infrequent, married women knew that they would need their relatives if their husbands died. Fears about their own mortality heightened women's sense of dependence. One study reports that 8 percent of white children born in 1870 lost their mothers before they were fifteen (cited in Motz, 1983:84). By providing care to a broad circle of relatives, women hoped to guarantee that their children would receive care in the event of their own deaths.

Women's responsibilities for rendering care thus extended very broadly. As Elaine M. Brody (1985) notes, care for elderly parents imposed fewer burdens in the nineteenth century than in the late twentieth. In 1900, the average life expectancy was 49 years; in 1983 it was 75 (Siegel and Taeuber, 1986:88). Demographer Peter Uhlenberg (1980:319) has concluded that the proportion of middle-aged couples with living parents was only 48 percent in 1900, compared to 86 percent in 1976. But responsibilities for the older generation were not restricted to parents. Women routinely nursed aunts and uncles who had been felled by disease. In 1867, Laura Stebbins explained why she could not join her friend in reform work: "My eldest Aunt, almost eighty, is so very frail and feeble, that I ques[tion] very seriously the propriety of my leaving—for both [aunts] are very helpless and in case of sudden illness—or of accident, they might suffer much; and then I should reflect upon myself exceedingly" (quoted in Chambers-Schiller, 1984:114).

And care for the elderly constituted only a small fraction of the overall care required. Because infectious diseases were rampant and antibiotics nonexistent, infants and children frequently became ill and died. Within a period of twenty-two months, Samuella Curd noted in her diary the deaths of eight of her friends' children (Arpad, 1984:151). Any illness could presage disaster (see Pollock, 1983: 133–34). In 1863, a woman in Georgia wrote in her journal: "Three o'clock A.M. finds me watching by the cradle of our dear baby. The dreaded hour has come! The hour I have feared must come, when we should see our little one prostrated by disease" (Dyer 1982:199). During epidemics, children's illnesses were particularly terrifying. When cholera struck Cincinnati in 1849, Harriet Beecher Stowe wrote to her husband: "Yesterday little Charley was taken ill, not seriously, and at any other season I should not be alarmed. Now, however, a slight illness seems like a death sentence" (Fields, 1970:117). It is true that, because the fertility rate of white married women dropped from 7.04 in 1800 to 3.56 in 1900 (Smith, 1974:123), this group of women had progressively fewer responsibilities for their own children. Nevertheless, women nursed nieces, nephews, younger siblings, and cousins in addition to their own offspring. "I watched last night with Cousin Ann's little boy who has been dangerously ill with lung fever," wrote Mary Low to her husband in 1828 (Loines, 1955:253). Samuella Card noted in her diary for August 11, 1863: "Spent the morning with Cousin Sue, nursed her sick baby" (Arpad, 1984:49).

Women also cared for nonrelatives. Neighbors and friends routinely attended the sick, sat up with the dying, laid out the dead, and comforted the bereaved. Women's journals were filled with references to "visiting the sick." Sarah Connell Ayer (1910:244) recounted the events of October 16, 1824:

> They sent in to me that Mrs. Appleby was dying. I hastened in, and found her in the last agonies of death, surrounded by her afflicted family. . . . I stood by her to the last, then closed her eyes, and assisted in performing for her the last sad office. Mrs. Appleby was one of my nearest neighbors; she had laboured under a long and severe illness, and I have often visited her during her confinement.

Eight days later, she wrote: "We had just sat down to breakfast, as Miss Jones ran up, to tell me Mrs. Emery, another near neighbour, was just gone. I got up from the table and went down" (Ayer, 1910:245). May Crane recalled her mother this way: "She would ride on horseback to the home of a sick neighbor, often taking with her the baby, if her services were required for a length of time. She assisted at births and deaths in many homes and in her calm way was a tower of strength to many in trouble" (quoted in Stratton, 1981:74).

Few medical services relieved the caregiving responsibilities of women. According to Charles Rosenberg, "Most Americans in 1800 had probably heard that such things as hospitals existed, but only a minority would have ever had occasion to see one" (Rosenberg, 1987:18). The situation had not changed greatly seventy years later. When the first government survey was conducted in 1873, the nation boasted only 120 hospitals (Vogel, 1980:1), most of which were custodial institutions, serving the "deserving" poor. Middle-class patients rarely entered hospitals. Although low-income people had fewer options, those with families to care for them avoided these institutions whenever possible. Even surgeries were performed at home, most frequently in the kitchen (Vogel, 1980). When a major train crash occurred in suburban Boston in 1887, ambulances transported the great majority of the victims to their homes rather than to either of the two major hospitals (Vogel, 1980:9).

Other institutions also were sparse. Although tuberculosis was a common scourge throughout the century, the sanitarium movement was not launched until the 1880s (Vogel, 1980:105). Reformers began to establish special institutions for the mentally ill as early as the 1820s and 1830s, but families frequently were reluctant to entrust ill relatives to their care (see Grob, 1971; Hatfield, 1987:15). In 1859, Abigail Malick described the problems caused by the mental illness of her daughter Jane:

> She distrois All that Come Before Her When She Has Her Crasy Spells on her And Wantes to kill All Derest Frendes And her Little Babe. And . . . I Have Had to Tak her Babe and Not let Her See it for two And thre dayes At A Time And tie her down on the Bed and it took Three of us to do it At that. So you May think I Have Had a hard time of it with her. (quoted in Schlissel, 1989:75)

Abigail explained why she nevertheless was determined to keep Jane out of the insane asylum: "That would Have Bin very hard for Her And us. For They Whip them Every Morning or When they do Eny thing, so I am told, And get hardley Eny thing to Eat" (quoted in Schlissel, 1989:78). In the absence of nursing homes, the sole facilities for the elderly were poorhouses; only the most desperate, however, sought refuge within their walls (Katz, 1986).

Family caregivers received little help from health professionals. Skepticism about medical interventions deterred some caregivers from relying on physicians. It will be seen that throughout the nineteenth century many family members had no confidence that physicians could deliver better care than themselves. In addition, some families could not afford the fees physicians charged. Without telephones and automobiles, summoning a physician involved considerable time and effort (Blake, 1977; Cassedy, 1977; Starr, 1982). Outside urban areas, physicians frequently were inaccessible. Although the population remained overwhelmingly rural during the early decades of the century, medical school graduates were concentrated in cities (Brown, 1979:61). Doctors were especially scarce on the frontier. When Ann Ellis's mother was dying in a mining camp in Colorado, a man volunteered to call for the doctor. Ellis (1929:166–67) later described his journey: "It is seventeen miles over Ute Pass—the snow in dreadful drifts, but he makes it, sometimes riding, other times leading his horse and breaking trail. He is all night, then starts the doctor, who has a horse and buggy, on his forty-mile trip around by the Grove." When a young woman had a miscarriage in Oregon in 1890, one of her relatives reported that the doctor "arrived in a wonderfully short time, about hours" (Donnell, 1982:290). In some cases, doctors came too late to attend the births or deaths for which they had been summoned (Bolsteri, 1982:99; Donnell, 1982:309; Leavitt, 1986:95; Springer and Springer, 1986:224).

Most family caregivers had even less contact with nurses. Nursing did not begin to organize as a profession until after the Civil War. The first nursing schools were established only in 1875 (Starr, 1982:154). The great majority of graduates worked as private-duty nurses, providing care to patients in individual households. Some families also relied on the services of untrained nurses. But hiring nurses was an option only for the very affluent; during the 1880s, a week's nursing care in Boston cost between $15 and $18, a sum far beyond the reach of most wage earners (Reverby, 1987:98). Even family caregivers who could afford to pay for nursing care often failed to purchase it. Some were unaccustomed to depending on strangers for care and fearful of allowing them into their homes (see Motz, 1983:105). Class prejudices may have heightened these anxieties. Although most families employing nurses were middle and upper class, nurses came overwhelmingly from poor backgrounds (Melosh, 1982:78; Reverby, 1987:15). Louisa May Alcott claimed that she intended to hire a nurse during her mother's long illness but could find none who met her standards. She subsequently employed a nurse to care for her father, but only because her own poor health prevented her from providing care herself (Saxton, 1978; Reverby, 1987:15). During the seventeen years in which he suffered from tuberculosis, Lucy Sprague Mitchell's father steadfastly refused to receive the ministrations of any but family members, even when his illness required surgical intervention (Antler, 1987:86).

The Work of Care

Despite the romantic glow with which popular writers tried to surround caregiving, women who cared for the sick were not simply angels of mercy. Before the advent of mass-produced labor-saving devices, most household chores entailed difficult and unremitting labor. Although manufacture of textiles, soap, and candles moved into the factory early in the nineteenth century, the great majority of households continued to lack indoor plumbing, gas, and electricity. Susan Strasser (1982:195) describes the drudgery involved in laundering:

One wash, one boiling, and one rinse used about fifty gallons of water—or four hundred pounds—which had to be moved from pump or well or faucet to stove and tub, in buckets and wash boilers that might weigh as much as forty or fifty pounds. Rubbing, wringing, and lifting water-laden clothes and linens, including large articles like sheets, tablecloths, and men's heavy work clothes, wearied women's arms and wrists and exposed them to caustic substances. They lugged weighty tubs and baskets full of wet laundry outside, picked up each article, hung it on the line, and returned to take it all down.

When families members fell ill, housewives had to bathe them, cook special foods, prepare medicines, and change sheets and bed clothes. At such times, the workload easily became unbearable. Marian Louise Moore (1977:176), an Ohio homesteader, remembered her experience nursing her mother: "In the Spring of the year 1872 . . . she was sick three months, part of the time helpless, typhoid inflammatory rheumatism. . . . This sickness of hers brought more work upon me, washing and other work, when I had more work of my own than I could possibly do well." Many women cared for others when they themselves were incapacitated by illness or childbirth (Myerson and Shealy, 1987; Nelson, 1977; Reid, 1936).

Women's Networks

If caregiving frequently was taxing, however, it was not a solitary endeavor. Several historians have argued that the rigid gender segregation of the nineteenth century helped to create a distinctive female culture. Although historians dispute whether women's intense personal ties ultimately promoted or impeded women's entry into the public arena, they agree that female networks sustained and supported women at critical times (Cott, 1983; Smith-Rosenberg, 1975). Mary Wilder Foote remarked that, when her baby was very ill: "My kind friend, Mrs. Peirson, sat with me *four* days, leaving all her family cares. Nobody ever tended a child so exquisitely, and in her lap I could place my darling, and feel at ease." When the baby lay dying, "Mrs. Peirson was with me all day, and, when night came, she would not leave me, but we watched over her together" (Tileston, 1918:92, 93).

A diary written by Nannie Stillwell Jackson in 1890 and 1891 portrays women's supportive relationships in unusually rich detail (Bolsteri, 1982). The wife of a small farmer in Arkansas, Nannie saw her close friend Fannie Morgan as often as four times a day. Nannie's entry for June 19, 1890, reveals their close interdependence: "I went up and washed the dishes for Fannie & helped her so as she could get an early start to washing for she had such a big washing. . . . I baked some chicken bread for Fannie & some for my self, & she gave me some dried apples & I baked 2 pies she gave me one & she took the other I made starch for her & me too" (pp. 30–31). Nannie also relied on Fannie for emotional support. Nannie wrote that she liked to tell Fannie "my troubles because it seems to help me to bear it better when she knows about it" (p. 35). When Nannie feared that she would die in childbirth, she asked Fannie to care for her two daughters. In addition, Nannie frequently exchanged goods and services with at least twenty other women, both white and African-American. Care for the sick and the dying was embedded in this collective female life.

"I have had a heap of company this week," wrote Nannie a week after giving birth. Her visitors included Miss Joe, Miss Ruth, Mrs. Chandler, and Fannie, who "stayed with me 4 nights" (pp. 60–61). When Mrs. Dyer "was terribly afflicted with boils," Nannie, along with several other women, visited her (p. 47). Fannie gave pills to Nannie's daughter (p. 56), and Nannie visited Fannie when the latter was "sick taking pills" (p. 46). Both women spent time at the home of Mrs. Caulk when her baby was ill (p. 41). When Nannie herself fell ill, Fannie cooked breakfast for her; Mrs. Gifford and Bettie Newby came by in the evening (p. 76). After Mrs. Hornbuckle's son died, Nannie and her husband stayed with her at night; the following day, Nannie returned to the Hornbuckle house, got material for the coffin, and went to the home of Fannie, who helped make "the pillow and face cover" (pp. 66–67).

Sickness at the Archdale house required a range of services from several women. On March 22, 1891, Nannie "set a while" with Mrs. Archdale's sons Bill and Lee, both of whom had pneumonia; she continued to visit the house regularly over the next few days, reporting on March 28 that the sons were better but that the daughter had fallen ill. On April 8, Mrs. Archdale herself became ill and sent for Nannie; the latter, in turn, summoned Fannie, and together they gave Mrs. Archdale "a dose of oil & turpentine & some gum camphor." Various other women spent the next few nights with the patient. Mrs. Archdale's son Lee came to the Jacksons' house for dinner, and he took food to Fannie, who also was not well. On April 11, all members of Mrs. Archdale's family appeared to be recovering. Nannie "cleaned up the dishes & stratened things about there some"; she also gave Lee Archdale two of his meals. The following day, Nannie had time to visit three women in addition to Mrs. Archdale. Then, on April 13, Mrs. Archdale took a turn for the worse; Nannie visited her "5 or 6 times," and she and Fannie spent the night. On April 14, Mrs. Archdale died: "Mrs. Morgan [Fannie], Mrs. Newby & I Mr. Jackson Kate McNiel & Fannie Totten all set up . . . & we dressed her and laid her out." Although a flood prevented the women from attending the burial, Nannie "fixed things about in Mrs. Archdale's house" (pp. 88–100).

When Nannie was too busy to engage in caregiving activities herself, she relied on her 12-year-old daughter Lizzie and her 9-year-old daughter Sue to fulfill her responsibilities; in this way, she was able to extend the range of her neighborly services. Thus, when Fannie had to spend the night with her sick mother, Lizzie "churned" for Fannie, ate supper at her house, and then accompanied Fannie to her mother's (p. 29). Nannie also sent both Lizzie and Sue to stay with Fannie when the latter was sick, and the two women who might have been expected to tend her had gone to spend the night at the home of a boy who had just died. The following day, Fannie took Lizzie with her to visit the bereaved mother (p. 53).

Nannie was intensely aware of sickness in her friends' homes, even when she was not directly involved in rendering care. She noted when Fannie's stepson Asher "took pills" (p. 41) and when he had a "chill" (p. 49). On July 9, 1890, she listed the women who visited Mrs. Hunley's "very sick" baby (p. 42). On January 5, 1891, she wrote that Fannie and Nellie Smithee "went down to set up with Mrs. Hunley" (p. 67). A few days later, Nannie "lent Nellie Smithee my shawl & Lizzie's bonnet for she & Fannie had to go down to sit up with Mrs. Maggie Stroud & Bettie Hunley they are both sick" (pp. 69–70). Fannie and Nellie returned to Nannie's house in the morning to report how the patients were faring (p. 70).

In short, care for the sick and the dying was part of the continual flow of services among Nannie Jackson's friends. It is, of course, impossible to determine the extent to which Jackson's experiences were typical. Certainly women in frontier areas often tended sick relatives without the help of neighbors or friends (see Everett and Everett, 1939; Snell, 1971; Reid, 1923). Nevertheless, births, illnesses, and deaths were communal events among many nineteenth-century women.

Relationships with Physicians

Women's relationships to the medical profession also shaped their experience of care. As noted, some women never consulted physicians. Those who did summon doctors in times of illness rarely considered themselves subordinate to these providers. Judith Walzer Leavitt (1986) demonstrates that the first physicians to attend births had to tred warily, deferring to the authority of the birthing woman's female attendants. In other arenas as well, family members felt free to disregard any advice physicians dispensed (Motz, 1983:102).

Before the twentieth century, doctors lacked the rewards and privileges of professional status. One problem was their inability to control access; they could prevent neither the proliferation of medical schools nor the rescinding of state licensing laws (Starr, 1982:58). Internal divisions also plagued medicine. Despite attempts by "regular" physicians to establish dominance, sects such as Thomsonianism in the first half of the century and homeopathy and eclecticism in the second attracted large and loyal followings. Nannie T. Alderson (Alderson and Smith, 1942:208) described the way she cared for her children's illnesses:

> On one of my visits east, a friend in Kansas had given me a kit of homeopathic remedies to take home. . . . The kit contained a number of bottles of little white sugary pills, and a book of directions telling you which to use in case of colds, fever, stomach trouble and so forth. Whenever one of the children was ill I simply consulted the book and gave a pill from the proper bottle.

Physicians could not claim special competence. Harold Wilensky argues that "if the technical base of an occupation consists of a vocabulary that sounds familiar to everyone . . . then the occupation will have difficulty claiming a monopoly of skill or even a roughly exclusive jurisdiction" (quoted in Larson, 1977:31). Before the rise of scientific medicine, physicians had no esoteric methods of diagnosis and treatment at their disposal. Lacking stethoscopes, thermometers, and X rays, they relied primarily on observation of patients. As Charles Rosenberg (1987:70) comments, "A flushed face and rapid pulse, a coated tongue and griping diarrhea would be apparent to laymen just as to physicians; and grandmothers as well as senior consultants could and did make reasoned prognoses." Even such "heroic" interventions as bleeding and purging bore a striking resemblance to many of the remedies of family members and were readily comprehensible to them (Rosenberg, 1987).

The locus of medical care bolstered the power of family members vis-à-vis formal health care providers. Physicians went to patients' homes to make diagnoses and administer treatments. Very few worked in offices or hospitals; Paul Starr (1982:162) estimates that just 2 percent of American doctors had hospital privileges in 1873. Instead of receiving clients in imposing and intimidating surroundings, physicians thus entered the family's turf. The need to board with family members also may have helped to erode status differentials. When physicians lived far from their patients, and illnesses required attention over lengthy periods, doctors often stayed in the homes of families. And physicians relied on relatives and friends for assistance, rather than on a staff of subordinates. In 1871, a physician operated on the thumb of a woman who was staying at a friend's home in Idaho. The friend later commented: "By the time it came to the tying of the stitches she struggled so that the doctor asked me to tie them while he held her and I did" (Reid, 1936:52).

Women's access to medical knowledge further undermined physicians' prerogatives. When accidents occurred, many women felt competent to act on their own. Maria D. Brown's son recalled: "I cut off three of [my fingers] one time when I was cutting sheaf oats for my pony in a cutting box. I rushed into the house with the ends of my fingers hanging by shreds. Mother washed them, fitted them together carefully, and bound them up so that they grew into perfectly good fingers again. Another time she saved my foot" (Brown, 1929:157). Some women were especially renowned for their knowledge and skills. Another son described his mother's medical prowess this way:

> One time a posse summoned her to treat a badly wounded prisoner. With a small vial of carbolic acid as an antiseptic, a knitting needle as a probe and a pair of common pincers, she removed the bullet and saved the man's life. At another time, with a razor as a lance and her embroidery scissors, she once removed three fingers from the crushed hand of a railroad brakeman. (quoted in Stratton, 1981:75)

Women also exhibited considerable self-confidence when illness struck. Many housewives had a stock of medicinal herbs, which they picked in the woods or their gardens during the summer and stored each fall along with other preserves (Riley, 1982:282; Starr, 1982:32). Writing in the mid-1940s, E. May Lacey Crowder remembered her mother's collection of herbs:

> Many wild plants were used as medicines, most of them steeped and drunk as tea. Among these were "Culver's root" taken, "for the liver." The dandelion, both as extract and as wine, was used for the same purpose. Tonics were made from the butterfly weed, sweet flag root, sassafras bark and boneset. . . . For colds, pennyroyal, prairie balm,

and horse mint were popular remedies. Mullen was used externally
for pleurisy. . . . Smartweed was used externally for boils. Cubeb ber-
ries were smoked for catarrh. (Quoted in Riley, 1982:282)

Mothers typically were the chief repository of medical wisdom for
their daughters. In 1873 Mary Cooley, living in Michigan, wrote to her
daughter that she should try to cure her child's earache by placing
paper filled with pepper on the ear (Motz, 1983:100–101).* Shared
responsibilities among communities of women also fostered the dis-
semination of medical knowledge and skills. A letter from Mary Paul,
a mill worker, to her father in 1855 illustrates women's confidence in
the treatments they learned from each other:

> Oh there is a remedy for rheumatism that a lady here told me of, I
> was telling her about your case & she told me to tell you to take *steam*
> baths, in this way. When you feel the lameness coming on, have a
> *sheet* wrung out of *hot* water and wrap it about you. Then over that
> put flannel blankets and dont spare the clothes. The object is to pro-
> duce heavy perspiration and thus throw off the disease. Half an hour
> is long enough to remain in the sheet. On coming out of it take a
> *warm* bath and rub till the flesh is dry. I have never heard of this rem-
> edy before but I have a great deal of faith in it, and I do wish you
> would try it. (Paul, 1981:122)

The domestic manuals that circulated during the middle decades of
the nineteenth century constituted still another source of medical lore,
containing remedies for illnesses alongside recipes for food. For example, *The Southern Gardener and Receipt Book,* which was published in
1860, included cures for cholera and consumption as well as for less
serious afflictions, including bee stings and colds (Motz, 1983:100).

During the middle of the nineteenth century, various entrepre-
neurs began to market patent medicines, and advertisements for their
compounds soon filled the pages of women's magazines (Cowan,
1983:76; Starr, 1982; Young, 1977). Although these concoctions
often consisted of little more than the herbal remedies that generations of housewives had brewed, they undercut women's traditional
skills, replacing folk remedies with commercially manufactured
products. Nevertheless, the availability of these nostrums enabled
many women to continue to circumvent physicians' authority. Companies producing patent medicines exploited the public's skepticism
of scientific medicine; they ridiculed the practices of physicians and

---

*Examples such as these remind us that, despite the confidence women placed in the
remedies they administered, many were ineffective.

proclaimed the superiority of their own productions (Stage, 1984; Starr, 1982).

In addition, dominant medical beliefs accorded a high value to aspects of care that lay almost exclusively within the province of female kin. Rosenberg (1979:117) elucidates the system of beliefs that dominated the first half of the nineteenth century:

> The body was visualized in terms of a central metaphor, one in which the organism was seen as a dynamic system constantly interacting with its environment. Diet, atmosphere and ventilation, psychic stress, all interacted to shape a patterned but continuously re-established reality. Within this framework of explanation, disease was no specific entity . . . but rather a general state of disequilibrium.

According to this theoretical framework, the restoration of health depended on controlling intake into the body and removing bodily discharges. Good housekeeping thus assumed enormous significance. Proper diet, adequate ventilation, and the regular emptying of bed-pans—aspects of care that women controlled—had a place alongside the drugs a physician administered or the surgery he performed (Motz, 1983:98). If the nineteenth-century obsession with order and cleanliness in the sickroom added to women's household chores, it also helped to define them as critical ingredients of medical therapeutics.

Nineteenth-century attitudes about the importance of personal ties also elevated the private world of caring. Assuming a close connection between the mind and the body, physicians were as concerned with psychic distress as with the external environment. Female kin were believed to be especially qualified to offer the attention, sympathy, and reassurance that alleviated emotional stress and facilitated healing (Ryan, 1982).

The strong moral component of contemporary medical beliefs further heightened the importance of informal care. Lacking knowledge about the causative agents of specific diseases, both physicians and laypersons believed that individuals bore significant responsibility for their afflictions. Lapses in self control were especially important. Catharine Beecher (1977:236) proclaimed, "All medical men unite in the declaration, that the grand cause of most diseases, is, excess in eating and drinking, united with too sedentary habits." A cardinal principle of the cult of domesticity was that women had the power to exert moral influence over others (Ryan, 1982). Women thus were indispensable not only because they provided the conditions necessary for recovery from disease but also because they prevented ill health by instilling proper habits.

Finally, because disease was believed to arise from the interaction of specific individuals with their environment, particularistic knowledge of patients and the context of their lives was considered critical. The intimate understanding of family members thus was as significant as the more detached universal expertise of physicians.

If traditional medical beliefs endowed women's household activities with significance, various sects were especially sympathetic to the work of family caregivers. Although they differed greatly among themselves, they shared a disdain for "heroic" medical treatments and a belief in the efficacy of folk practices (Numbers, 1977). Thomsonians, for example, touted the superior safety record of family health care. One member of the sect argued: "It has been generally remarked that those families that employ no physicians, in cases of scarlet fever, canker rash, measles, and &c, lose a less number of children, than those who employ them" (quoted in Numbers, 1977:56).

The Impact of Care

Although women's responsibility for care tied them to a broad network of family and friends, it also helped to bind them tightly to the home (Lerner, 1977:150). After providing a litany of the ills that had afflicted her children, Rachel Simmons, a Quaker living in Ohio in the 1830s, wrote to her mother: "I have been confined at home nearly two months. . . . It is 8 weeks this day since I have been to meeting or anywhere" (quoted in Heiser, 1941: 113). Other women complained that caregiving obligations prevented them from attending church or participating in social gatherings.

Caregiving had an equally profound impact on the lives of single women. In some cases, demands for care determined marital status: youngest daughters were especially likely to sacrifice marriage in order to remain at home and tend their parents in their old age (Yalom, 1981). As noted, after the death of their parents, single women lived with other kin, providing a range of services in exchange for room and board. "The single woman," Lee Chambers-Schiller (1984:112) observes, "remained 'on call' throughout her life."

Young unmarried women who left home during the 1820s and 1830s to seek paid employment frequently relinquished their jobs when family members became sick. Mary Hall, who worked in a store in Exeter, New Hampshire, for seven months, returned home when several relatives required her care (Cott, 1983:137). After Malenda

Edward quit her job in the mills to care for her parents, she wrote to a friend that she was serving as "physician and nurse too" and that she would travel west were it not for the need to provide care (Edwards, 1981:85–86).

Caregiving responsibilities curtailed other types of public activity as well. During the 1830s and 1840s, large numbers of single, middle-class women enlisted in social reform movements. Although they rarely rose to positions of power, they provided essential services to an array of antislavery, temperance, and medical reform associations. But even the most prominent women reformers abandoned their work when relatives fell ill. Some shuttled back and forth, interspersing reform activities with stints at home. After vacillating for several years between her work with freed slaves and caregiving, Emily Howland finally renounced her career as a reformer and dedicated herself to the care of her aging parents (Breault, 1976; Chambers-Schiller, 1984). Sarah Pugh, another leading antislavery activist, spent two years working in the British abolitionist movement, served as an editor of the *Anti-Slavery Advocate*, and organized local abolitionist societies. Summoned to care for a dying cousin, she soon discovered that other relatives also required her assistance. She never resumed full-time involvement in the cause (Chambers-Schiller, 1984:109–10).

The opening of higher education to women after the Civil War promised a broadening of women's sphere. But caregiving obligations prevented some women from taking advantage of this opportunity. Frances Marion Eddy, for example, gave up her plan to enter the University of Michigan in 1881 at the behest of her father, who was stricken with Bright's Disease (Eddy, 1981). Women who did receive college degrees often lacked a sense of direction. Without clear career possibilities, they were extremely vulnerable to parental demands that they return home and minister to the sick. Shortly after graduating from Radcliffe in 1900, Lucy Sprague Mitchell went back to California and resumed her place as the family nurse (Mitchell, 1953). Jane Addams did not pursue her ambition to enter medicine after graduating from college partly because her family thrust a variety of domestic responsibilities upon her. Although she was not asked to provide direct nursing care, she took charge of the arrangements for the care of an older brother who had suffered a mental breakdown (Addams, 1910; Davis, 1973). Years later she drew on her own experiences in writing a famous essay entitled "Filial Relations," in which she criticized parents who fail "to regard the daughter as otherwise than as a family possession" (Addams, 1972:308).

Even entry into a career did not excuse single women from the duty to care. The history of women teachers in the late nineteenth century is filled with stories of women who left their posts to nurse family members (see, e.g., Dodge, 1901:xi; Lensink, 1989:333; Yzenbaard and Hoffmann, 1974:272). Mary Holywell Everett was a successful physician when her sister became ill. A male colleague to whom she had written counseled her this way: "Even at the risk of losing your practice entirely, duty commands you to remain by the side of your old mother and help her to carry the burden" (Everett, 1977:179). At least one of Everett's female patients concurred with this advice. Writing to Everett about her absence from her practice, the patient commented, "Being that you have no husband, your dear mother has the first claim to you" (Everett, 1977:179).

To be sure, some single women did resist the presumption that they would be available to any family member who needed their help. Immersing themselves in other endeavors, they refused to be trapped by caregiving responsibilities (Chambers-Schiller, 1984). At a time when few formal services substituted for family care and women had virtually no way to achieve economic independence, however, most women felt powerless to resist their relatives' claims. As a result, demands for care dictated the patterns of their lives.

Varieties of Care

Because the writings of white, middle-class, eastern women provide the easiest entry to nineteenth-century women's lives, it is important to direct particular attention to the experiences of other groups. This section examines two varieties: women who emigrated to the West Coast during the middle decades of the century and slave women in the antebellum South.

Pioneer Women

Between 1841 and 1867, 350,000 people traveled westward along the Overland Trail to California and Oregon (Faragher and Stansell, 1979:246). John Faragher and Christine Stansell (1979:247) provide this description of the journey:

> From present-day Idaho . . . to their final destinations, the pioneers faced disastrous conditions: scorching deserts, boggy salt flats, and rugged mountains. By this time, families had been on the road some three months and were only at the midpoint of the journey: the environment, along with the wear of the road, made the last months difficult almost beyond endurance. Finally, in late fall or early winter

the pioneers straggled into their promised lands, after six months and over two thousand miles of hardship.

Domestic tasks tended to be grueling along the road. Cooking involved collecting buffalo dung and weeds for fuel and keeping fires going during wind and rainstorms. Although health care advocates preached the virtues of cleanliness, water was unavailable at many points. When parties passed rivers, women lugged kettles, tubs, and loads of clothes to wash (Myres, 1982; Schlissel, 1982). Rebecca Ketcham's diary reveals the hazards this activity could entail: "Camilla and I both burnt our arms very badly while washing. They were red and swollen and painful as though scalded with boiling water" (Kaiser and Knuth, 1961:283). Esther Hanna, an eighteen-year old bride, described her daily travail:

> Had to haul our water and wood for night as in many places there is none for miles, and then it is not good. I have had to bake also tonight. It is very trying on the patience to cook and bake on a little green wood fire with smoke blowing in your eyes so as to blind you, and shivering with cold so as to make the teeth chatter. But this is one of our crosses and we must bear it! (Allen, 1946:29)

The major migration occurred during the height of the cholera epidemic. Although travelers believed they were escaping the worst of this scourge, they carried the disease with them. Other serious illnesses that stalked the route were measles, typhoid, smallpox, and dysentery (Schilissel, 1982:15, 59–60). In addition, accidents frequently befell the emigrants.

Women's meticulous recording of the graves that they passed provides haunting testimony of the heavy loss of life. Here is a passage from the diary of Cecilia McMillen Adams, who traveled from Illinois to Oregon with her family in 1852: "Child's grave . . . smallpox . . . child's grave. . . . [We] passed 7 new-made graves. One had 4 bodies in it . . . cholera. A man died this morning with the cholera in the company ahead of us. . . . Another man died. . . . Passed 6 new graves. . . . We have passed 21 new-made graves . . . made 18 miles. . . . Passed 13 graves today. Passed 10 graves" (quoted in Schlissel, 1982:112).

Not surprisingly, women frequently noted that family members were sick. "My baby was sick all the way across," Margaret Hecox recalled. "I was so afraid that he would die and we be obliged to leave his little body in that strange country for the Indians to dig up or wild beasts to devour, that I hardly knew a moment's peace" (Hecox, 1966:26). When Elizabeth Smith Geer reached Oregon Territory in

November 1847, she had a dying husband and seven children. She wrote in her diary that she "found a small, leaky concern with two families already in it. I got some of the men to carry my husband up through the rain and lay him in it." A later entry read: "I have not undressed to lie down for six weeks. Besides all our sickness, I had a cross little babe to take care of. Indeed, I cannot tell you half." She continued to sit up "night after night, with my poor, sick husband, all alone and expecting him every day to die." She buried him in February (quoted in Schlissel, 1982:55). One woman's attentiveness to her seriously wounded husband won praise from another woman: "To add to the horrors of the surroundings one man was bitten on the ankle by a venemous snake. Although every available remedy was tried upon the wound, his limb had to be amputated with the aid of a common handsaw. Fortunately, for him, he had a good, brave wife along who helped and cheered him into health and usefulness" (Haun, 1982:178). Margaret A. Frink found herself alone with a sick husband at a particularly desolate spot along the trail:

> Mr. Frink had been taken sick during the day, and when he got to the foot of the bluffs, he was no longer able to walk, and with difficulty climbed into the wagon. . . . We had to stop in that miserable desert of dust until late the next day. . . . Our boy, Robert, remained with us; but, excepting him, Mr. Frink and I were entirely alone. The situation was a serious one. I was frightened at feeling we were almost helpless, a thousand miles from civilization. (Frink, 1897:62)

Most women, however, did not tend sick relatives by themselves. Accidents, arguments, and illnesses occasionally ruptured parties of travelers, but families made every attempt to travel in the company of others. Of the ninety-six emigrants whose diaries Lillian Schlissel examined, thirty-six crossed the country in extended kinship groups (Schlissel, 1982:153). Thus, although the trip fractured women's ties with women at home, they often created new support networks along the road. "Late in the afternoon a group of women stood watching Mrs. Wilson's little babe as it breathed its last," wrote one female traveler (quoted in Jeffrey, 1979:41).

Women's responsibilities for care typically extended to other members of the train. Mary Stuart Bailey (1980:73) recounted the events of July 17, 1852: "Found Frank Farewell very sick. His brother was taken the night before, mountain fever I suppose. Took them into our tent & took care of them both." Because many female travelers were of childbearing age, and families embarked on the trips even when wives were pregnant, births occurred frequently. Of the 122 families whom John Mack Faragher studied, sixteen included wives who delivered en route (Faragher, 1979:139). Caroline Findley gave this account of assisting at a delivery during a storm: "Within a tent, during the storm, were nurses *wading* around a bedside placed upon chairs ministering to a mother and new born babe" (quoted in Schlissel, 1982:57). Catherine Sager noted that, when her mother became ill after childbirth: "Her babe was cared for by the women of the train. The kindhearted women were also in the habit of coming in when the train stopped at night to wash the dust from her face and other wise make her comfortable" (quoted in Schlissel, 1982:41). Camilla Thomson Donnell (1896:13) cared for an ailing child: "A man of our party named Craig, whose wife died on the trip, was too worn out and weak . . . to care for his small child, who was also very sick. I took charge of the child and floated over the Cascades in an Indian canoe, manned by Indians. The child died about two weeks after this."

Women also stopped to assist strangers they passed along the way. Charlotte Stearns Pengra rode with women from other parties to help a woman afflicted with "camp colic": "I thought her case almost helpless, but after applying numerous remedies we succeeded in relieving her" (quoted in Faragher, 1979:140). Others went on similar missions of mercy. Frances Sawyer noted in her diary, "Tonight we visited an adjoining camp to see a lady and her little daughter who had been turned over in a carriage today while coming down a steep mountain-side" (quoted in Faragher, 1979:138). And Lydia Allen Rudd reported, "I went a few rods to a train this evening to see the sick There was two that were very sick" (Rudd, 1982:191). Merritt Kellogg wrote with pride of his wife's readiness to aid others in times of need, despite her own infirmity:

> [A man] said that this company was ten miles ahead and that with them was a young woman who was about to be confined. He said that she was the only woman in the company. Her husband was a young man, and they had not been married quite a year. . . . He said he had come back in search of a woman to help the young woman in her trouble. [The story] touched my wife's heart and she said, "I am lame, and ought not to go, but that woman needs help." She then slipped on a pair of my trousers under her dress, then mounted the mule man-fashion, and galloped away with the man. (quoted in Farragher, 1979:139–40)

When Helen Carpenter's family passed a train in which a woman had just delivered a premature baby, her mother "at once took the baby and is nursing and caring for it" (Carpenter, 1980:164). Deaths as well as births required women's assistance. "This day closed sadly for us," began an entry in Lucy Ide's diary. A woman traveling in a train of strangers had recently died:

> We advised them to hitch up their teams and come over to us and we would do all we could for them. They did so. She had no lady friend with her, but her friends did all they could and seemed almost heart broken. . . . Lucinda and Mrs. H. Hunter washed and dressed the corpse. She was a nice looking lady, very poor and looked as though she had been sick a long time. I went to her trunks and got out her clothes; she had everything very nice,—had suit after suit of under-clothing, and one suit beautifully made and laid by itself I thought, especially for just this occasion; it so impressed me that I took it. We put it on her, and the men went to town and purchased a coffin, in which she was gently placed. You can scarcely imagine how sad we felt, as we lay camped by the river bank, with this strange lady lying dead, dressed for burial in a covered wagon, a few steps away. Lucinda, Lena and Nellie Egar sat up by the wagon (occasionally wetting her face) all night. (Oliphant, 1927:279–80)

Female solicitude was hardly boundless. Virginia Wilcox Ivins later wrote that, after she gave birth to a child when she and her husband were alone one night, "My husband inquired of the first train that came past for some elderly woman to come in and see me and the somewhat unexpected guest. About ten o'clock a good Samaritan came in, looked at the baby, said a few kind words to me and left me to my fate" (Ivins, 1905:110). After recovering from a brief illness, Rebecca Ketcham complained about receiving inadequate compassion from her friend: "After stopping our tent had to be mended before it could be put up, so I had to sit in the carriage nearly two hours with as hard a headache as I most ever had. Oh, how I thought of Cynthia and her dear Mother! If they had been with me I don't believe I would have sat there all that time without a word of care or sympathy. Camilla is kind but she has her hands full" (Kaiser and Knuth, 1961:338). The exigencies of the trip had far more drastic consequences for some invalids. After riding with another women to attend a woman dying from cholera, Lydia R. Cooke commented, "Did what we could. But the next day, the woman's husband had died and there was no one to stay and care for her. Hated to leave her but . . . [we] went on" (quoted in Schlissel, 1982:114). Mary Stuart Bailey (1980:70) recorded a similar incident: "A company passed us from Cold Water, Michigan. . . . A lady with them was so sick that she could not travel. . . . The ladies left her at Willow Spring to die. Oh how sad."

In some cases, illnesses dissolved the gender division of labor. When Charlotte Pengra suffered from dysentery, her husband took care of her, administering opium, preparing wet bandages, and making "a good bed in the wagon." In turn, when her husband fell ill, she drove the team. She commented in her diary, "I have suffered much pain and feel a good deal reduced but all are sick and I must keep up to the last" (quoted in Schlissel, 1982:98). Another woman recalled: "My husband was taken sick and I had to drive the team. At that time there were nine women who were driving—not well men enough in the company to drive the teams. Well, that was a sad day for me. I had never done anything in that line and was very awkward" (quoted in Myres, 1982:131). At most times, however, gender lines remained intact. Throughout the journey, women remained, in Lillian Schlissel's words, the "ritual caretakers" (Schlissel, 1982:15).

Although women often helped each other care for the sick, they had few other types of assistance. Doctors were few and far between. "Poor Sim, he is very sick," wrote Sarah Raymond Herndon (1902: 236) in her diary. "I do wish we could come across a physician. We have administered simple remedies, but seemingly without effect." One woman later recalled her mother's fears: "I know how worried my mother was when any of us got sick. There were no doctors in the party and we all had to doctor ourselves with the few medicines we brought along and the home remedies we knew about, such as tying a strip of bacon around our necks when we had a sore throat or blowing sulphur down our throats" (quoted in Myres, 1982:129). Some women who nursed relatives also lacked their usual supply of medicine. Mary Stuart Bailey (1980:49), for example, lost a satchel containing all her medicines shortly after embarking on the trip.

In short, the need for care frequently arose during the journey, and it occurred in extremely difficult situations. As Lydia Allen Rudd (1982:192) wrote on the way to Oregon in 1852, "Sickness and death in the states is hard but it is nothing to be compared with it on the plains."

Slave Women

A host of illnesses including dysentery, typhus, diarrhea, rheumatic fever, diphtheria, and whooping cough ravaged slave communities in the American South. Slave quarters were overcrowded and lacked proper sanitation and ventilation; hard physical labor, combined with inadequate, rest, diet, and clothing, heightened vulnerability to disease. In addition, disabilities frequently resulted from accidents and brutal punishments (Jones, 1985; Mintz and Kellogg, 1988; Savitt, 1985). Not surprisingly, slaves had higher rates of mortality than whites; the infants of slaves were twice as likely as white babies to die in the first year of life (Mintz and Kellogg, 1988:73).

Jacqueline Jones (1985:4) observes:

> Throughout American history, the black family has been the focus of a struggle between black women and whites who sought to profit from their labor. . . . To slaveholders and later to white employers, the black family offered a steady and reliable source of new laborers. . . . Yet women's attention to family duties represented a drain on their time and physical resources that might otherwise have been expended in the work force. Slaveholders callously disregarded black familial relationships in order to advance their own financial interests.

Slave women could eke out time to care for their families only when they returned at night, exhausted from work in the fields or big house. Care for sick members of slave owners' families invariably took precedence over care for the slave women's kin. The conditions of the slave quarters, which abetted the spread of disease, also made caregiving a herculean endeavor. A cabin consisted of one room with a dirt floor, no window, cracks in the walls, and a chimney made of clay and twigs. Two or more families frequently shared such cabins, which measured between ten and twenty-one feet square. The great majority of slaves lacked privies and any sanitary means of disposing of garbage (Mintz and Kellogg, 1988:73).

Jones argues that caregiving represented a way in which slave women asserted their autonomy. Because all slaves were viewed as labor power, women promoted their owner's economic interests by tending their own families. But women viewed themselves as struggling to preserve their communities in the face of a system that constantly threatened their survival. The nurturance women provided for their families thus reaffirmed their sense of humanity and afforded them a measure of personal fulfillment (Jones, 1985).

Slaves also resisted owners by relying on their own methods of healing. Owners typically demanded that slaves report any illnesses they or their families experienced; many hired doctors who were responsible for overseeing the health of the slaves. But many slaves preferred their own medical practices over the harsh treatments these doctors employed; some tried to prevent owners from knowing when they or their relatives fell ill (Savitt, 1985).

The few slave women who survived to old age tended to be responsible for caring for sick members of their communities (Mintz and Kellogg, 1988). In turn, by displaying medical knowledge, they gained respect from others. Their remedies drew on both African traditions and local folk beliefs. Sally Brown, an ex-slave, recalled that older slave women taught her to use medicinal herbs, including peachtree leaves for upset stomachs and cow manure flavored with mint for consumption. Brown told an interviewer, "I still believes in them ole ho-made medicines too and I don't believe in so many doctors" (quoted in Fox-Genovese, 1988:169). Other ex-slaves similarly asserted their faith in women's traditional cures. R. S. Taylor, who stated that his mother "looked after most of us when we were sick," concluded, "When my mother got through rubbin' you, you would soon be well." Bob Mobley noted that although his owners employed a doctor to care for sick slaves, "my mother was a kind of doctor too." When other slaves were ill, she would "ride horseback all over the place an' see how they was gettin' along. She'd make a tea out o'herbs for them who had fever an' sometimes she gave them water from slippery elms" (quoted in Fox-Genovese, 1988:171).

It was common for slave women to care for members of an extensive network of kin. Herbert Gutman has demonstrated that a web of mutual obligations bound adults to grandparents, grandchildren, aunts, uncles, nieces, nephews, and siblings. In addition, the concept of "fictive kin" linked unrelated individuals to each other, enhancing communal solidarity (Gutman, 1976).

Ties of reciprocal support continued after emancipation, as large networks of ex-slaves exchanged services and pooled resources. Although broad ties of kinship and community were essential to survival, this family structure earned the contempt of whites, who regarded it as a sign of pathology and used it to blame African-American people for their plight. John DeForest, an agent of the Freedmen's Bureau, denounced African-Americans who cared for "a horde of lazy relatives" and thus forfeited their chance of individual success. He used as an example the case of Aunt Judy, a washerwoman and the mother of small children, who was delinquent in her rent to a white woman but nevertheless had "benevolently taken in, and was nursing, a sick woman of her own race. . . . The thoughtless charity of this penniless Negress in receiving another poverty-stricken creature under her roof was characteristic of the freedmen. However selfish, and even dishonest, they might be, they were extravagant in giving" (quoted in Jones, 1985:66).

The Changing Context of Care

1890–1930

A constellation of factors altered the nature of caregiving between 1890 and 1930. Large corporations began to mass produce goods and services for private households; as electricity, gas, indoor plumbing, ready-made clothing, and store-bought foods reached increasing numbers of families, the individual tasks of caregiving became progressively easier (Strasser, 1982). At the same time, urbanization and geographical mobility weakened the bonds of kinship and community that had sustained women responsible for care (Leavitt, 1986:176). Caregivers who previously might have drawn upon a web of support increasingly found themselves in isolated dyads. The control of infectious diseases both lessened the burdens of care and changed the shape of the dependent population. Such fearsome diseases as cholera, typhoid fever, and smallpox, which had reached epidemic proportions in the nineteenth century, were virtually eliminated by 1930, and other common killers, including tuberculosis, rickets, syphilis, and dysentery, had lost much of their menacing power. In a world less marked by disease and disability, caregiving obligations grew lighter. But responsibilities for care also shifted to the latter part of the life course, as chronic diseases replaced acute ailments as the major cause of death.

During the same period, the gap between family caregivers and physicians widened dramatically. Advances in laboratory science during the second half of the nineteenth century radically altered concepts of disease. "Regular" physicians capitalized on these breakthroughs to assert their dominance over the rest of the medical community (Brown, 1979; Starr, 1982). They first reorganized the American Medical Association by linking it more closely with local and state medical societies; by 1910, over half of all physicians had become members (Larson, 1977:162). This newly reconstituted body then took steps to limit access to the profession. Joining forces with the Carnegie Foundation, it helped to produce the Flexner Report in 1910, calling for a drastic reduction in the number of medical schools (Brown, 1979; Starr, 1982). Within the following decade, the number of schools plunged from 155 to 85 (Numbers, 1985:192).

The metamorphosis of hospitals helped to consolidate the transformation of medicine into a privileged and powerful profession. As Paul Starr (1982:145) writes, hospitals developed "from places of dreaded impurity and exiled human wreckage into awesome citadels of science and bureaucratic order." Although hospitals existed on the periphery of health care throughout much of the nineteenth century, they moved to the center after 1900. A survey conducted in 1909 found 4,359 hospitals with a total of 421,065 beds (Rosenberg, 1987:5).

The biological advances that contributed to the ascendancy of physicians also helped to inaugurate the reign of hospitals. Lister's discoveries in the field of antisepsis revolutionized surgical procedures by the late 1880s; after the turn of the century, surgery replaced custodial care as the central function of hospitals. The development of X rays and clinical laboratories also improved care in hospitals and enhanced their social legitimacy. In turn, as the reputation of hospitals rose, growing numbers of physicians sought to affiliate with them, gain a voice in their governance, and bring patients to fill their beds (Rosenberg, 1987).

It has become almost commonplace to note that the growth of social institutions, such as schools, prisons, and hospitals, removed critical functions from the home. Some evidence suggests, however, that families did not readily relinquish jurisdiction over members who entered hospitals; relatives often expected to follow patients inside and continue to care for them. In 1876, a prize-winning essay by Dr. Gill Wylie warned that hospitals "tend to weaken the family by separating the sick from their relatives, who are often too ready to relieve themselves of the burden of the sick" (quoted in Starr, 1982:151). But a major reason families increasingly abandoned patients at the hospital door was institutional compulsion.

To understand how hospitals disrupted contact between families and patients, it is necessary to return briefly to the 1870s, when hospitals still served a predominantly low-income population. Charles Rosenberg (1987:286–87) describes the life on a typical hospital ward during that decade:

> Patients hoped and expected to find relatives and friends a source of emotional support in strange and threatening surroundings; visitors not only smuggled in forbidden food and drink but milled about in large numbers and with casual disregard for stated visiting hours. On one occasion, the harried Officer of Hygiene reported eleven visitors at a bedside and another day, four men and a dog sitting on a bed.

According to Marilyn Ferris Motz (1983:102), when Winnie Parker entered a hospital in 1897, her sister believed that she had a "right and duty" to accompany the patient into the operating room and was shocked to discover that the physicians would not permit this.

Because hospital administrators viewed themselves as agents of moral uplift, they sought to impose strict discipline on patients and sever their connection to family and friends. This goal was clearly expressed by policies at Children's Hospital in Boston, which stipulated that parents could visit their children only one hour three days a week. As a result, the trustees hoped, the children would be improved by their hospital stay, having been "carefully taught cleanliness of habit, purity of thought and word" (quoted in Vogel, 1980:24–25). Even after the missionary ardor of hospital administrators waned, they remained convinced that the internal order of their facilities demanded strict regulation of visitors. Thus, Massachusetts General surrounded its grounds with a high wall and stationed guards at the gates to carefully screen visitors (Vogel, 1980).

The removal of wealthy families from hospital premises followed a very different path. As a result of the economic depression of the 1890s, many hospitals faced financial crisis. In response, they launched campaigns to attract an increasing proportion of private-pay patients. The centerpiece of these campaigns was the argument that changes in living arrangements prevented families from caring for the sick. Crowded urban apartments, it was claimed, could not provide an adequate setting for the delivery of care. In addition, administrators asserted, health care was best delivered by those who were not emotionally involved (Rosenberg, 1987; Rosner, 1982). One hospital superintendent intoned: "It can be put down as one of the advantages of a hospital that the relatives and friends do not take care of the patient. It is much better for them [patients] not to be under the care of any one who is over-concerned for them" (quoted in Rosner, 1982:78). If Wylie had argued that hospital care would destroy bonds among kin, hospital administrators now asserted that emotional intimacy hindered the delivery of good care.*

At the same time, however, because administrators sought to promote the home-like qualities of their facilities, they advertised their willingness to include family members in the life of their institutions. Extensive visiting hours and special rooms to accommodate relatives

---

*In the 1950s, this view received the stamp of approval of Talcott Pasons and Renée Fox, two sociologists who wrote an article asserting that institutional care prevented the overindulgence of family members in times of sickness (Parsons and Fox, 1952). The contradictions in the arguments about the value of emotional intimacy in care of the sick suggest that most assertions are rationalizations for other purposes. Similarly, today policy analysts with opposing political perspectives clash about the benefits of family care for the disabled elderly.

at night were among the inducements held out to affluent patients (Rosenberg, 1987; Rosner, 1982).

But hospitals failed to fulfill their promises. As administrators sought to impose greater order on hospitals, they subjected all patients to impersonal and rigid routines. In highly bureaucratized institutions, solicitous relatives could have no place. Although private-pay patients continued to enjoy greater freedom than others, their access to family and friends was substantially reduced (Rosenberg, 1987).

Family members not only were expelled from hospitals; they also ceased to control medical decisions. Historians do not fully understand the process by which women lost faith in traditional methods of healing and surrendered authority to physicians; it is clear, however, that the Progressive period was a time when scientific and technological progress in all areas was glorified. The accumulation of bacteriological breakthroughs was particularly dazzling. Although historians now debate the extent to which these advances contributed to the decline in infectious diseases, contemporaries were convinced that the credit belonged to medical science alone. In addition, a broad-based movement for scientific housekeeping encouraged women to disregard the advice of female relatives and friends and turn instead to experts for guidance (Apple, 1987; Rothman, 1978; Strasser, 1982). As noted, hospitals attempted to attract a broader clientele; many pitched their appeals specifically to birthing women. Hospital maternity wards, in turn, helped to educate new mothers about the importance of professional expertise (Leavitt, 1986).

It is not surprising that immigrants tended to remain more skeptical than middle-class Americans about the efficacy of scientific medicine. At the turn of the century, between one-third and one-half of the residents of major East Coast cities were immigrants (Kessler-Harris, 1982:121). Living in squalid and overcrowded tenements and working in dangerous occupations, they continued to experience high rates of morbidity and mortality (Ewen, 1985). Distrust of health care institutions was common in many immigrant communities. Rose Cohen (1918:233), a Jewish immigrant in New York City, later remembered her family's reaction to the suggestion that she enter a hospital:

> It was not an easy thing for my people to send me to the hospital. For the very word filled us with fear. How could a helpless sick person be trusted to strangers! Besides, it was quite understood that in the hospital patients were practised upon by hardened medical students and then neglected. . . . We saw our neighbours all about us borrow and pawn but keep their sick at home.

The harsh treatment immigrants received in dispensaries and hospitals served to heighten fears (Rosenberg, 1974, 1987; Starr, 1982). Most immigrants also lacked the resources to pay health care providers. Recalling that a physician came to the home to treat her younger sister, Kate Simon, another Jewish immigrant, commented, "It must have been an affluent time to afford doctors' visits" (Simon, 1982:78). Notwithstanding the increased prominence of hospital care during this period, even patients suffering from such serious diseases as typhoid fever and tuberculosis remained at home. And, despite the increased medical management of illness, immigrant women relied heavily on folk remedies and treatments (Ewen, 1985:141). One Jewish woman later recalled the treatments her mother employed: "My mother had me urinate and rubbed it on my forehead and my fever subsided. Another time I had fever so my mother ripped the top of my ear and let the blood flow and the fever subsided too" (quoted in Ewen, 1985:141).

Because immigrants did not immediately seize the new medicine, they were the object of various public health reforms. Officials sought to impose change on immigrant communities through such measures as school medical inspections and compulsory vaccination programs (Baker, 1980; Cornell, 1912; Reese, 1986). In many cities, these programs met widespread resistance. When authorities in Milwaukee attempted to vaccinate German and Polish immigrants and remove sick children to the hospital during the smallpox epidemic of 1894, mothers rioted (Leavitt, 1982). A riot also erupted in a Jewish neighborhood in New York City in 1906, when physicians removed adenoids from school children (Baker, 1980:140–42; Ewen, 1985; Reese, 1986).

Nevertheless, many immigrants did accept the precepts of scientific medicine. Some were desperate to find new ways to prevent the illnesses that devastated their families. In unfamiliar environments, old methods of cure no longer seemed reliable. Some families also suffered from diseases that were uncommon in the communities they had left. If many physicians and social workers viewed the immigrants with hostility and suspicion and denigrated traditional community values, others exhibited genuine concern about the well-being of their clients; as a result, many immigrants were willing to believe that they held out the promise of better health. As immigrant communities became less cohesive, women found it more difficult to rely on a network of neighbors. And the process of assimilation weakened attachment to traditional practices (Ewen, 1985).

In short, the emergence of a powerful health-care industry meant that the great majority of women gradually delivered care under the supervision of scientifically trained experts. Although women gained greater confidence in the ability of formal providers to cure sick family members, they lost the sense of mastery they previously had enjoyed. In addition, as a result of the new understanding of disease processes, family caregiving was stripped of its medical significance. Once researchers had identified the pathological organisms that caused specific ailments, technical expertise eclipsed personalized care. The new reductionism rendered irrelevant the moral state of the individual, the quality of the interaction between patient and provider, and the nature of a patient's physical surroundings—aspects of healing in which family members had specialized (Rosenberg, 1987).

1930–Present

Although caregiving underwent the most radical transformation between 1890 and 1930, more recent developments also have left their mark. This section will briefly outline some of these changes. As life expectancy has continued to grow and fertility to drop, there has been a shift in the composition of the dependent population. The elderly, who were 8 percent of the total population in 1950, increased to 12 percent in 1984 (Siegel and Taeuber, 1986:77). The rate of increase of the very old, who are at the highest risk of illness and disability, has been particularly dramatic. The number of those 85 and over rose 154 percent between 1940 and 1960 and another 142 percent between 1960 and 1980 (Rosenwaike, 1985:189).

Because caregiving increasingly is focused on the frail elderly, changes in the material condition of older people constitute an important part of the history of family care. The establishment of publicly funded income maintenance programs and private retirement plans has altered the relationship between adult children and their parents. Although Title I of the 1935 Social Security Act (the Old Age Assistance Program) was predicated on the assumption that children have an obligation to support their parents financially, Title II (the Old Age and Survivors Insurance Program) calculated benefits without regard to the income level of adult children. Moreover, after the 1930s, family assistance for the elderly gradually dwindled. By 1976, just 1 percent of the elderly received any income from personal contributions, whether from their families or others (Crystal, 1982:52). Thus, although the responsibility to care for the elderly has continued to rest with adult children, the financial burden has been lifted from them.

The increasing economic independence of the aged also has enabled them to live apart from their children. The proportion of people 65 and over sharing households with adult children was 60 percent in 1900, 40 percent in 1960, and just 22 percent in 1984 (Congressional Budget Office, 1988:xi; Smith, 1986:95). We saw in the introduction that family members continue to provide extensive help to disabled elderly people living by themselves. Nevertheless, caregivers who live separately from the recipient provide fewer services than those who share homes (Soldo and Myllyluoma, 1983).

The growth of the service sector also has had a major impact on family caregiving. The nursing home industry emerged after World War II and expanded rapidly after the passage of Medicare and Medicaid in 1965 (Vladeck, 1980). Although only a fraction of frail elderly persons reside in such facilities, they represent an important alternative to family care. Board and care homes, other congregate living arrangements, and home health care services also have helped to remove responsibilities from private households.

The continued expansion of acute-care institutions has had a similar effect. By the mid-1930s, hospitalization had become routine for a broad range of afflictions, and over a quarter of all deaths occurred in hospital settings (Stevens, 1989:172–73). Two subsequent developments helped to ensure the dominance of hospitals in health-care delivery. First, the growth of hospital insurance plans made these facilities accessible to the middle class. Although the poor remained unprotected against the cost of hospital care until the establishment of Medicaid in 1965, the clientele of most institutions both grew and diversified. Second, the Hill-Burton Act of 1946 provided for a vast infusion of federal funds into hospital construction. Between 1947 and 1971, the program distributed a total of $3.7 billion (Starr, 1982: 350). Within the first six years after the passage of the Hill-Burton Act, admissions to hospitals jumped 26 percent (Stevens, 1989:220).

Nevertheless, the movement of care between the home and medical institutions has not been unidirectional. If the expansion of nursing homes and hospitals transferred care from private households to the public arena, a combination of economic and humanitarian factors oppose this trend. By shifting responsibility for care back to families, policymakers can respond simultaneously to demands for reduced public spending and to the widespread disenchantment with technologized and impersonal medical care (see Zola, 1988).

We saw in Chapter 2 that policies increasingly seek to keep the elderly out of nursing homes. By 1989, thirty states had instituted preadmission screening programs, which determine the extent to which nursing home placement is appropriate before people gain admission (Special Committee on Aging, 1989:245). Other methods of reducing the nursing home population include certificate-of-need programs, the expansion of home health services, and prospective reimbursement programs under Medicaid for nursing homes (Special Committee on Aging, 1989:245; Swan and Harrington, 1986).*

The deinstitutionalization of mental patients began even earlier. After the discovery and introduction of antipsychotic drugs, the total patient population of the nation's mental hospitals plunged from 559,000 in 1955 to 193,000 in 1975 (Starr, 1982:365). A 1978 study reported that two-thirds of discharged patients returned home to receive care from their families (Minkoff, 1978; see Goldman, 1982). One observer notes: "Over a period of nearly 3 decades of deinstitutionalization, mental health professions were . . . oblivious to what it might mean for families to replace the ward staff without the training and resources ordinarily available in the hospital" (Hatfield, 1987:8).

Family members rarely receive the assistance they want. One of the major advocates of managing the mentally ill outside hospitals was President Kennedy, who called for a "bold new approach" based on establishment of a vast network of community mental-health centers. Adequate funding never was forthcoming. Fewer than half the mental-health centers required to serve deinstitutionalized patients were built; those that were typically fail to provide the full range of services originally envisaged (Starr, 1982:365). Other services are equally scanty. Relatives often search unsuccessfully for adequate halfway houses and day hospital programs and for such nonmedical services as rehabilitation programs in housing and employment (Vine, 1982).

Acute medical care also is undergoing deinstitutionalization. As a result of the creation of outpatient surgical facilities and the enormous expansion of home health care, an increasing number of patients receive treatment outside hospitals. Moreover, in 1983, the federal government introduced a prospective payment system under Medicare to reduce the high cost of hospital care. The average length of a hospital stay dropped from 9.5 days in August 1983 to 7.5 days in

---

*The extent of institutionalization of course is a function not only of government policies but of the preferences of disabled elderly people and their families. Many frail elderly people are strongly motivated to stay out of nursing homes. Chapter 8 will demonstrate that many daughters do not want even to contemplate residential placement for their parents.

August 1984 (Stevens, 1989:326). In 1984, it was estimated that between 3 and 4 million days of care had shifted from hospitals to the community and home (Estes and Arendell, 1986). Although many patients released from hospitals early receive home care services, home health agencies cannot accommodate the growing demand for their services. Family members make up the difference (Sankar et al., 1986).

The prospective payment system also has meant that family members must render more care to hospitalized patients. Some hospitals have responded to greater fiscal constraints by reducing nursing staff (Glazer, 1988; Sacks, 1990). At the same time, early discharge has contributed to a rise in the level of patient acuity. Because patients are sicker and staffing levels lower, nurses have increased workloads. Many find that they no longer are able to respond to the social needs of patients (Glazer, 1988:133–34). From a longitudinal study of a large suburban hospital in Minnesota, Lucy Rose Fischer and Nancy N. Eustis (1988) reported that more family caregivers in 1986 than in 1982 complained that the staff failed to perform such activities as answering call bells, assisting patients to get to the bathroom on time, and helping them to eat. As nurses withdraw social support services, the participation of family members becomes crucial. Thus, although hospitals sought to expel family members at the turn of the century, some now encourage their involvement in patient care.

If family caregivers must provide more personalized care in hospitals, they also must furnish more medical services in the domestic domain. Because patients are discharged earlier than they were before the establishment of the new payment system, they tend to be sicker when they arrive home. It is not uncommon for patients to leave the hospital when they still are in a sub-acute stage. Family members must exercise discretion previously the exclusive province of registered nurses, determining when pain or bleeding from a wound is serious enough to warrant immediate medical care (Glazer, 1988). Families also are responsible for managing advanced technology. Just as the deinstitutionalization of mental patients depended on the discovery of psychotropic drugs, so early discharge from the hospital followed the development of sophisticated technology for the home. A recent article in the *New England Journal of Medicine* reports: "Techniques previously used only in institutions have been adapted for use at home. Intravenous lines, both central and peripheral, for the administration of parenteral nutrition, chemotherapy, antibiotics, narcotics, and occasionally, cardiac pressor agents have become commonplace in home care" (Koren, 1986:917). Some relatives of the frail elderly are responsible for care that not even licensed vocational nurses are permitted to administer in hospitals (Estes and Arendell, 1986). Although family caregivers lost confidence in their medical skills and judgment at the turn of the century, they increasingly are compelled to acquire highly specialized medical knowledge.

In reimposing care for the sick and disabled on private households, policymakers are not simply returning to nineteenth-century methods of caregiving. For one thing, the content of medical care has changed. Until the rise of scientific medicine at the end of the nineteenth century, family members relied on traditional methods of healing, which they learned from each other and which permitted them to maintain distance from the authority of physicians. Today, caregivers increasingly are responsible for complex technological procedures that they can perform only under strict medical supervision.

The conditions of women's lives also have changed. In 1900, the 5 million women workers were just 20 percent of the adult female population. By 1985, the 48.5 million women workers constituted 53 percent of all adult women (Bianchi and Spain, 1986:141–42). Many women thus are not available to tend sick relatives around the clock. Moreover, a large proportion of female workers have entered caring occupations, where they provide the same services to strangers that women previously rendered only to neighbors and kin. Workers who continually meet the needs of others on the job may feel especially overwhelmed when expected to fulfill caregiving obligations in the home.

The steep rise in the divorce rate also has affected women's ability to care for sick and disabled people. Increasing numbers of women are single heads of household who must work full-time to support themselves and their children. Women with very onerous responsibilities at home and at work often have little time and energy to respond to the needs of others.

Conclusion

Because caregivers deal with fundamental aspects of human existence—birth, pain, infirmity, and death—we might expect their experiences to remain constant over time. However, a complex series of historical changes have profoundly altered the content and meaning of care. Policymakers who tout the superiority of family care and seek to return care to the home cling to a romantic vision of a world that has ceased to exist.

The past hundred years have seen both losses and gains. The

dispersion of household appliances and the emergence of a formal system of health-care delivery have altered the nature of caregiving. Almost no women still carry tubs of water inside in order to bathe patients or care for very sick family members without the help of doctors and hospitals. But the developments that have lightened caring work also have undermined women's traditional skills. Moreover, time spent shopping for household goods and arranging for medical services has partially replaced the time previously devoted to home production and direct patient care. Because women increasingly work for pay, they have growing economic independence. Consequently, more women can exercise at least some control over the amount and type of caregiving responsibilities they assume. But women who hold paid jobs can less easily fit care for dependent relatives into their lives. As a result of the loosening of the bonds of kinship and community, women are less likely to feel responsible for ensuring the well-being of an extensive network of relatives, neighbors, and friends. When women do care for the sick, however, they frequently cannot rely on community structures of support.

Historical analysis also reveals the legacy of the nineteenth century. Although the context of care has been transformed and the cult of domesticity no longer governs gender relations, we still allocate caregiving responsibilities inequitably between men and women and assume that there is a necessary connection between caregiving and self-abnegation. Caregiving thus continues to disrupt women's lives and restrict their participation in the public arena.

But caregiving in the late twentieth century also has a number of distinctive features. Caregivers are far more likely than ever before to tend elderly persons suffering from chronic conditions rather than children with acute illnesses. Caregiving also has become an extremely lonely endeavor. As Hilary Graham writes, caring in our society "is something women do as an expression of their connectedness with others, yet it is something they invariably do alone" (Graham, 1983:26). If most caregivers lack a support network, however, they interact regularly with the formal health and social service system. Brokering the services rendered by paid providers increasingly dominates caregiving work. Finally, women responsible for care at home frequently hold waged jobs. It is critical that policymakers base their recommendations for change on an understanding of the reality of contemporary caregiving rather than on nostalgia for a mythical past.

4

Methods of Studying Caregiving

A Critique of the Literature

The literature on informal care of the frail elderly has grown dramatically during the past decade. As recently as 1980, all but a tiny fraction of investigators ignored this topic; however, research reports have become common in the annual meetings of such associations as the Gerontological Society of America. Leading professional journals frequently include articles on family caregiving.

As a result, we now have a wealth of studies documenting the magnitude of informal caregiving and the nature of the problems experienced by family members who deliver care. We know that long-term care in the United States rests on a vast network of informal providers and frequently imposes numerous costs on family members. But this literature remains incomplete. Most studies are based on structured interviews, which are analyzed statistically, and they focus on two issues that lend themselves to quantification—the chores caregivers perform and the stress they experience. Both are important; but if we continue to restrict our scrutiny to these topics, we will miss essential aspects of the caregiving experience. Moreover, the current preoccupation with caregiver stress restricts the range of policy recommendations.

Researchers frequently conceptualize caregiving behavior in terms of specific tasks. For example, the Health Care Financing Administration 1982 Long-Term Care Survey divides caregiving into personal care tasks (including hygiene and mobility), administration of medication, household tasks, shopping and transportation, and handling of finance (Stone, Cafferata, and Sangl, 1987). Although some researchers establish slightly different categories, most use a task-based definition of caregiving (see Horowitz, 1985a).

This approach makes good sense. Gerontologists typically consider people to need care if they have functional limitations that prevent them from conducting activities of daily living (including bathing, eating, dressing, and walking) and what are called instrumental activities of daily living (such as doing housework, preparing meals, going shopping, managing money, taking medicine, and using the telephone). Almost by definition, then, caregivers are relatives and friends who help impaired persons with such tasks. This approach also illuminates the importance of endeavors previously dismissed as routine domestic activities. By analyzing the chores caregivers perform, researchers have demonstrated that informal caregiving is labor-intensive. Family members shop for elderly persons, dress them, cook their meals, help them in and out of bed, and administer their medications. Viewing caregiving in this way has made it easier to recognize that informal care is socially necessary work and has an important place in the long-term care system. The gerontological literature thus inadvertently contributes to the feminist project of revaluing women's work at home. Some researchers have been able to attach a price to informal caregiving by calculating the market value of the particular tasks family members perform. According to one study, the annual cost of replacing the services now provided informally in the United States would be $9.6 billion (Paringer, 1983).

The division of care into specific tasks also enables us to compare the intensity of work caregivers perform. It clearly is important to stress the difference between relatives who run occasional errands for the elderly and those who provide round-the-clock care for bedridden persons. In addition, a task-oriented approach has provided a framework for differentiating various subgroups of caregivers. Studies have found, for example, that neighbors and friends undertake far fewer tasks than family members (Horowitz, 1985a). As the introduction noted, spouses are more likely than adult children to assume responsibility for intimate personal care, and daughters are more likely than sons to perform chores that keep them constantly on call. Not surprisingly, the level of material resources available to caregivers also influences the allocation of tasks. One researcher found that adult daughters who lack access to formal services are more likely to provide direct, hands-on care themselves. Daughters who are able to purchase outside help tend to relinquish the tasks they find especially difficult (Archbold, 1983).

If the focus on specific tasks has many merits, however, it also limits our understanding of the endeavors of caregivers (Hasselkus,

1988).* The chores family and friends perform do not exist in a vacuum; rather, they are embedded in intimate personal relationships. A British sociologist argues that concentration on tasks may blind us to what is most distinctive about this activity:

> Stripped of the emotional bonds which encompass it, caring becomes redefined as 'tending,' 'the actual work of looking after those who, temporarily or permanently, cannot do so for themselves.' . . . But caring is more than this: a kind of domestic labour performed on people. It can't be 'cleaned up' into such categories without draining the relationship between carer and cared-for of the dimension we most need to confront. Caring cannot be understood objectively and abstractly, but only as a subjective experience in which we are all, for better or worse, involved. (Graham, 1983:27–28)

Task-oriented research may be particularly inappropriate for an activity dominated by women. It has become almost a truism to note that men and women experience personal relationships very differently. Men are more likely than women to take an instrumental approach toward their children and grandchildren, reducing caregiving to a series of specific activities and remaining somewhat distant and detached. Women are more apt to emphasize the relational aspects of care—to feel submerged in caregiving, experience emotional closeness and connectedness with the recipient of care, and express empathy (Cherlin and Furstenberg, 1986; Rossi, 1985). There is some evidence that these generalizations apply to caring for elderly relatives. A few researchers report that women are less likely to establish limits and more likely to assume responsibility for improving the overall quality of the lives of the elderly (George and Gwyther, 1986; Miller, 1990; Robinson and Thurnher, 1979; Zarit, Todd, and Zarit, 1986). As mentioned in the introduction, adult daughters are more likely than sons to undertake personal care tasks, which require attentiveness to individual needs.

If we were to extend our focus beyond specific tasks, we might ask how various types of relationships affect not only the allocation of specific chores but also the nature of the care that is rendered. According to one of the few studies employing in-depth, qualitative interviews, wives caring for husbands with dementia find it especially

---

*Irving Kenneth Zola (1988) has criticized functional assessment tools from the point of view of disabled people. These tools focus exclusively on the performance of concrete tasks, which can be easily measured. As a result, the tools tell us little about the quality of life disabled people actually experience.

difficult to assert control because they are accustomed to defer to their husbands' authority (Miller, 1990). A British researcher using qualitative methods found that adult daughters often are particularly overwhelmed by the emotional aspects of care and can continue to render services only by ignoring the intense feelings aroused (Ungerson, 1987).

If we learn only that a woman prepares meals for her mother, we know very little about her work as a caregiver. Is she assuming this task despite her mother's objections? Is she trying to please her mother? Is she cooking in order to avoid talking with her mother? Whose kitchen is she using? Is anyone else around? Is she cooking for herself and other members of her family at the same time? Is she following her mother's instructions? Those of a physician? Answers to such questions would dramatically enlarge our understanding of the experience of caregiving.

The major focus of researchers, however, is to analyze the impact of caregiving on family members rather than to describe caregiver behavior. Various studies have found that caregivers experience a range of physical, emotional, social, and financial problems. In many cases, caregiving responsibilities reignite family conflicts, impose financial strains, and encroach on both paid employment and leisure activities (Brody, 1981; Cantor, 1983; Horowitz, 1985a; Horowitz and Dobrof, 1982; Lang and Brody, 1983; Montgomery, Gonyea and Hooyman, 1983; Pearlin, Turner, and Semple, 1989; Robinson and Thurnher, 1979; Scharlach and Boyd, 1989; Stephens and Christianson, 1986; Stone, Cafferata, and Sangl, 1987; Travelers Companies, 1985).* Researchers repeatedly report that caregivers experience stress because they perceive their responsibilities to be burdensome. Numerous studies also examine the mental and physical health outcomes of stress. Some rely on self reports of symptoms of mental health problems, others on clinical assessments of caregivers (see Schulz, 1990:40). Both types of studies find that caregiving increases the incidence of psychiatric disorders, such as depression (Fiore et al., 1983; Haley et al., 1987; Gallagher et al., 1989; see Schulz, 1990; see Tennstedt and McKinlay, 1989). Two researchers compared caregivers of memory-impaired adults with age peers unburdened by such obligations and concluded that the caregivers also are very likely to use psychotropic drugs (George and Gwyther, 1986). Although the evi-

---

*Most studies focus on caregivers of elderly persons suffering from Alzheimer's Disease and related disorders.

dence about the impact of caregiving on physical health is far more fragmentary, a few studies do suggest that caregiver stress can create physical problems (see Koin, 1989; see Schulz, 1990; see Tennstedt and McKinlay, 1989).

Because stress has critical implications for public health, researchers have attempted to identify caregivers most at risk. They have correlated caregiver strain with factors such as the recipient's impairment; the level of support available to caregivers; the amount of care they deliver; the quality of the relationship between caregiver and recipient; and various caregiver characteristics, such as age, gender, race and ethnicity, marital status, employment status, and income (Braithwaite, 1990; see Horowitz, 1985a; see Ory et al., 1985). Researchers also have evaluated interventions. Investigators have assessed the reduction of stress associated with a variety of programs, including respite care, counseling services, caregiver support groups, educational and training programs, and assorted in-home supportive services (Burdz, Eaton, and Bond, 1988; Greene and Monahan, 1989; Haley et al., 1987; Lawton, Brody, and Saperstein, 1989; Montgomery and Borgatta, 1985; Scharlach and Frenzel, 1986; Toseland, Rossiter, and Labrecque, 1989; Zarit et al., 1987; see Gallagher, 1985; see Kane and Kane, 1987: 175–84). Finally, studies have examined the extent to which individual coping strategies and social support moderate the effects of stress on caregivers (Morycz, 1985; Pearlin, Turner, and Semple, 1989; Zarit et al., 1980). These various types of studies have provided useful information for practitioners.

Nevertheless, many studies of stress have serious deficiencies. Those seeking to correlate stress with various aspects of caregiving suffer from the shortcomings common to positivist social science. To establish connections between two variables, it is necessary to abstract these variables from the context that gives them meaning. I have noted the importance of examining the complex web of relationships within which caregiving is embedded. In many studies, however, relational aspects of care are considered part of the background researchers seek to control (often unsuccessfully). Thus, even researchers who wish to explore the subjective responses of family members may fail to capture the emotional dynamics of caregiving.

To engage in quantitative analysis, researchers often construct simplistic measures of complex phenomena that cannot easily be scaled. For example, some studies seek to measure the quality of the relationship between caregiver and recipient. A recent study of the role stress experienced by middle-aged daughters caring for elderly mothers assessed relationship quality by means of a scale including questions such as the following: "How well do you and your mother get along together?" "How much do you enjoy your visits together?" and "How satisfied are you with your relationship?" (Scharlach, 1987:628–29). It hardly bears repeating that the mother/daughter relationship frequently is characterized by deep ambivalence (Chodorow, 1978). Women may find such questions meaningless or provide very different responses at different points in time.

Studies investigating the relationship between social support and caregiver stress are equally problematic. Although some researchers have concluded that social support helps to shield caregivers from stress, they fail to provide an adequate conceptualization of social support. Richard K. Morycz (1985) defines social support as caregivers' perception that they can rely on others to provide backup help. This definition, however, ignores several critical dimensions of social support (see Chapter 9). Steven H. Zarit and colleagues measured social support by assessing the frequency of household visits by other relatives and friends (Zarit et al., 1980). But numerous researchers have faulted studies that rely on the quantity rather than the quality of personal interactions (see Rook, 1984). In a study based on participant observation of and focused interviews with a support group of caregivers of Alzheimer's patients, Jaber F. Gubrium found that caregivers occasionally viewed visits by other relatives as intrusive rather than helpful. If some subjects bemoaned the absence of friends and family to share their responsibilities, others complained that contact with other family members exacerbated their stress (Gubrium, 1988).

Studies of the mental and physical health status of caregivers have still other disadvantages. Although they are useful for demonstrating that responsibilities for care of the elderly can expose family members to serious risks, these studies impose a medical model on caregiving. Critics of medicalization argue that whenever the problems of a group (such as women or aged people) are defined in clinical terms, we tend to ignore the social and economic forces that create these problems and focus narrowly on medical solutions (Estes and Binney, 1989; Riessman, 1989). It will be seen that some of the most popular proposals for ameliorating the lot of caregivers involve medical management and treatment.*

---

*One group of researchers argues that the high prevalence of depression among caregivers should not cause serious concern because depression is a problem that can be cured. The interventions they mention include cognitive/behavioral therapies, antidepressant medication, psychotherapy, and caregiver support groups (Gallagher et al., 1989:231).

The focus on stress also seriously restricts our understanding of the experience of caring for a disabled elderly person. Because studies assume that hardships are converted automatically into strain, they ignore a range of other possible responses. Thus, researchers have correlated stress with the degree of intimacy between caregiver and elderly relative (Cantor, 1983; see Miller, 1989), but none has examined whether a strong sense of affiliation and attachment simultaneously imbues caregiving with meaning and purpose. One unusual qualitative study of the members of a caregivers' support group found that caregiving not only imposed burdens but also offered a sense of worth and accomplishment:

> Support group proceedings showed that at least two images of the personal side of the caregiving experience underpinned participants' offerings and exchanges. One image was the version that informs existing studies of the burden of care. . . . Another image was strikingly different. In this version, what the patient presented was not so much a burden but a challenge, for some, part of the wider range of lesser or greater challenges of human experience. As such, the orientation to the challenge was not one of personal tribulation but of successful confrontation and eventual triumph. Caregiving was something to behold, to be proud of, a sign of effective human stewardship. (Gubrium and Lynott, 1987:279)

Although other researchers occasionally note that caregiving can be gratifying as well as stressful (see Subcommittee on Human Services, 1987; see Horowitz, 1985a), very few examine in depth the rewards to caregivers (Motenko, 1989; Miller, 1989). Nor do studies explore aspects of the caregiving experience that cannot fit neatly into a cost-benefit calculus.

If we expand our inquiry beyond stress we may fall into the trap of romanticizing family caregiving. Furthermore, by emphasizing the rewards of caregiving, we may imply that family and friends can manage on their own and might even be able to shoulder additional caregiving responsibilities. But discussions of stress do not necessarily lead to the conclusion that caregivers need greater assistance. I hope to show that evidence of caregiving strain has been used to advance the goal of reprivatization, not only to advocate relief for caregivers. By deepening our understanding of the experience of caregivers, we may be able to respond more appropriately to their needs.

Although stress research has a number of practical applications, it also may limit the range of policies discussed. I noted that researchers have evaluated various programs in terms of their potential for reducing stress. Proposals calling for a broader social transformation, however, cannot be assessed in this way. As long as we concentrate on proposals that are amenable to conventional evaluation, we will continue to disregard structural reforms.

The emphasis on stress narrows policy concerns in other ways as well. Although stress often results from social structures (see Pearlin, 1989), it is a property of individuals. Consequently, most remedies focus exclusively on personal change (Young, 1980). Stress management techniques, for example, seek to help individuals cope better with adverse situations. As noted, education and counseling programs geared toward increasing adaptive capabilities of family and friends dominate the policy agenda. Even such remedies as respite care and supportive services, which seek to alter the context within which care is delivered, tend to focus on individuals. The overriding issue is not how to relieve stress but how to organize society to make care for the dependent population more just and humane.

In addition, because evaluators typically view interventions primarily as stress-reduction mechanisms, they ignore other benefits these programs may provide. Some studies, for example, suggest that training and education programs and family support groups have little impact on the level of caregiver stress (Haley et al., 1987; Zarit et al., 1987). Yet these programs nevertheless may be useful because they increase the effectiveness of caregivers and help them to deliver better care (see Haley et al., 1987). One observer recently argued that, because studies consistently find that home care services do not reduce stress, public expenditures on these services no longer can be justified (Callahan, 1989). But it is not surprising that these services have little impact on the level of caregiver stress; as numerous researchers report, the stress of caregivers varies primarily with their emotional response to caregiving and their relationship to the recipient rather than with the amount of care they render or the disruption in their lives (Braithwaite, 1990; Gwyther and George, 1986). Home care services have no direct impact on the subjective or relational aspects of caregiving. Nevertheless, services *can* enable caregivers to remain in the labor force, engage in leisure activities, and retain links to friends (see Chapter 8). The critical question for evaluators is not whether various programs make caregivers feel better about themselves but whether the programs can improve the quality of caregivers' lives and minimize the sacrifices caregiving requires. By using stress reduction as the only outcome measure, we reinforce the belief that our main concern should be to help caregivers adjust to their unavoidable burdens.

The focus on stress also deflects attention from the way particular groups are disadvantaged by our insistence that caregiving is an individual, rather than a social, responsibility. For example, although researchers have asked how the conflict between waged work and caring for elderly relatives engenders stress (e.g., Scharlach, 1987), they often fail to consider how this clash heightens the subordination of women as a group. As discussed in the introduction, daughters are more likely than sons to quit paid employment in order to provide care. More daughters than sons also reduce their work hours, re-arrange their schedules, and take time off without pay (Stone, Cafferata, and Sangl, 1987). Like child-rearing obligations, women's responsibilities for the care of the elderly may reinforce the notion that they are intermittent workers and thus serve as a rationale for employment practices that maintain their lower pay and status.

In addition, we should note that some stress is inherent in caregiving. Above I criticized researchers who view mental-health problems as inevitable outcomes of caring and fail to recognize how social and political forces contribute to these problems. Nevertheless, even if we alter the context of caregiving, some stress may be unavoidable. Conflicts between the needs of caregivers and those of the elderly they tend commonly engender stress. Caregivers must confront their own fears of disease, disability, and death. When the elderly suffer mental impairments, family members may engage in anticipatory mourning. Adult children must forge new relationships with the parents they tend. Then, too, caregivers frequently are assisting someone with overwhelming needs that can never be met. And stress can result from the effort to individualize care. From a qualitative, in-depth study of spousal caregivers of elderly persons with dementia, Miller found that wives were more vulnerable to stress than husbands because they were more concerned about treating their spouses with dignity and more willing to respond to their changing needs (Miller, 1990). Certainly it is critical to provide services that can help to reduce some of the stress caregiving engenders; however, because the experience of providing care touches some of our deepest emotions, the eradication of stress never should be our primary policy objective.

Finally, it is important to challenge the instrumentalist view, which underlies much research on caregiving. Some policy analysts do use evidence of caregiver stress to caution against imposing additional burdens on individual households. Taking the needs of caregivers as the starting point, they urge that the government acknowledge greater responsibility to care for its elderly citizens. Many other policymakers, however, argue that we should encourage increased caregiving by families. Pointing to studies that report that the timing of nursing home placement is related more to the intensification of caregiver stress than to changes in the condition of the care recipient (see Horowitz, 1985a:199), this group also seeks to alleviate the stress of family members. But they do so to prolong family caregiving, not to promote the well-being of caregivers as an end in itself.

A report by consultants to the Health Care Financing Administration in 1980 illustrates the prevailing perspective. The report declares: "There must be caution not to widen too broadly the use of funds for home care purposes other than those related to cost containment." Assuming that families have primary responsibility for the delivery of care, the authors recommend the provision of just enough publicly funded services to encourage households to keep elderly relatives at home. Access, they insist, should be limited to persons "at imminent risk of institutional care." Determination of need should rest not with relatives of care recipients but rather with professionals, who are uniquely equipped to assess the level of disability and the amount of informal care family members "can reasonably and fairly be expected to give" (Callahan et al., 1980).

As numerous observers have noted, positivist social science tends to view human beings as objects rather than active agents; therefore, it is particularly conducive to a policy science based on technical control (Fay, 1975; Habermas, 1971; Stacey and Thorne, 1985). I argue that we should attempt to understand the experience of caregivers and help to articulate their concerns, rather than seek to manipulate family members in pursuit of "economic efficiency." This project would require us to investigate areas too often dismissed as "soft," employing qualitative as well as quantitative methodologies and incorporating the theoretical insights of a wide range of disciplines.

Feminist Analysis

The following chapters are based on my study of women caring for frail elderly parents. In conducting this study, I was concerned with several issues that feminist scholars have raised but that tend to be absent from research on caregiving. One is mother-daughter relationships. I have noted that women constitute over three-quarters of adult children providing care. In addition, the elderly population is predominantly female. In the group 65 to 69 years old, there are five women for every four men. In the group 85 and over, there are five women for every two men. Moreover, elderly women are far more likely than elderly men to be indigent, living alone, and in poor health, and thus to require assistance from their children (Rix, 1984). As a result, when we speak about parent care, we often are referring to daughters caring for mothers. To what extent are recent writings about mother/daughter relationships relevant for understanding the experiences of daughters who render care? Do adult daughters providing care revive old patterns of behavior, or do they establish new ways of relating to their mothers? How does the experience of caring for mothers differ from that of caring for fathers?

Feminist writers also have called into question the conventional opposition between public and private. They note first that political and economic forces affect even the most intimate relationships at home; as we saw in Chapter 2, public policies shape the nature of family care. Second, feminists challenge the notion of the domestic domain as a refuge from the public world. Highlighting the tensions within individual households, they point out that personal relationships in the private arena are not invariably governed by warmth, concern, and affection (see Thorne, 1982). While some policy analysts exhort us to return care to the home in order to strengthen intimate ties, feminists argue that the intensity of family relations can create conflicts and even violence. To what extent can caregiving be construed as a labor of love? Is it possible that strong bonds between adult daughters and aging parents hinder as well as foster the delivery of good care?

In addition, feminists have called attention to class and race divisions among women. I have pointed out that deficiencies in long-term care services have the most profound impact on poor women and those who belong to ethnic and racial minorities. It also is important to note that privileged women who "buy out" of their caregiving responsibilities frequently do so by hiring low-income and minority women. Several researchers have analyzed the complex and often exploitative relationships between female employers and domestic servants (Colen, 1986; Dill, 1988; Glenn, 1986; Palmer, 1988; Rollins, 1985; Romero, 1988). To what extent do caregivers view the aides and attendants who tend their parents any differently from other household workers? Are they willing to treat aides and attendants with the same respect they expect these workers to accord to the frail elderly?

The relationship between women and professional expertise is another topic of feminist scholarship. The previous chapter argued that, as a result of biological breakthroughs at the turn of the century, physicians were able to undermine folk methods of healing. Numerous observers contend that professionals attempted to impose even broader authority during the Progressive period. Imparting advice about proper child-rearing methods, they devalued and dismissed women's experiental knowledge as mothers (Ehrenreich and English, 1978; Lasch, 1977). The direction of expert advice has followed the changing contours of women's caregiving responsibilities. As care for the aging gains a major place in women's lives, a new enterprise has been created, devoted to counseling and educating relatives of the frail elderly. But some feminist analysts challenge the relevance of all expert advice to caregivers. They argue that caregivers employ a distinctive pattern of thought, which differs sharply from scientific rationality. Rather than learning through instruction, they apply knowledge gained through example and intimate understanding of a particular individual (Ruddick, 1982; Waerness, 1983). Hilary Rose (1986:165) writes, "The increasing tendency to make caring 'scientific' has eroded women's confidence, delegitimizing the knowledge they have gained individually and inter-generationally from the practice of caring." To what extent is informal care of the elderly being subjected to scientific control?

Women's coping strategies also are an important issue to researchers in women's studies. A variety of feminist analysts argue that women respond to difficulties by seeking to absorb the costs themselves. Laura Oren (1974), for example, has shown that, when food was scarce in nineteenth-century Britain, working-class women routinely gave relatively generous portions to their husbands while skimping on their own share. The distribution of such resources as leisure and medical care followed similar patterns. Hilary Graham (1985) contends that women continue to sacrifice their own health in order to promote the well being of other family members. In a very different arena, some researchers conclude that, because women view conflicts between work and family as personal rather than public problems, they search for solutions that do not involve imposing on others (Gerstel and Gross, 1987; Hochschild, 1989). Do caregivers who hold paid jobs press for special consideration from employers? To what extent do women seek help with the burdens of care from the larger family circle? To what extent do they try to shield their relatives from the consequences of caregiving?

Finally, although feminist scholars have directed little attention to the specific topic of care for the elderly, they debate the place of caregiving in women's lives. Since the publication of "The Female

World of Love and Ritual: Relations between Women in Nineteenth-Century America," by Carroll Smith-Rosenberg in 1975, some feminists have sought to describe a unique women's culture centered around caregiving. More recently, Carol Gilligan's book, *In a Different Voice: Psychological Theory and Women's Development* (1982), has sparked a line of writing concerned with elucidating women's special connection to an ethic of care. Many scholars emphasize the positive aspects of women's involvement in care. First, they argue, as a result of dominant patterns of female identity formation in this society, many women find personal fulfillment in caregiving. In addition, they assert, women's experience as caregivers makes them better people— more attuned to the needs of others, more socially responsible, more capable of sustaining a variety of intimate connections. Some commentators have gone so far as to view caregiving as the model on which to reconstruct society. The characteristic thought and practice cultivated by caregivers, they contend, should be extended to the larger social arena (Ruddick, 1983).

But others caution us against enshrining activities that are entwined with women's subordinate status. As Eli Zaretsky (1982:193) comments, "It is a tragic paradox that the bases of love, dependence, and altruism in human life and the historical oppression of women have been found within the same matrix." Some observers also argue that the emphasis on the personal fulfillment women derive from caregiving shades easily into a celebration of differences that serve as a rationale for women's inferior position. How do women caring for aging parents understand the nature of their caring work? What meaning does it have for them? To what extent does women's participation in care for the elderly clash with other goals they have for their lives?

5

The Caregivers' Perspective

When we hear women talk about the experience of caring for elderly parents, it is clear that caregiving does not conform to the classic distinction between instrumental tasks and affective relations. Caregivers try to provide love as well as labor, "caring about" while "caring for" (Graham, 1983; Ungerson, 1983). We saw in the last chapter that researchers frequently define caregivers in terms of the tasks they fulfill because tasks are the feature of caregiving that can be quantified most easily. This chapter will explore the various ways caregivers themselves understand their endeavors.

Not surprisingly, the importance that women in this study accorded to chores depended partly on the amount they performed. Women whose parents required few services or who had delegated the most difficult chores to paid helpers tended to speak dismissively of the tasks involved in care. The following are two representative comments by women who had hired aides to help tend their mothers with Alzheimer's disease:

> The direct care isn't really anything. Anyone can dress, give medication. What is the big deal? That is physical. The hardest thing is talking to someone who no longer can respond, where there is no reaching with one another. That's the part that really hurts.

> The instrumental kinds of things—finding places and buying her things—that's not what I find so difficult about caring for her. What I find the difficult part is coming to terms with the course of a human being's life at this point.

Women without onerous practical responsibilities occasionally saw helping with household tasks as a way to escape what they considered the more emotionally demanding aspects of care. One woman described visits to her mother's home: "I start cleaning her house the minute I go there, making food, cooking things in her refrigerator, making the food that's rotting away. I'm not my best self. I find that I do things rather than talk to her." Women who cared for seriously impaired parents with little outside assistance were far more likely to focus on concrete tasks. One of the five women living alone with parents reported, "My day is filled up with little chores—non stop, no break until the night, when I fall asleep in front of the television." A second woman, interviewed a few weeks after the death of her father, described the daily grind in a similar way: "A typical day was complete drudgery, from the time I got up in the morning until I went to bed."

Nevertheless, even women whose days were consumed by a range of chores stressed other aspects of the caregiving experience. When asked to estimate the number of hours they devoted to caregiving tasks, most women responded that it would be impossible to make such a calculation, explaining that they remained preoccupied with their parents' well-being even when not actually rendering instrumental assistance. In their eyes, caregiving was a boundless, all-encompassing activity, rather than a clearly demarcated set of discrete tasks. The dominant element in caregiving was their overall sense of responsibility for their parents' lives, not particular chores.

Responsibility

Because the phrase "filial responsibility" appears frequently in the writings of policy analysts, it is important to understand how caregivers themselves defined this term. When some women said that they felt responsible for their parents, they meant that they had taken charge of decisions affecting their parents' lives. Some still were pondering decisions they had made months and occasionally years before, and they used the interviews as opportunities to reassess their choices.

But the meaning of responsibility typically extended much farther. Once women had begun to make decisions on their parents' behalf, they felt accountable not just for the consequences of these decisions but for virtually every aspect of their parents' lives. Several believed that they should be able to protect their parents from all physical harm. Two, for example, viewed themselves as culpable when their parents hurt themselves in falls, although they acknowledged that they could not possibly have prevented such mishaps. One woman, interviewed a few months after she and her husband had moved into her mother's house, remarked: "I felt really bad one day. I came home from work, and she'd gone in her bedroom, and I heard her fall down.

It was such a shock because I thought, if I'm living here, I can protect her from this. It was so shocking to just hear her fall, and I was twenty feet away, just in the next room and not be able to do anything." Three others faulted themselves for not having been able to halt or at least slow the progress of their parents' disease. A woman whose mother suffered from episodes of depression stated:

> When she goes to the hospital, I seem to think there should have been something I could have done to stop that from happening—that I should have better control of the situation; I should have called the doctor sooner; I should have gotten her more medicine; I should have told the other doctors to stay out of things; I should have been able to help her more, somehow.

Despite the reassurances she received from others, a woman whose mother was in an advanced stage of dementia could not rid herself of the belief that she had enabled her mother to relinquish whatever abilities she retained:

> One of the things I might have done—but everybody says no, it doesn't matter—is that at the very beginning, because she seemed so frail, I might have overprotected her by having things done for her and doing things for her, and maybe she just decided that she shouldn't keep trying to do things. But I felt that she wasn't able to do a lot of things, it was such an effort, so I did a lot for her. And nobody knows whether that's good or bad. I felt so badly that she had to have this problem, and I just wanted to do everything I could to make it easier for her. That might have been a big mistake.

Several women considered themselves answerable for any deficiencies in medical or social service programs they arranged. And in some cases the daughters' sense of responsibility encompassed their parents' emotional as well as physical well-being. Although their parents suffered from intractable physical or mental health problems and had experienced losses that could not be repaired, the daughters believed that they should be able to make their parents happy.

How can we account for the overwhelming sense of responsibility these women felt? Nancy Chodorow argues that because women in this society fail to differentiate themselves from others, they often assume responsibility even for events they could not possibly control (Chodorow, 1974). According to Elaine M. Brody (1985), women caring for aging parents measure themselves against the all-embracing care they received as children. Hilary Graham (1985:35) offers a very different explanation. Women consider themselves responsible for anything that befalls the recipients of their care because caregiving is defined as a private endeavor. In the absence of governmental responsibility for care of dependents, "experiences become personalized with problems seen as self-inflicted and failures seen as a cause for self-recrimination and blame."

The chasm between women's overriding sense of responsibility and their ultimate powerlessness was one of the major difficulties caregivers experienced. One woman recalled: "In the beginning, I cried every night. Because you feel so powerless to do anything. And I think that's the worst thing, to see a person who's been very active, very personable, and all of a sudden, right in front of your eyes, they're just totally deteriorating." Policymakers frequently exhort adult children to display greater responsibility toward their aging parents. We will see, however, that the women in this study frequently expressed a desire to do just the opposite—to reduce their sense of involvement in their parents' lives and lower their expectations of what they could accomplish.

Dignity

Daughters also refused to define caregiving as a series of concrete chores because their primary objective was to preserve their parents' dignity. In a study of daughters caring for aging parents, Barbara Bowers (1990:279) concluded that women "conceptualized their caregiving work in terms of purpose, rather than tasks. The adult daughters . . . placed a priority on protective care (protecting or preserving the parent's sense of self and the parent-child relationship). This was especially true when their parents had either a mild or moderate form of dementia." This analysis illuminates the experiences of the women I interviewed. As Chapter 6 will discuss, many women had their own reasons for seeking to protect their parents' individuality and self image. Some also invoked the authority of experts to support their definitions of good care. Books and lectures counseled them to preserve their parents' sense of competence and uniqueness and not compel them to confront their disabilities. The women interpreted this injunction in various ways.

When parents suffered little or no mental impairment, daughters defined their goal as respecting their parents' autonomy and encouraging them to remain in control of their lives. Thus, although some caregivers tried to protect their parents from all hazards, others deferred to their parents' judgment and refrained from intervening, even when the parents placed themselves in dangerous situations.

When dementia progressed, women found it more difficult to view their parents as self-governing and to leave major decisions in their hands. The daughters thus increasingly viewed their mission as pretending that nothing had changed. One woman who spoke emphatically about the need to respect her mother's dignity explained that this meant preventing her mother from realizing that she had lost control over decisions affecting her life: "I let her think she had made the decision, or that she was taking care of herself. I don't ever let her feel that she couldn't survive if she wasn't here with me. To some people, that would be a comfort, but not to someone like my mother. If she could really come back and look and see, it would be the worst thing in the world." The daughters tried to conceal other changes in their parents' status. Women whose parents had been professionals sought to create the illusion that the parents continued to command the respect they previously had enjoyed. One woman was pleased when an aide was willing to cater to her father's professional pride, despite his severely impaired mental capacities: "This man makes an effort to be sensitive, and he is very willing to say, 'Yes, sir,' and 'Doctor this' and 'Doctor that,' kind of play to my father's authoritarianism." Another woman asserted: "My mother had been on the faculty at the university. I didn't want her ever to know that she is losing her memory, which she is; that she is losing her hearing, which she is; because her conception of herself is someone still on the faculty. I won't allow her to see that anything is wrong."

Women caring for mothers who had been housewives encouraged their mothers to believe that they still could make valuable contributions to household services. One woman discussed her mother's visits to her house:

> Part of what I try and do when she's here is make sure that I have accumulated things she can do so she feels useful. For example, I may just leave a pile of laundry totally unfolded, because that's something she can do and do easily. Last time she came, I was trying to iron, and she insisted she wanted to iron, so I let her, and she ironed. I will let her do whatever I feel she can do. Sometimes it interferes because it's not exactly what I had planned to do that day, but that's the way it is.

When this woman returned from the hospital after a serious illness, she worked to foster the pretence that her mother could care for her in meaningful ways:

> By the time I came home, I could cope with her trying to take care of me. She could bring me a cup of coffee and she could bring me some food, because I made sure everything was prepared. She had the feel-

ing she was helping because I set it up, knowing what she could do, and I think that helped her. I could just as well have gotten up and gotten a drink as have her bring me a drink, but she felt better because she was bringing me the drinks.

But women not only tried to prevent their parents from acknowledging their disabilities. Those who believed that the disease had ravaged their parents' sense of personhood viewed themselves as guardians of the people they remembered. One woman recalled a ritual she conducted during the two years she tended her mother, who suffered from Alzheimer's disease: "I kissed her goodnight every night, but it was never returned. I always felt like I'm just doing it because when she was herself, she liked that." A second woman demonstrated her protectiveness toward her father's former self in a very different way:

My father was extremely able in all kinds of household fix-it-ups and things like that, and he had built a house and then when they lived out in the country he did all kinds of work on the house, so that he had every kind of plumbing tool and every kind of carpentry tool and every kind of electrical wiring tool and every kind of car fix-it tool. Somebody had to deal with all of the stuff, and they had skis—my father skied until he was in his seventies, and so he had skis and old tennis rackets. He just had unbelievable stuff that he had saved and not thrown away. So basically I had to pull the garage apart and sort everything and organize a garage sale. . . . It was just exhausting and time consuming, a garage sale is, because you're just parting with things, which is hard. But at some point I was going to sell this beach umbrella and I could just see my father's young physique, maybe in the forties, so this is forty years later. I could see him opening this wonderful old beach umbrella, and I just sort of fell apart and started sobbing and said, sorry I can't sell it, so we called it the end of the garage sale. I just felt like such a traitor. I was there, and my father was wandering around the house without his brains, and I was sort of selling off all these memories and his abilities to do things. I just felt like I had betrayed him. . . . I never did sell the beach umbrella.

Two women asserted that caregiving was a means of expressing loyalty to the mothers they had known. Said one:

I loved my mother a lot when I was growing up. . . . When her memory went so poor, I realized that I really loved the lady she was. This is a different lady. This is not the mother that was, this is someone else. I can't really say that I love this person that is now, but what I do love is the memory of the person that was before, and because of that love, I have a tremendous sense of obligation to her, and I'll take care of her till the day she dies. Sometimes there's guilt involved because I don't love her in the way that I did. And sometimes I'm sad about it because I really remember the way that she was, and that's a curse and a blessing at the same time.

The other commented: "I try to validate some of the things she tried to raise, ideals in me, things that she tried to teach us as we were growing up, that it was important to care about other people." By acting in accordance with the ideals her mother had sought to instill in her, this woman reaffirmed her bond with a mother she feared she had lost.

Finally, daughters viewed themselves as promoting their parents' self-respect when they helped their parents conceal evidence of physical frailty. It will be seen that a key reason some women hired aides was that they did not want their parents to be compelled to reveal the extent of their physical impairments to their daughters. In addition, many daughters did not insist that their parents use walkers or wheelchairs, even when their parents had serious problems with ambulation. In a society that places a high value on independence, weakness of any kind is considered shameful; caregivers promote the dignity of recipients by hiding all signs of dependence.

Medical Diagnosis

In trying to foster their parents' dignity, the daughters in this study were following one line of advice frequently offered to caregivers. But daughters of parents with dementia also received a contradictory message—to define their relatives in terms of their diseases. Such popular advice books as *The 36-Hour Day* (Mace and Rabins, 1981) stress the importance of viewing the behavior of demented adults as symptoms of disease rather than as deliberate acts. Women whose parents suffered from some form of dementia thus faced a problem that has been common since the rise of scientific medicine at the end of the nineteenth century and the new understanding of disease specificity. To what extent should patients be viewed as a configuration of symptoms and to what extent as whole and unique individuals? Because a diagnosis of dementia can call into question an individual's sense of self, this issue emerges in particularly urgent form for their caregivers. This section thus will focus on women caring for parents with dementia.

Diagnosis typically follows an evaluation by a physician. In most cases, family members initiate the process of obtaining an evaluation.

One daughter in this study, however, had not even considered the possibility of dementia until she saw her mother's insurance form and learned that her mother had sought a consultation for memory loss.

Obtaining the diagnosis marked a turning point for many women. Three who had hoped that their parents had problems that could be treated (such as depression or alcohol or drug-induced dementia) were shocked to learn that their parents were suffering from an irreversible form of dementia. The reactions of two others revealed the stigma attached to Alzheimer's disease; they stated that they were relieved to learn that their parents had other types of dementia, although there still was no possibility of a cure.

But the precise designation was less important than learning that something was the matter. Although the diagnosis often confirmed daughters' worst fears, it also could be a source of reassurance. One woman explained why she and her siblings had insisted that their mother receive an evaluation:

> We suspected, and we didn't think we had a right to suspect without a professional opinion. . . . We used to swap stories of "guess what mother did now?" and it wasn't cruel. [The diagnosis] reconfirms that it's not you, because sometimes when you're in with someone who's not dealing with things properly, you begin to feel: "Was it me? Did I hear that? I don't believe she said that."

A second woman also initially had considered it improper to question her mother's mental capacities: "We just didn't know what was going one. She would say things that were strange, and I thought, 'My mama has really been very bright and now. . . .' I didn't say the word 'stupid,' but you get the idea. I really thought that was not the respectable thing to say because it was my mother." Once their parents were labeled sick, women could trust their own instincts, make sense of their parents' behavior, and consider the best way to provide care.

After receiving a diagnosis, most women tried to learn more about the nature of their parents' impairments, seeking information from books, friends, support groups, and professionals. As their knowledge grew, many increasingly interpreted behavior in light of the disease. Some began to associate their parents with other victims of dementia. In answer to questions about their own parents, they discussed adults with dementia in general, occasionally referring to "them" or "these people." One woman lamented her inability to spend more time talking with her mother "because this is what an Alzheimer's disease patient needs." Another woman explained why she had found the right aide for her father: "She is aware of how to take care of Alzheimer's people. It would be a real problem for some if they didn't understand Alzheimer's disease and the nature of it and how people are when they have that disease. She knows never to confront my dad head on, that there are other ways of getting him to do what you want." The women also used their new understanding to develop techniques for dealing with their parents themselves. One woman explained how she coped with her father's repetitive questions:

> His memory is so poor that he'll ask me the same questions over again, like, "What are you doing in your life now?" and "Do you have a job?" So I have to answer him a lot. And one thing I feel proud of myself is that, because I understand his situation, I don't put a lot of energy into answering the questions, I mean I just say the same thing over and over again. And people have said, "You're incredibly patient that way, I can't believe that you can say the same things over and over to him and not get furious." He'll ask my mother something, and she'll put a lot of energy into trying to explain it, and she'll say, "Well, this is why we're doing it, and . . ." and then he'll ask the same thing five minutes later, and she'll get irritated. Because he didn't understand. But I don't expect him to understand. I just answer it so he'll get the answer at that moment, but I don't expect him to remember five minutes later, and I expect it to come up again and again and again.

Another woman realized that, because her mother had the same disease as members of a day care center she observed, the daughter could learn techniques from the center staff:

> I learned so much about what must be the fright or the fear that the old people feel, the threat at the loss, even if they don't know what they're losing or what they lost. There's something that's so interesting that happens. If there's stress in the room, they pick it up like children. And what I saw at the day care center were the workers always touching the people. They give them a hug, or a pat, or hold their hand, or a kiss. Lovely, lovely. And I've learned to do that with my mother. When she's real agitated or upset, if I just sit down and put my arm around her, she calms right down.

Several women also claimed that information about the genesis of behaviors helped them to gain greater control over their own emotions. Thus one woman reported:

> We always viewed my mother as somewhat crazy and tried to get her to see a psychiatrist, but to have it be a clear dementia in some ways

makes it easier to relate to her. Even though some of the things she does it's hard not to take personally, it's clearly not personal and doesn't have anything to do with me and who I am. . . . My coping mechanism had always been to distance myself, but there was always some doubt that maybe that was invalid, it always got to me eventually. This way, it's objective, so there is no way it could get to me.

When caregivers learned that their parents' actions were unintentional, some of their anger faded. One woman recalled:

I took [my mother] to the doctor, and he's the one who told me about the book, *The 36-Hour Day.* I went and got that book, and I read it from cover to cover. And after I read that book, I started to understand some of the things that were happening to me. I started to understand why it is when she calls me and I would have her come here that she would want to go home again. It was because she felt totally uncomfortable, she wasn't in surroundings that she's used to, she would forget where rooms were. Just all these things started to come together, and I started to understand. Because I went through a real difficult time. It was so difficult not to be mad. I would say, "Mom, don't you understand?" or "Don't you see this?" or "Don't you know when you're doing something?" or "Don't you understand, you've always done this?" or "What is wrong?" It was so hard. And then when I read the book, I realized that she was just like a model case. I mean, all these things that were in this book were happening to her. I was seeing she can't help it, and I think once I realized in my own mind that, yes, this is what is happening to her, then our whole relationship and my attitude to her really changed.

A second woman initially had been enraged by other types of behavior, but she learned a similar lesson:

I had a lot of hostility towards [my father] in the beginning, because I just got so furious that he wouldn't take care of himself, and he wouldn't make decisions. I think probably the memory was starting to go, and I wasn't understanding how bad off he really was. I would just get angry a lot. . . . I read *The 36-Hour Day,* which really helped understand how scary it is to lose your memory; it's like your mind gets out of control. That's a real basic part of your life, to have your mind, and to be able to understand things, and to control your life with it. It just seems like it would be real scary to lose control of your mind. Ever since I've read that book, I've changed my attitude. I used to get real angry at him, because I didn't realize that he couldn't do all these things. After I realized he couldn't do them, I just take it.

Not all women found it so easy to translate information about dementia into appropriate emotional responses. Arlie Russell Hochschild (1975:289) has coined the phrase "feeling rules" to describe rules that "define what we should feel in various circumstances." An understanding of the relationship between parental behavior and disease processes convinced women that they should not be angry; but many acknowledged the difficulty of conforming their feelings to the knowledge they had gained. Looking back on the two years she spent caring for her mother, one woman stated: "I wish it hadn't upset me. I wish that I could have coped with it. I wish I could have just said, 'She can't help it,' and that was that, but I couldn't. I couldn't do it." Another woman noted that it was "hard to put insights into practice." Nevertheless, a medical label did help women gain at least some of the emotional distance they considered critical.

Caregivers also noted the importance of learning what to expect. A diagnosis of dementia leaves many questions unanswered: How rapidly will the disease progress? What symptoms will emerge? To what extent will the individual's disease follow the widely recognized stages? Nevertheless, most women believed that the diagnosis dispelled some of the uncertainty surrounding their parents' care and enabled them to make preparations for the future. One woman remarked: "At the hospital, there was a wonderful doctor, and he said: 'Watch for these signs. When you come to pick her up and she has to brush her hair or brush her teeth, she's beginning to deteriorate. And then watch for her doing this and wandering off and not being able to get home.' So we watched for all the signs to come." Because many women insisted that their parents' illness had caught them by surprise, their ability to make plans gave them a sense of greater control over their lives.

Finally, women who attached a medical label to their parents found it easier to consult physicians about a broad range of issues. Aside from prescribing medications to control agitation, there was little that medical science could do in most cases. Physicians could neither cure the disease nor slow its progress. As one woman said, "You can't put the mind back." Nevertheless, many women sought guidance from physicians for problems that required human, not technical solutions. Women invoked physician recommendations to explain such varied steps as consulting a psychiatrist, joining a support group, enrolling their parents in day care centers, bringing their parents to live in the same city as themselves, and hiring aides and attendants.

But it is important to note that the comments of several women revealed that women were motivated less by trust in professional judgment than by their desire to use physicians to bolster their own authority. They sought professional advice in order to justify actions they already had decided were correct. Asked whether she had considered placing her father in a nursing home, one woman responded:

> I don't think he's quite ready yet, and I don't want to move him until he really is, because I think once the move is made, that will be it, that will be where he'll remain. And I just feel that right now, it's just much more pleasant for him to be where he is. This is why I think I've been so insistent on finding one of these geriatric assessment services and doing the tests again, to try to get someone else to say to me, "He's not ready to go yet. He's not ready to move yet." I just wanted to put that burden, that responsibility on someone else. I'm half-way through one of these assessments, and they agree that he should stay where he is for now. And I'm relieved to hear them say that. I would like to keep him where he is as long as I can.

A second woman wanted a physician not just to justify particular decisions but also to validate her entire behavior as a caregiver:

> The doctor really made me feel very good because he would always talk to me after he spoke to her and say, "Well, it looks like you're doing a good job, and she seems to be very well adjusted." And they know. I guess they can read a lot more than we can. That would make me feel good, that's where I got my gratification, in that I was doing something that was helping her. It was through the doctor at the hospital.

Although this woman did believe that physicians have superior insights—"They can read a lot more than we can"—she did not alter her actions to suit this doctor's advice.

Several other women relied on doctors in order to avoid conflicts with their parents. As the next chapter will discuss, caregivers often must assert authority over parents and prevent them from engaging in certain activities traditionally considered basic to adulthood in our society. When physicians recommended that parents stop driving or managing their own money, the daughters were relieved of responsibility for the decision. And one woman used a consultation with a physician to puncture her brother's denial about their father's condition:

> My brother kept insisting that my father's just having anxiety attacks. So I made my brother go to the doctor with my father. And he sat and watched how his father could not remember to do three things that the doctor had told him to do and how he couldn't do things properly. And he watched the whole process, and then he was willing

to accept the fact that he was really sick, that there was something wrong with him. Then my brother was willing to set up a conservatorship.

In short, a diagnostic label served women in various ways—enabling them to muster resources for dealing with their parents' problems, helping them develop techniques for coping with bizarre or troublesome behavior, permitting them to gain critical emotional distance from their parents, and enabling them to rely on the authority of physicians. Nevertheless, the women in this study resisted reducing their parents to a set of symptoms. If they "watched for all the signs to come," they also continued to respond to their parents as individuals. One woman commented:

> I've just realized that there are things [my mother] can't grasp. My dad set up a trust in his will when he was ill, and I explained it to her so many times over so many months, and she still doesn't understand it. My husband finally just said, "Listen, let's just tell her it's just complicated legal stuff and you're never going to understand it, and just don't worry about it. Your husband took good care of you, and you don't need to worry about any of it." But my first impulse is always to treat her the way I've always treated her. I still try and get her preferences for things. She can't try on anything in stores anymore, it's just too hard, so I just charge everything and take it home so she can try it on. I kind of say, "Well, which one do you think looks better on you, and which colors do you like best?" I'd also like to ask her advice. I think in matters of the heart she probably could still advise me. She just can't balance her checkbook very well.

As this woman struggled to accept the fact that her mother's mental capacities had diminished, she remained attentive to her mother's wishes and sought to convince herself that her mother still possessed wisdom. Another woman described her determination not to treat her mother like every other victim of Alzheimer's disease, even as the progression of the disease threatened to destroy her mother's uniqueness:

> What I find difficult is trying to figure out what's best for her, which is what a parent does for a small child, but there are many more clear directives for a parent than there are in this situation. And it's hard to separate what I would want for me in that situation [from how she might] choose for herself in a former time or now. We are dealing with a person that is different from the person that I know how to make choices for. I can't easily say that my mother would like this, this, and this, based on what she appears to want, because she can't

communicate. . . . I was clear that I wanted her to have as much of her own furniture in her place around her as possible, because furniture was a big part of her life, and she loved antiques, and she got her self worth from her surroundings. There was a three-week delay in getting her furniture to where she was staying, and she'd forgotten it all. There was just that much progression of degeneration in that time. When she was in her own house, she got a lot of pleasure out of it. In fact, just slightly before she moved out here, she got most of her pleasure driving around Palm Beach and then going into her house and saying, "Isn't this a nice place, my this is nice." So I thought that would be what she'd want in a new environment, and she'd forgotten it all, which people had told me, but I still was making decisions on the basis of what I thought she would want. I didn't want to have to acknowledge that she's no different from X, Y, or Z who also has Alzheimer's, that there's no individual distinction making her the mother that I knew.

Jaber F. Gubrium and Robert L. Lynott (1987:271) argue that medical assessments of demented adults serve to construct as well as detect disease. Once evaluations have been conducted, caregivers tend to "see impairment everywhere." But a study by Betty Risteen Hasselkus (1988) suggests that family members are less easily swayed by medical labels. The caregivers she interviewed occasionally used their special knowledge of elderly relatives to cast doubt on their diagnoses. A few women I spoke to pointed to faculties their parents retained in order to question a medical diagnosis. One expressed doubts about whether her mother actually had Alzheimer's disease because she still could play the violin so well. Some who accepted the diagnosis nevertheless argued that certain behaviors experts attributed to disease actually were exaggerations of lifelong personality traits. The comments of one woman illustrate the difficulty of determining which behaviors should be attributed to a disease and which to a parent's distinctive personality:

When my mother's brother was visiting, my father had no idea who this man was, but he was quite indignant that this strange man had come to visit. My mother left the car lights on in the car, and my uncle said, "Give me the keys and I will go and turn them off," but my father said no. He told my mother that she had to go out, that she was the one who left them on, and she was going to have to turn them off. This kind of behavior was a side of him always, but it was not always so naked in front of my uncle. He would not have been totally unconscious about it. He would have veiled it in the past. But he never was a good person to get along with. It's hard to tell now when his personality is deteriorating. It is very difficult to tell whether or not it is the crankiness they talk about or the nastiness related to Alzheimer's disease or if it is just him.

A second woman noted that as long as she could remember, her mother had had angry outbursts, although they now seemed to take an exaggerated form. A third was uncertain that even more aberrant behavior could be classified as a disease symptom:

> The first hint that she was sick was an incident that clearly had a paranoid element because she imagined helicopters landing in her yard. But the distinction was very difficult, because she always had crazy-making behavior. For example, she changed her will and gave all her money to Harvard. It always was hard to know how much was her craziness, which always was there, and how much was a definable diagnosis. . . . She does very inappropriate things. For example, she'll say in a loud voice: "There's Helen. Don't talk to Helen; she has nothing going on upstairs." It's embarrassing. What's so funny is she might have said the same thing toned down six levels when she was more coherent. She used to say obviously embarrassing things in the middle of large groups. So in that sense it's just an exaggeration of how she is or was.

Many women also asserted that their parents' personalities transcended the disease. One woman explained why she enjoyed the time she spent with her father: "He's real sweet, he's not like sometimes Alzheimer's people get, kind of angry. He was a real sweet person to begin with, and he's still really nice. I mean, to me, he's fun, and even with his Alzheimer's, he'll say really funny things." Finally, rather than assuming that the disease had transformed their parents' personalities, three women reassessed their prior view of their parents in light of the changes that had occurred. "It's as if I've been fooled all these years," one said.

Women who emphasized their parents' uniqueness tended to be less impressed by advice books than others. One, for example, had little praise for *The 36-Hour Day:*

> There's nothing human about it. The discussions about how you pick a place are all very instrumental, and none of it deals with the concerns about how you know what's good for a person. Nobody has described to me what would be the impact on me of walking for the very first time into a nursing home, the impact of seeing these very old women who were sitting and kind of nodding. I would see *my* mother in every single one of the women, and it's very hard.

Some women considered other types of professional expertise equally irrelevant. One mentioned that her husband had suggested that she consult a geriatric specialist to give her guidance about the way to care for her father. She explained why she had demurred: "We're dealing with a uniquely strong personality."

Women also gained the confidence to override physicians' advice by relying on their own intimate knowledge of their parents. Some argued that physicians, acting on the basis of universalistic knowledge, missed unique aspects of their parents' experiences. Thus one woman scoffed at a physician who recommended that she give her mother a sense of security by imposing routines on her mother's life, "My mother never has lived by routines." The recommendation most commonly rejected was that parents be placed in nursing homes. As Chapter 8 will discuss, virtually all women in the study were staunchly opposed to institutionalization. One woman who did accept a physician's counsel to put her mother in a home told an unusually harrowing story:

> My husband started getting terrible pains, just unbearable pains, and we went for months to doctors. They all said, "Your husband has terrible headaches because your mama is living with you." Finally, we went to a neurologist for my mother, and he examined her and took a CAT scan and he gave us the verdict that she had Alzheimer's. He said, "Let me tell you what that means." I will never forget those words. He said to me: "You have to put your mama in a nursing home because if you don't your marriage is at risk. Your husband is suffering very much. It's going to destroy your marriage." I want to explain that our marriage was fine, except that we were in pain about my mom. It hurt us because we didn't know what her behavior was about. We called in a professional counselor to come and see my mom here and see how she behaves and all. We ended up putting my mom in a nursing home about ten minutes away. I went to see her every day, and I couldn't bear seeing my mama in the situation they had her in. . . . I'll never forgive myself for letting her go there, but I was so desperate and my husband was getting worse. A few months later he collapsed, and then he found out that it was a brain tumor, and he had twelve and one-half hour surgery and we almost lost him. . . . The worst thing I ever did was to put her in a nursing home and not let her stay with me anymore. I was given advice by professional people that I respected. I went to doctors and I went to counselors, and they all said to me: "Your mom needs to leave the house. You have to come ahead of her. How much can your husband take?" . . . The doctors convinced us that this was the only thing that we

could do. . . . So it wasn't a question of listening to ourselves, it was a question of listening to professionals tell us that this was the way it had to be or should be.

During a period of enormous stress, she had allowed the judgment of physicians and other professionals to prevail, disregarding her own knowledge about both her husband and her mother. She bitterly regretted acquiescing in professional expertise and remained convinced of the importance of personalized, as opposed to scientific, knowledge.

Role Reversal

If caregivers of persons with dementia viewed their parents simultaneously as disease victims and unique individuals, they also referred to their parents as both adults and children. A cardinal principle of gerontology is that the elderly should not be considered children; despite any disabilities they may experience, they should be accorded all the rights and privileges of other adults in our society. But Karen Lyman (1988) found that at least some staff in adult day care centers for dementia patients violate this principle; believing that demented adults degenerate by regressing to the level of young children, the staff members she observed routinely infantilized their patients. From a study of fifteen women caring for frail elderly parents, Lucy Rose Fischer (1986:165) reported: "All but one of the daughters declared specifically that they had experienced a role reversal."

In this study as well, women labeled their relationships as "role reversal," said "I'm the parent now," and described the "childlike" qualities of their parents. Women used such phrases to signify that their parents depended on them for care. One commented: "The day that he couldn't find his way to my house in his car was when I felt like I had really lost my father. It was almost like a dying of my father. And it was sort of like all of a sudden, I'm the big one now, and he's the little one, and I've got to take care of him." Women who were mothers themselves reported that certain caregiving activities—tucking their parents in at night, bathing them, and hiring sitters—were reminiscent of their experiences as mothers of small children: "A couple of years ago, my mother was in the hospital, and she kept climbing out of bed and would fall. It was very difficult. I had to tell them it was O.K. to tie her down. That was so hard for me. I remembered having to make similar decisions when my child was young. Something just has to be done. I immediately went into that mode." Women without children were convinced that they would be better equipped to give directions and make decisions if they had raised children. One said:

> My sister told me that when she was visiting here that she just went back to her days of having a toddler and treated Mom very much in the same way. She'd say, "Well, it's time for your bath now" and "Dinner's ready." Because she's raised a child, that's a posture she's more familiar with. For me, this has been a little harder because I haven't had any kids. I wonder if you find that women who have had children, if it's easier for them somehow.

Defining parents with dementia as children also may have enabled the women to deny some of the emotions the experience of care provoked. One woman stated: "The problems may just be me and my reactions to things. If I can try and keep the attitude that she's really just a little girl who needs to be treated gently and lovingly, then I kind of have fun with it. But if I expect her to be an adult and fend for herself, then it's much harder."

Nevertheless, all the women I interviewed emphasized the vast differences between caring for children and aging parents. Instead of fostering growth and development, they witnessed deterioration:

> When my mother first came to live with me, I thought: "Oh, this isn't going to be difficult. I can manage this, I've raised six kids." I kept seeing the relationship in terms of that, she acted very much like a 3- or 4-year-old. And, goodness, I had six children, ten grandchildren, and so I could handle this. And it wasn't the same, because with children you know they're going to grow, and you know there's a future, and with this you know it's the opposite.

Caring for the elderly also lacks familiar milestones; thus, although caregivers typically have an enormous investment in providing good care, they have few ways of evaluating their work:

> You expect small children to show progress. If small children don't show progress, then you really have to take steps to see what's wrong with them. The difference is that here there is no progress, there's only a slow deterioration, almost an invisible deterioration, but I know it's there. It's very different from taking care of kids. If you're doing a good job with kids, they move along, they progress, their world expands. My mother's world is contracting.

Women also pointed out that, although parents seek to produce socially acceptable children (see Ruddick, 1982), they were not trying to mold their aging parents.

But the major reason women did not confuse parent care with child care is that, as Chapter 6 will discuss in greater detail, caregiving often revived powerful elements of the original parent-child relationship; several women reported that the emotional relationship with their parents remained unchanged. The term "role reversal" thus can be considered more an indication of women's discomfort at the inversion of responsibilities than an expression of their belief that they actually had traded places with their parents (see Brody, 1985).

Reciprocity

It often is assumed that care for elderly parents is rooted in reciprocity—children repay parents for the care they received when young (see Bulmer, 1987; Qureshi and Walker, 1989; Ungerson, 1987). The notion of reciprocity meshes with social exchange theory (Blau, 1964). As Tamara Hareven (1987:73) writes, "The classic exchange along the life course is that between parents and children, based on parents' expectation of old age support in return for their investment in childbearing."

Six women in this study explained their motivation in terms of filial gratitude. Said one, "She was there for me, I'll be there for her." Another woman felt an obligation to repay her mother for services the daughter received when she already was an adult:

> She made me go back to college after I had graduated to become a teacher because I didn't take my education courses, and she came an hour and a half train ride to take care of my kids in the morning so I could go to school. It was three different trains for her. In snow and sleet, she carried food, and she cleaned my house and my windows and everything while I was in school, so I really owe her. I wanted to pay her back.

But, just as adult children do not simply reverse roles when caring for parents, so most women I interviewed did not perceive themselves as giving payment for services rendered. As noted, all discussed the enormous differences between parent care and care for children. Moreover, eight stated that they were rendering care in spite of rather than because of their treatment as children. They claimed that their parents either had given them insufficient love or had entrusted their care to outsiders, such as nannies or governesses. One woman mused, "My brother says to me, 'She was so awful to you, why are you so interested in taking such good care of her now?' and I can't really answer that."

Most women also did not believe that their parents had a special right to care because of the services they had rendered their own parents. The great majority asserted that they were the first in their families to care for elderly parents. And, just as some women said that they cared for their parents despite the poor care they had received as children, so some women claimed that their parents' treatment of their own parents constituted a negative, rather than a positive, model. One woman explained why she brought her mother with her when she moved across the country:

> We were originally from southern Germany, and my mother cared for her mother. By the time we emigrated from Germany, which was in the spring of [19]38, very late, my grandma had had a stroke, and my mother left her behind, and she ended up in a concentration camp, and she was killed, as far as we know. It was something my mother never talked about. But I certainly don't want to treat my mother the way she treated her mother.

Nor did women believe that they could expect payment in the form of services from their own children when they themselves grew old. Although two women asserted that they were setting an example for their children, most were far less sanguine about their future. All the childless women expressed fears that they would have no one to care for them in old age. Most mothers shared these fears, either because they had sons rather than daughters or because they were convinced that all young people had rejected an ethic of care. "We're the last generation to provide this care," one woman asserted.

By emphasizing the reciprocal nature of caregiving, we miss its essential meaning. The notion of reciprocity rests on the assumption that individuals view each other as instrumental resources for discrete tasks, coming together primarily to exchange specific goods and services (see Glenn, 1987; see Hartsock, 1983). By contrast, writers such as Nancy Chodorow (1974) and Carol Gilligan (1982) argue that women experience themselves as embedded in social relationships and derive their sense of identity from such relationships. According to most women I spoke with, caregiving flowed from a sense of connection to their parents, not from a desire to repay services previously rendered or to make an investment in their own futures.

Appreciation

Partly because these women did not view themselves as either returning services or accumulating credit for their own old age, they believed that their care deserved appreciation. One woman who recently had moved with her husband into her mother's house was dismayed to discover how desperately she sought thanks:

> I think people have told her that it's good for the kids, that we won't have to pay rent, that we'll be able to save money. So I think in some ways she didn't see that it was a sacrifice for us. . . . One day she could tell I was just upset, I was kind of banging dishes around when I was cleaning up, and it's terrible, she was saying, "Well, if you don't want to be here, you don't have to be." It was strange for me, because I realized I wanted her to be grateful, I wanted her to appreciate the sacrifice I was making. It sounds terrible. She just kind of said, "If you don't want to live here, you can leave." She's never brought it up again, but it's like she was doing us a favor. I don't like that in myself, that I want her to be grateful. I feel like a real jerk to want her to be grateful, to just kind of acknowledge that this isn't all fun and games and that I was happy with the life I had before, that I liked my privacy and my freedom, and it's a sacrifice.

A woman caring for a father also revealed an intense desire for appreciation:

> Once he said to me, after we had a very good day together, he said, "Thank you for everything." I cried all the way home. It touched me, because he doesn't say thank you and sometimes I don't believe that he's aware of what's happening. Just having him say that meant that he was aware, that he appreciated it. It was such a nice thing that it moved me to tears, it doesn't happen often. In fact I even had talked to a close friend of mine, "If once he'd say thank you, if he'd say thank you just once, I would feel somewhat that he was cognizant of what was going on." And it was several days after that, that he said that. So it was very poignant. It was striking at the time he said that, although he has no idea that he has turned my life absolutely upside down, that he's caused such an upheaval and disturbance to my life.

These women were not alone in receiving less gratitude than they wanted. The great majority of women in the study complained of inadequate appreciation. Some explained that, because their parents suffered from dementia, they had little conception of what was being done for them. As we have seen, some women also took pains to conceal their contributions in order to foster their parents' self-image. In addition, women noted that their parents resented their dependency and resisted all offers of help; they could not show gratitude for services that were being rendered over their objections. Finally, some women believed that their parents simply took their daughters' efforts for granted. One woman commented:

I keep expecting her to see that it's too much for me, that's what I'd like. My aunt and uncle do that. They fuss and fume and take care of me and say, "This is just too much for you." But the more I do for mother, the more she seems to expect. I'd like even a little concern that I'm doing too much. One day I was lugging all these groceries up the stairs, and she looked at me and said, "Smile when I smile at you." Every time you look at her she smiles, and she wants a smile back. And I didn't smile. I said, "I'm tired," and her response was, "Well, sit down." She thinks it's that easy, you just sit down. But it's not that easy.

A second woman voiced a similar complaint: "From time to time she expresses her appreciation, but on the whole I think she expects it. She expects me to be there for her. I think she does appreciate what my husband does, and she says thank you to him. I think she thinks I'm her daughter, and I should just be there for her." Women like these tended to interpret their parents' failure to appreciate their efforts as evidence of their own worthlessness in their parents' eyes.

Responses to Care

When women assessed their responses to caregiving, they agreed that stress was a major component. I have noted that stress consumes much of the attention of students of informal caregiving. Comments about stress also were constant refrains in the interviews I conducted with caregivers. As Allan Young (1980:133) writes: " 'Stress' and ancillary concepts such as 'coping' have permeated everyday discourse. . . . Information on stress is now widely available to lay audiences . . . through frequent articles in mass circulation magazines, self-help books, television programs, lectures, and pharmaceutical advertising for vitamins and sleep preparations." Although the women were not asked directly about the stresses of caregiving, nine volunteered that they had consulted therapists to help cope with the problems of caregiving, and another commented that she was considering doing so. Twenty-four women also were members of support groups, where they discussed the strains involved in rendering care. Several women attributed physical problems to stress. Three stated that the stress of caregiving created fatigue, and three others claimed that it contributed to eating problems. Four women believed that stress had precipitated even more serious health problems, including chronic back pain and cancer. Two additional women wondered if stress had exacerbated their difficulties with infertility. Women who lived apart from their parents described physical symptoms that occurred either while visiting their parents or after returning home. One woman, for example, remarked:

> I had a bad experience a couple of months ago. Boy, it taught me a lesson. I thought my mother would enjoy going to the arboretum. They had a special spring show of flowers, and I wanted to see them myself. The only problem is that it was fifty minutes in the car. I didn't realize that I couldn't sit in the car with her for fifty minutes. She talked on and on, and she says the same things over and over and over again. What happens to me when I am stressed out or anxious is I get very sleepy. I almost couldn't make it home. There were times on the freeway coming back where I thought, "If I don't pull over and take a nap, I'm going to fall asleep." If she drove, I would have said, "Please drive." I really almost couldn't make it. I'd never gotten that bad before. I got her home and I sat in the car and took a little nap before I came back home, which was only another ten minutes. I realized I can't do that anymore.

Another woman noted: "I find the day is better if I visit mother in the morning and then go about my business, and then I come home refreshed. But the majority of days I go toward the end of the day, and then I come home beaten because it takes a lot out of me. I normally am very organized, but I am not then. I drive very carefully because I'm just not all there." A woman interviewed a few days after institutionalizing a mother with whom she had lived for two years reported:

> When I woke up, I thought, oh, another day, and when I went to bed, it was the same thing. All day I could keep busy, coping, but at night it was terrible. It got to the point where I was not myself any more. One of my daughters said, "You were just driving a car with empty," and that's the way I felt. Any little thing that happened was a major catastrophe to me, and I'm not that way. I'm an easy-going person. Usually I'm not a worrier, but I couldn't relax. I was becoming uptight, neurotic. I felt someone else was coming inside and controlling me.

But, if stress was a key concern of women in this study, most insisted that it did not define their experience of caregiving. When asked how life would be different without the responsibility of care, one woman caring for her mother responded:

> I think I could plan more trips. I like to travel. I could think about moving away, which I would never do now, moving to a quieter, simpler community. I guess I'd eventually feel less burdened. But I also think that I'd miss her very much, and her presence and all the cher-

ished moments that you have. All the family occasions and the times you want to share with a parent, that you want them to be there to see and be a part of.

Another commented: "I'd have a lot more free time and a lot more freedom of movement. I think I'd feel a lot more carefree. But, you know, it's like this is thinking back to the past, because in the future, if I'm not caring for her it means that she's not well enough for me to care for her anymore, and so I'm sure there's going to be a lot more sadness mixed in with it." And a third remarked: "It would be one less responsibility but also one less joy. I am just lucky to have her." To women such as these, a one-sided focus on the problems of caregiving denied the value of their parents' lives. They viewed caregiving as the inevitable consequence of having elderly parents and an expression of their attachment to their parents. As a result, it was a privilege as well as a burden.

When asked if caregiving offered satisfactions, a few women laughed dismissively. One angrily retorted, "you don't expect rewards for caring for your mother." Nevertheless, most women identified at least some gratifications from caregiving. Although many women said that they felt uncertain about how best to proceed when they first assumed caregiving responsibilities, four said that caregiving eventually provided them with an opportunity to display competence. Several women also took pride in making an important difference in their parents' lives. A woman who was interviewed shortly after she placed her mother in a nursing home assessed her contribution this way:

> I think I helped her just to retain her dignity a little longer, just to hang onto it a little bit. She was always a very dignified lady. It's sort of like seeing your mother stripped naked when they don't care for themselves. Their clothes are dirty; they have this look on their face of total rejection. It's like seeing them standing there naked. So I was able to, in a way, clothe her for two years.

If some women had grandiose expectations about what they could accomplish, this woman believed that she had fulfilled her desire to foster her mother's self-respect. In addition, caregiving enabled women to reaffirm their sense of themselves as good people. For example: "I don't know if I would be doing all this if I didn't get some sense that I'm helping and that I'm worthwhile for doing it, that I'm a good person, that I'm someone that can be relied on." Some women asserted that caregiving was a humanizing experience. Said one, "You gain a lot of wisdom and insight and compassion for other people's suffering and problems." Another commented: "I've always been very religious all my life, but I've always had a very wonderful life. I haven't had any massive burdens or catastrophes, just your normal things that happen in life. But because of this problem with my mother, I've had to search and realize what my faith means to me. I look at it like this was mother's final gift to me."

Conclusion

This chapter suggests that many of the concepts commonly used to describe caregiving fail to capture the experience of women engaged in this activity. Rather than perceiving caregiving as a series of chores, the women I interviewed emphasized their overall responsibility for their parents' lives and their determination to foster their parents' self-respect. Although several spoke in terms of role reversal and reciprocity, these terms did not adequately describe the way most daughters defined their endeavor. And, despite their emphasis on the strains that caregiving generated, the majority of women resisted viewing caregiving solely in terms of stress and burdens.

This chapter also demonstrates the complexities of women's relationship to professional expertise. Although some daughters whose parents suffered from dementia believed that the jurisdiction of physicians extended very broadly, most did not simply relinquish authority. Instead, they used professional opinion to enhance their own authority over their parents. Because they viewed their parents as unique individuals rather than simply victims of disease, they retained faith in their own ability to determine how care should be rendered.

6

Mothers and Daughters

Although researchers in women's studies devote substantial attention to relationships between mothers and daughters, few examine how these change when daughters provide care. Caregiving often reactivates daughters' feelings of dependency and interrupts workplace achievement that confers a sense of competence and adulthood. It also demands that women adopt a new stance toward their mothers. Daughters who render care must simultaneously revive and reconstruct intergenerational relationships.

In discussing their interactions with their parents, many of my respondents stressed the idiosyncracies of their families. Nevertheless, a number of patterns can be discerned. Although these characterized the majority of the women I interviewed, future studies should explore why some women exhibited different responses. I will begin by looking at the experience of caring for mothers and then contrast the different interpersonal and intrapsychic factors that shaped the experience of caring for fathers.

Relationships with Mothers

Reviving and Reconstructing Relationships

Caregiving brought women into intimate contact with their mothers, often for the first time since they had been adolescents. Issues they assumed had been fully resolved suddenly reemerged. Several women were shocked by the intensity of the feelings this experience provoked. Although a few viewed caregiving as an opportunity to master old conflicts, many stated that they simply slipped back into old patterns.

One of the five women living alone with severely disabled parents represents an extreme example of emotional responses that were common, if less intense. She had lived on her own for many years before moving into her parents' house to care for them. She first nursed her father; when he died, she became responsible for her mother, who had dementia. At the time of the interview, the daughter no longer could leave her mother alone. She did not work for pay, rarely saw friends, and had time to herself only during the few hours a week when her mother attended an adult day care program. She described her life this way:

> My struggle is that because I'm sequestered with my mother all the time, I feel that I'm reverting back, I don't feel like an adult. This could be my chance to grow, but in the process I'm regressing. I had overcome an eating problem, and I'm going back to it now—eating a lot at night and then not being able to get up in the morning. Boundaries are hard. Which part is me? And it's hard because mother always is talking about me as a child.

Because other women in the study had been far more successful in carving out adult identities, prolonged and intense contact with their mothers did not threaten their sense of self so profoundly. Those who were not living with their mothers were better able to distance themselves emotionally. Most women who shared a residence with their mothers retained at least some links to jobs and other adults. Nevertheless, the majority of women stated that they reestablished old modes of interacting with their mothers and reexperienced feelings that were appropriate to an earlier period. Several mentioned specific incidents that evoked childhood experiences. One woman said, "Sometimes she'll say, 'Wait a second. Who's the mother here?' and I still get that feeling of when I was little, and she'd say, 'Wait a second. I'm the mother here, and I'll decide.' " Another woman described her experience taking her mother shopping: "We had a problem because things cost too much. She made a scene in front of a sales girl, although I took her to the May Co. Budget Store and looked at the sales table. Mother was outraged that shoes cost $12. I felt like I was about 15 years old again."

Old resentments suddenly had renewed force. Some women became preoccupied with the ways their mothers had hindered their growth and development or failed to love them adequately when they were children. Many women also acknowledged that they found themselves once again looking to their mothers for approval and striving to please them. A few expected to receive the approbation and affection that previously had been withheld. A woman who perceived herself as having been her mother's least favorite child realized that she harbored a persistent fantasy that caregiving might alter her mother's assessment: "I keep thinking that there is a chance that I will do these wonderful things, and then she'll love me." A second women spoke in similar terms: "I'm still working on the relationship with her, in that I'm still trying to be the daughter she expected me to be, and I'm still seeking after some kind of recognition from her, still wanting her approval." And a third said: "Whatever I do, it's not the right thing. And I keep having the expectation after all this time that one of these days it's going to be the right thing."

If caregiving reawakened childhood feelings, however, it also compelled these women to acknowledge how much had changed. In some cases, the mothers appeared very different from the women whom the daughters remembered. Many women spoke of the difficulties of watching the deterioration of a person to whom they felt intimately bound. One woman commented: "Having just lost my dad, I'm real grateful she's still alive, but it's sad. It's hard to have a positive attitude, just watching her get frailer and more forgetful. In a week or two you can see the difference, that she's walking with more difficulty, and she remembers less. It's hard to see at such close quarters."

Fears of aging and death surfaced. Identifying closely with their mothers, many women were terrified by their mothers' infirmities, which foreshadowed their own old age. One woman put it this way: "You realize your own vulnerability. Without being entirely aware, you think, 'Am I going to be like this? Are my children going to worry about me?'" Caregivers whose mothers had Alzheimer's disease worried about inheriting a propensity for the illness: "Aging never bothered me before. Now I wonder if I will inherit this, if I will do this to my own children. If I forget something, it's not just a funny matter any more. I wonder if this is how mama started. It's made me more aware of growing older, and it's not such a wonderful thing any more."

Alterations of affect and behavior were both painful and confusing to children of mothers with dementia. Many acknowledged anger at their mothers. As the disease progressed and personalities changed, some women felt that they had been abandoned.

Caregiving itself accentuated the sense of loss. The presence of mothers reminded women continually of the former person. One woman, who lived with a mother suffering from Alzheimer's disease, said: "The person I loved isn't there. It's just a body sitting there. The terrible thing is that she looks like the same person, but she doesn't share my joys or my sorrows or anything. It isn't the same person, but

I still have to look at that person that looks like the mother I loved. And it just tears me apart." In some instances, the level of lucidity fluctuated. When mothers afflicted with dementia sounded more coherent than usual, hopes were raised that they would recover; the sense of loss thus was recurrent.

Regardless of whether parents suffered from dementia, daughters must relinquish the illusion that their mothers are omnipotent and still can offer protection.* The great majority of women stated that they were shocked when the need for care arose because they had assumed that their mothers somehow were insulated from illness and dependency. Asked whether she had expected to care for her mother, one woman answered:

> I suppose in the back of your mind, you always think, what if anything happened. But my mother was such a powerhouse all of her life, beyond the norm, that it seemed very farfetched to me. Hardly anybody at 67 says, "I'm going to join the Peace Corps and go to Africa and build mud huts and teach children out in the bush country." I mean, that takes a bit of courage. She traveled all over Europe and stayed in tents and bicycled. She had raised all these children, and then she decided that she would like to do some things, and she set about doing them. We all thought it was wonderful, and her health has always been wonderful.

Another woman spoke in a similar vein:

> I don't think I ever expected to have to care for either one of my parents. They always seemed to be so self-reliant and independent and outgoing and had all these plans for their lives. We never talked about illness. My father was a physician, and yet we never talked about the possibility that he might become ill. And then, that my mother would become ill. I just never saw my mother as a person who was ever ill. She was never in bed with any problem. She was always a well person. So I think the idea that I would ever be responsibile for caring for her, I don't think it entered my mind at all. So maybe that's why it was such a shock when she just fell apart when my father died, and then she was just so dependent on me. She always looked to me like a very strong, together person.

Even a woman whose mother was 96 when the two began to live together recalled: "It never entered my mind that I'd be caring for her. When you live with somebody who's healthy and independent, you

---

*Over twenty years ago, Martha Blenkner (1965) coined the phrase "filial crisis" to describe this realization.

can't look that far ahead. It just never occurred to me. She was always a very active woman. Running to her lunches and her card games and everything. A simple thing like a bone fracture, a couple of cracked ribs, that started the whole thing." In rendering care, these women were forced to acknowledge that their mothers were vulnerable to infirmity and old age and could not remain independent forever.

If mothers were not invincible, they also no longer could be relied upon. A woman who had been caring for her mother for two years still had not reconciled herself to the impossibility of turning to her mother when she was in need:

> Sometimes I just want my parents. I have my own problems, and I want my mother and she's not in there and it looks like her but it's not my mother anymore. That's the hardest part, I think, when I just want to be a little girl. Sometimes I try to imagine what it would be like to have parents you can go to and ask help of and maybe that would be nice, to have a relationship with your parents where they were still your parents and you were still their child. I have friends who still can leave their children with their parents on the weekend or borrow money or ask advice. I can't do those things.

Still wanting support from her parents, she had to care for them instead.

Moreover, caregiving demands that women redefine their roles vis-à-vis their mothers. Nel Noddings (1984) has commented that "apprehending the other's reality, feeling what he [sic] feels as nearly as possible, is the essential part of caring. . . . Caring involves stepping out of one's own personal frame of reference." Ideally, then, before a woman cares for her mother, she should be able to view her mother as separate from herself and understand the reality of her life. An article by Judith Kegan Gardiner about the school of self psychology also helps to explain what is called for. Gardiner (1987) writes that members of this school "see empathy as an adult process in which one mature self takes the position of the other person. . . . From this perspective, empathy is not the same as but opposite to projective identification in which one person insists that the other is an extension of the first. This self psychology view of empathy entails no merging, blurring, or loss of self for adults." Such empathetic understanding is a critical aspect of caregiving, but it requires that a woman cease viewing herself as a child in relation to her mother. Nancy Chodorow (1987) argues that, as a result of dominant patterns of child rearing in our society, many women experience themselves as being intimately

connected to their mothers. This sense of fusion, however, is antitheti-
cal to the stance women must adopt as caregivers.

Most women I interviewed found caregiving particularly difficult
because it required them to exert authority over their parents. Many
women were acutely aware that their mothers resented filial assertions of authority. These caregivers feared they were wounding their
mothers further by taking control. One woman viewed caregiving as
an aggressive act: "Maybe I'm just getting even with my mother. I
have a guilty feeling because I enjoy being in control. It always was a
problem that my mother was over-controlling." A woman who acknowledged that she could not forgive her mother's past treatment of
her took pains not to use caregiving as an opportunity to settle old
scores: "There's probably some really quirky part of me that says, 'I
have the power, ha, ha, ha.' And yet I really don't think I'm doing that.
But I think that's why I'm having to be so careful when I do things like
taking away her money and making her do things that I want her to
do." Asserting control was especially difficult for women who still
were seeking to please their mothers and win their approval. These
women felt torn between the need to assume responsibility and the
desire to oblige their mothers by acceding to their mothers' wishes.
One woman who lived with her mother initially stated that caregiving
was not hard for her because her mother had had recurrent psychotic
episodes throughout much of her life, and the daughter had had to
render care when still young. Later in the interview, she revised her
opinion:

> I said that I was comfortable taking care of my mother because I had
> been doing it all my life. That's not true. I used to care for her the way
> she wanted me to take care of her. I used to do what she wanted me
> to do. Now I have to make decisions for her and say no. This is terri-
> bly, terribly difficult for me. I have to do what she doesn't want me to
> do. I'm not used to saying no to my mother. "No, you can't have co-
> deine pills," and I'm working up to saying, "No, you have to live in a
> board and care facility." I've been a good girl all my life, even though
> I'm 46 now.

Several women explained their reluctance to assert authority by stat-
ing that their mothers were entitled to refuse to surrender control
because they were adults, not children. In addition, some women
defined good daughters as those who respect the wisdom of their
parents:

> My difficult problem over the last two years has been trying to get my
> mother's cooperation in doing the things I have to do to make her life

better, and that's not been easy. Like when she has to go to the doctor when her foot is sore and she wants to go to the doctor and then at the last minute, she won't go. I just talk to her till she agrees to go. She has no choice. I yank her out the door and at times she will be very angry and be sputtering at me when I put her in the car, saying she doesn't have to go and she doesn't understand why, and she can't afford it, and all sorts of strange things that she would not say if she was well. But she is the parent, I have always been trained to respect that role, and so when she says get out of my life, she has a right to say that in a sense. You feel that a person in old age should be at the most wise point of their life in a sense, and in your head that means control of every situation.

Although caring demanded that she seize the reins, this woman was loath to dishonor her mother.

But, if women employed the language of rights and obligations, they also used terms that betrayed the sense that they still were operating within the framework of filial relationships. One woman explained her reluctance to wield authority by saying that she couldn't "cross" her mother. Three others described themselves as being "mean" to their mothers. Such words suggest that these women viewed themselves as daughters rebelling against their mothers, not simply as adults responding to the needs of others. When asked how her relationship with her mother had changed since she began rendering care, one woman responded: "I don't know how to answer that. I suppose it has changed in the sense that I have become bossy and say 'you have to do something my way, and I don't care what you say,' which I never would have said before. In a sense I exert outward kinds of control and maybe that is a difference. But emotionally the relationship is the same still. I am the child." A second woman, queried about whether caregiving made her feel more like a child or an adult, answered this way:

> It's a very tricky thing. I think I went between those two. I would feel one and then just the opposite. My mother was a very strong person, and I was a very easygoing person. It was very hard for me to be the strong one. Even in all her dementia I never felt she was that child-like. I felt that underneath, that personality of her was still there, like I'd help her down the stairs, and she'd pull back.

These women found it hard to tell their mothers what to do because they still felt their mothers' power over them.

Some women avoided challenging their mothers' authority. I noted in the previous chapter that several women hesitated to intervene when their mothers acted in ways that jeopardized their health or safety. One woman described her predicament: "Because she's heard there have been a lot of robberies, she has put a big heavy chair in front of the door of her bedroom, which is dangerous in case of a fire. What can I do? My mother's 82 years old, she's lived her whole life, she's done whatever she's damned well pleased, and I can't make her change. She's very set in her ways." A second woman explained her refusal to act by noting the importance of preserving the mother-daughter relationship:

> In addition to the mental problem, she has diabetes, chronic hypertension, and high blood pressure. I'm kind of worried right now about her physical condition. She doesn't follow any guidelines for diabetes, in terms of what she's supposed to eat. She just eats what she wants to eat and takes her pills and thinks that that's going to keep her going. You see, when someone's 79 years old, you can't really say, "You need to go on a diet now, Mom, and you need to stop eating all those sweets." This is a lifetime pattern, and you just can't change someone's lifetime pattern. And I think my biggest struggle has been trying to keep from becoming her mother. I don't want to be her mother. I'm her daughter, and I don't want to ever make her feel as though I'm trying to tell her how to live her life. So I try to be as low key as possible about whatever help I do offer her.

Taking control of mothers' financial affairs, preventing them from driving, and hiring aides and attendants were critical junctures that aroused profound anxiety. One woman confiscated her mother's car keys only after her mother had had three accidents. A second hesitated to hire an aide to tend her mother although she suspected that her mother occasionally lost her way when returning home from shopping. Two other women were reluctant to begin managing their mothers' finances even after insurance salesmen had convinced their mothers to enroll in worthless plans. Yet another woman refrained from setting up a conservatorship despite her mother's increasing propensity to make serious financial mistakes.

Other types of control were more subtle but equally problematic. One woman gave this account of taking her mother shopping:

> I was always on edge. I lost her four times. They were the worst things in my life. So there always was that fear. I wanted to hold her hand, but I didn't want to rob her of her dignity and make her feel she was demented to that extent. I tried always to let her have her self-respect, but always there was a very fine line of where and what to do. So it was very stressful.

To this woman, holding her mother's hand meant crossing a sensitive boundary in parent-child relations.

Women who did manage to assume responsibility over their mothers' lives tried to shield mothers from awareness of the shift in roles. The few women who helped their mothers financially were careful to conceal their contributions. Women also failed to inform their mothers when they took control over their financial affairs. One woman hid car keys from her mother rather than confront her about her dangerous driving and demand that she stop.

Some women acknowledged that it was as important to themselves as to their mothers to create the illusion that the original parent-child relationship remained intact. Thus, one woman who eventually hired an aide for her mother, an Alzheimer's patient, explained her previous reluctance to do so this way:

> The concern for all children is treating this person with dignity and respect and trying to keep them intact for as long as possible. So you are always looking at it from that perspective. You are altering your behavior. You are trying to maintain this in everything that you do. You try to have them keep their independence, but it can be a trap. When the dementia gets to a certain point, you finally realize that it doesn't make any difference, because whatever cognition she had a minute ago, she's not going to remember it. . . . You gradually realize that you are trying to maintain the status quo for yourself because it may not matter to them any more.

Nevertheless, it would be wrong to suggest that caregivers practiced deceptions solely to satisfy their own needs. I have noted that the great majority of women in this study took as a given that their primary mission should be to protect their mothers' individuality and self-image. Some invoked the advice of experts to support their own definitions of good care and justify their behavior. They also expected others to adhere to their own standards of care. Several expressed fury at relatives and professionals who failed to respect their mothers' worth and humanity.

If their own desires meshed with the requirements of good caring, however, their attempts to preserve their mothers' identity also conflicted with their needs in two ways. First, because they tried to maintain the pretence that the mother-daughter relationship had not changed, they failed to dislodge their mothers from positions of power. But the more they viewed their mothers as retaining their former characteristics, the easier it was to lapse into familiar patterns and the more difficult to exert their own authority. Second, because they rendered their own work invisible, they made it difficult to receive the appreciation they longed for. We saw in Chapter 5 a variety of reasons that parents did not show gratitude, including, in many cases, their cognitive impairments. Nevertheless, an important factor may well have been the daughters' determination to render their assistance inconspicuous. Jean Baker Miller (1976:64) argues that women who serve the needs of others frequently have the illusion that their own needs, even when unarticulated, "will somehow be fulfilled in turn." Several women in this study hoped that their mothers would appreciate the daughters' sacrifices even though the daughters strove hard to conceal them. When thanks were not forthcoming, the daughters felt angry and resentful.

Responding to Demands for Care

Although most caregivers believed that their mothers resisted even essential help, several women also portrayed their mothers as making impossible demands. Some women complained that their mothers expected them to spend inordinate amounts of time with them. The following comment was typical: "She's not saying it in so many words, but she wants more of my time and energy, which I can't give her. I have a home and a husband and two children, a 15-year-old and a 10-year-old. . . . She keeps wanting more. I feel like it's a bottomless pit." Caregivers believed that their mothers assumed that the daughters would take responsibility for decisions the mothers easily could make on their own. Caregivers also pointed to instances in which their mothers had summoned them for crises that turned out to be imaginary or for trivial reasons: "She'll call me whenever she wants. Sometimes it's because she doesn't have a postage stamp and wants me to mail something." In addition, many women believed that their mothers had boundless expectations about what their daughters could accomplish. Some mothers appeared to hold their daughters accountable for any plans that went awry or any unsatisfactory program or service.

But few daughters perceived their mothers' demands as clear-cut. Many daughters complained that their mothers rebuffed any assistance offered. Those who asked for a great deal of help often seemed ambivalent about receiving it. For example, some mothers urged their daughters to take charge of certain plans for them but then proceeded to make their own arrangements. Some daughters stated that their mothers gave them overly precise instructions about how chores should be carried out and carefully monitored performance. One woman said, "Mother treats me like I'm 6 years old. She will literally tell me what to do every step of the way, and she will repeat it several times." Daughters also stated that their mothers expressed disapproval about the ways their daughters assisted them. One woman interpreted her mother's criticisms this way: "I just get complaints when I do things. Every time I take over and make a decision that happens because deep down my mother wants control over her life, and she still wants to be in charge of it, but she doesn't know how."

Several researchers have argued that disabled elderly women strive to retain their sources of power in the family (Evers, 1985; Fischer, 1986; Lewis and Meredith, 1988; Matthews, 1979). Many women in this study interpreted their mothers' demands as manipulative attempts to remain in control. Many also related their mothers requests to personality changes caused by dementia (see Mace and Rabins, 1985).

In addition, these women frequently stated that they considered their mothers' demands unreasonable. Two contended that their mothers clung to an idealized notion of caregiving relationships in the nineteenth century, which was inappropriate to the 1980s. Three complained that the care their mothers expected from them far exceeded what these mothers had provided their daughters when they were young. Said one:

> My mother is just a critical woman. She is terribly selfish. And now she expects me to give my whole life to her, and all the grandchildren should devote themselves to her. She never devoted herself to others. . . . To this day when I walk in, she's straight as a ramrod, and she turns her cheek for me to kiss. She's not embracing or spontaneous. Very cold and stiff, and yet she wants all of your affection. It's terrible.

Still other women felt that their mothers should have been satisfied because the care their daughters rendered already had improved their lives dramatically. One woman remarked:

> On Sunday Mother was very depressed and had nothing to do. This has been going on for months, and she complains bitterly. Sunday is the day with nothing to do. My brother was supposed to take her to dinner, but he had to cancel. This threw my mother into a depression, she was all teary. There was no consoling her. Considering that she spent all her time before she moved out here doing nothing, it seems strange. When she was alone it never even occurred to her to go out, to look at a tree. And all of a sudden this woman is frantic because she has nothing to do. And she has the busiest schedule she's had since her children were small. So I'm constantly reading it as, you don't do enough for me, or you should be taking me someplace on Sunday.

In short, these women believed that their mothers were ambivalent about receiving assistance, perceived their mothers' demands to be unreasonable, and attributed them both to illness and fears of losing control. Why, then, did these demands exert such a powerful influence over the daughters? Why were they so likely to "read" their mothers' complaints as requests for more help?

One explanation may lie in the daughters' sense of identification with their mothers, which may have permitted them not just to share their mothers' pain but also to anticipate their mothers' needs and grant them primacy. In addition, many women interpreted their mothers' continuing requests as evidence that they had fallen short as caregivers. I noted in Chapter 5 that most women in this study embraced a notion of caregiving that required them to improve the overall quality of their mothers' lives. They viewed their mothers' complaints as evidence of their own failure to do enough. One woman lamented: "No matter how much help I gave her, I can't seem to give her what she needs, and I can't seem to reconcile it with myself. That's the hardest part. I know I've done a lot of good for her, but she seems so unhappy no matter what I do. I keep wanting to fix it, and I can't, I really can't."

Such attitudes may help to explain why caregiving fails to resolve residual conflicts between mothers and daughters. Had this woman succeeded in her goal of restoring her mother's happiness, she might have demonstrated her worth to her mother and earned the latter's approval. Instead, she felt continually rebuffed. Nancy Chodorow (1978) argues that the ambivalence mothers feel about being women in this society colors their behavior toward their daughters. As a result, mothers often fail both to nurture their daughters adequately and to encourage their autonomy. If Chodorow is correct, then women who perceive their mothers as simultaneously demanding and ungrateful may feel that they are replaying earlier dynamics.

Establishing Limits

Because this study was cross-sectional rather than longitudinal, it was not possible to trace the evolution of the women's responses to caring for their mothers. Nevertheless, most women who had been providing care for at least a year stated that they experienced the greatest difficulties during initial stages. Several women pointed with pride to their increased ability to draw boundaries around caregiving responsibilities. They had reduced both the time spent with their mothers and their emotional involvement in their mothers' lives.

Some claimed that they no longer responded to each crisis that arose with the same urgency.

Women who had attended support groups or sought individual therapy reported that they had been counseled to establish limits to the obligations they assumed, and they were attempting to follow this advice. As noted in the previous chapter, caregivers whose mothers suffered from some form of dementia gained distance by learning more about the nature of their mothers' impairments. Although no woman had succeeded in disengaging entirely from the relationship, many claimed that issues that had consumed them when they first began caring for their mothers persisted only in an attenuated form.

Relationships with Fathers

Fourteen women in the study were caring for fathers. Although women struggled with issues of authority in relation to fathers as well as to mothers, the experience of caring for fathers differed from the experience of tending mothers in two important respects. First, caregivers were less likely to perceive their fathers as making extravagant demands. Although fifteen of the forty-four women tending mothers complained about their mothers' demands, just two of the fourteen women caring for fathers reported that their fathers placed impossible demands on them.

Second, caregivers of mothers and fathers responded to personality changes of their parents in very different ways. Women caring for mothers with dementia stated that, as the edges of their mothers' personalities eroded, the intensity of their own feelings also waned, and they were better able to extricate themselves from the morass of the relationship. One woman was relieved to realize that her mother no longer remembered their arguments; this allowed her to forget them as well. Women caring for fathers, by contrast, reported that, as their fathers became more vulnerable, they ceased to be objects of awe. As a consequence, the daughters were able to express affection they previously had been afraid to demonstrate and to establish a close connection, often for the first time. One woman discussed her experiences this way:

> My father has always been a very difficult person to get along with. I mean it sounds really perverse, like I am glad that he is sick or something, but there has been this period of time where I have a feeling that I can be nice to him and be sweet and give him kisses and be affectionate in a way that is not at all threatening. It was horrible grow-

ing up with him. We were always afraid that he was going to be angry if we had done something wrong. So this is this kind of process of
making my peace. When I see my friends whose parents have died
suddenly and they have not made their peace, I realize I am in a way
very lucky. I have the perception that he is nicer most of the time, and
maybe it's because people can without any terror give him more emotional support and attention. Unlike the past I can laugh with my father and give him little kisses on the cheek and I can rub his arm or
rub his knee and just be affectionate.

A second woman also spoke of forging a closer relationship with her
father:

When he got sick, my feelings started changing. I started worrying
about him, and realizing I really did care about him. I feel closer to
him now than when I was a kid. I didn't get it as a kid, but I'm getting enough now that I feel if he dies I will have felt like I was close
to my father. Sometimes if someone's ill or sick, you can give to them
more than if they're healthy. If they're healthy, they won't take it or
it's harder. Like before he was real sick, there was that clash of me
wanting to give and he not wanting me to. When he's sick, I can give
him more. I feel less inhibited.

In short, the personality changes of frail elderly parents enabled caregivers of fathers to develop a greater intimacy and caregivers of mothers to establish critical detachment. This divergence is consistent with
theories arguing that women experience relationships with mothers
and fathers very differently. According to Chodorow (1978), women
remain enmeshed with their mothers but idealize their fathers, viewing them as clearly differentiated from themselves.

Conclusion

Parent care involves a constant tension between attachment and
loss, pleasing and caring, seeking to preserve an older person's dignity
and exerting unaccustomed authority, overcoming resistance to care
and fulfilling extravagant demands, reviving a relationship and trans-
forming it. Some of these contradictions are built into the experience
of caring for any person at the end of the life course. When adult
children are the caregivers, however, services are rendered within the
context of relationships that already are characterized by deep ambivalence.

Although residues from the past shape the experience of caring for
elderly mothers, daughters discover that they cannot go home again.

Even caregivers who feel most like children must have the personal strength to make decisions about what they perceive their mothers' needs to be. Moreover, caregiving punctures the illusion of maternal omnipotence. Although many daughters continue to look to their mothers for protection and security, they must acknowledge their mothers' growing infirmities and dependence. Even before a mother's death, the need to render care may signal the end of childhood.

Few daughters receive the affirmation they seek. Because their own notions of good care compel them to camouflage their activities, they discourage rather than invite gratitude. In addition, although their mothers often have needs that can never be fully satisfied, many daughters interpret any complaints as indictments of themselves.

Some policymakers argue that returning care to individual households will reinforce traditional values and strengthen intimate bonds. The women to whom I spoke felt overwhelmed by the intense emotions this experience provoked, and a few felt that this diminished the quality of care they rendered. We will see than many wanted outside help not only to gain relief from caregiving tasks but also to achieve emotional detachment.

7

Work and Leisure

Policies that seek to reimpose care for the elderly on private households assume not only that families deliver superior care but also that women easily can absorb additional obligations. But women rarely are free of competing demands. In fact, because care for the elderly is intrinsically unpredictable, women often find that responsibility particularly difficult to accommodate. Reproductive technology has enabled many women to exercise greater control over the timing of childbirth, but they never will be able to determine when a parent needs care.

The great majority of women I interviewed had not anticipated caring for their parents. Many remarked that "it never had occurred" to them that they would need to provide care or that caregiving responsibilities "seemed to come out of the blue." Several stated that, if they ever had thought about their parents' old age, they simply had assumed that their parents would die quickly. Those who had considered the possibility that their parents would need help were shocked by the type of disease that struck. A woman caring for a mother with Alzheimer's disease noted:

> I really thought that, in my mother's old age, if she ever needed me, I'd be there 100 percent. My husband and I discussed it, oh, many times, way back when my father died. We used to say, "She could come and live here, and she'd just love it. She loves flowers, and she loves to go, and we'd take her here, and we'd take her there." It was always with that thought in mind, if she needed us. I certainly never dreamed that she would suffer anything mental. It was just beyond me.

Eight women had assumed that the other parent would be the one who required care.

Many women had to be available at short notice because they had little warning that they would be called upon to provide care. One woman whose mother suffered a stroke commented, "If you plan to have a child, you get pregnant, and even if you don't plan at least you have that nine months. But this was a real surprise situation." Although the onset of other diseases was more gradual, nine women had lived far from their parents and did not learn about parental impairments until they had become severe. Six women discovered the extent of one parent's disabilities only after the death of the other, who had shielded them from the initial stages. Recent writing has emphasized the need for predictability; we can cope better with events that arrive at scheduled times and for which we have prepared (Hagestad, 1986). But caregiving obligations often occur precipitately, catching family members by surprise.

Some women stated that the need to provide care occurred at particularly bad times for them. Four assumed caregiving responsibilities for one parent just after they had begun the process of mourning the other. Two suffered from serious disabilities themselves; six others developed serious health problems after they had begun rendering care.

Care for elderly parents often coincided with other caregiving obligations. Several women had heard the terms "sandwich generation" and "woman in the middle" and believed that they applied to their own plight. Just two had children under the age of 18 at home, but many felt responsible for the well-being of older children. One woman had to take charge of her disabled brother because her mother could no longer care for him. A woman caring for both of her husband's parents as well as her own mother stated: "I feel constantly as though I'm treading water just as quickly as I can. And I frequently have dreams where I'm on a carousel, and these things are going too quickly, or people are literally throwing things at me on the carousel and saying, 'Catch this, catch this, take care of this, do this, do that.' "

When caregiving responsibilities were sequential rather than concurrent, other problems emerged. Women whose children were independent had looked forward to a period when they would be free of the demands of care; they felt cheated as parental care increasingly dominated their lives. Some already had devoted many years to caring for other parents, husbands, and in-laws. A sixty-year old widow with a particularly long caregiving career behind her stated:

> This has affected my social life because I have no patience for developing a relationship with a man, whereas five years ago I had a lot

of fun. We're getting too old, or I can see the handwriting on the wall, and I don't want to take care of anyone again. I have taken care of too many people, and I'll date some guy that's 65, 70 years old, and I think how many good years does he have? And it could be me, but it also could be the other way around. I'd rather be alone and also have my freedom because I don't want to take care of anyone else again.

Although personal disabilities and competing caregiving responsibilities contributed to many women's sense of overload, those who worked for pay were especially likely to believe that parental care imposed excessive burdens. Like child rearing, care for the elderly clashes with labor force participation in various ways. Waged work and family care confer different rewards, operate according to different clocks, and are guided by different value systems. Demands in one arena frequently are incompatible with those in the other. One recent study found that those caring for the disabled elderly have the same number of absences and take the same amount of time off work as parents of young children (Scharlach and Boyd, 1989). Because an unprecedented number of women are entering the work force just when the frail elderly population is growing rapidly, the conflict is intensifying between paid employment and informal care. This chapter examines the difficulties of combining outside jobs and caregiving responsibilities at home. It also briefly discusses the impact of caregiving on women's ability to engage in leisure activities. Many observers fear that women cope with excessive demands by sacrificing their personal needs (see Hochschild, 1989).

Care and Career

Full-time Workers

Twenty-one women in this study (42 percent) were employed full time when they were interviewed. Seven were professionals (two nurses, an elementary school teacher, a writer, an interior decorator, a professor, and a policy analyst); five had managerial positions; and nine worked in administrative support occupations (such as secretarial work and bookkeeping). These women clearly had it easier than the great majority of female workers. None was employed in a highly supervised blue collar job or in the rapidly expanding low-status service sector, where workers rarely remain long enough to obtain special treatment (Smith, 1984). Most exercised at least some control over their hours.

Nevertheless, like many other employed caregivers (see Brody et al., 1987; Scharlach and Boyd, 1989; Stephens and Christianson, 1986; Stone, Cafferata and Sangl, 1987; Travelers Companies, 1985), these women reported that responsibilites for care encroached on their work lives in various ways. Five (36 percent) said that obligations for their parents affected their occupational placement. One, a public health nurse, passed up an opportunity for advancement: "I had made an appointment for a promotional interview in September, but when I brought my mother here I canceled it, and I have not accepted any more interviews, because I have all I can handle right now. The idea of taking on a new job in a different location is too much for me. I just can't deal with anything new right now." Another woman refused to be considered for a promotion that would have required her to work swing shift; she lived with her mother and wanted to be home each evening to care for her. Three other women changed jobs in order to be more available to their parents. A systems analyst recently had switched firms so that she no longer had to travel. A representative for an insurance company had sought a job that would give her more leeway to respond to her mother's needs:

> Caring for my mother is one of the main reasons I went into this work. Before this, I was an administrator running a program. I worked very long hours and many weekends, and I never really got away from my work. I brought it home in my head, and it was like a tape spinning all night long, in my sleep. I took this job because it's more self-directed. I can do a lot of paperwork at home, and I make my own appointments and schedules, and so if I need to be with my mother to take her to a doctor's appointment, which I have done many times, or to visit her in the hospital, or to take her to the hospital, or bring her home, or be there when she has these tests in the hospital, I can just schedule my time to be available for those things. One of the main reasons I'm staying with this work is that it's flexible, and that if she needs me in a crisis, I'm there. I can be there, I can go anytime.

An interior decorator explained why she left her position in a firm and began to work on her own: "The only way I've been able to manage is to be self-employed, because the last time I worked for a firm, my working day was constantly being interrupted with emergencies."

Caregiving also intruded on the work lives of women whose employment status remained stable. Women in professional or managerial positions reported that they had wanted to make a total commitment to their careers. Preoccupation with their parents' difficulties often prevented them from taking the initiative or exercising their intelligence. A woman with a managerial position in a company remarked:

> I'm just drained and run down and tired and just burned out by caring for my father, and I don't have that much left to give to my job. It's not my primary focus right now. It is not something that I'm directed towards right now. The job is really a very self-motivating position, and I'm not motivated. I would say that the quality and the motivation of the work have changed drastically. I don't think that the interest level is there. When I had no other responsibilities, my career was the motivating force for me. This is something that I feel very dissatisfied with. I have really lost interest in it.

An elementary school teacher reported a similar experience: "I don't have the same energy and the same enthusiasm for the class. I find that certain projects I might have wanted to do, that I change the scale, certain new activities which I enjoy doing for myself. I don't like constantly repeating the same curriculum year after year, but certain new activities I am not able to develop."

Women working full time also stated that phone calls from their parents or paid helpers interrupted their work. In addition, these women took time off from their jobs when their parents became ill, saw doctors, or visited possible residential facilities.

Women's responses to such intrusions were influenced by the nature of their relationships to their parents and their attitudes toward their parents' requests. Women who felt their parents' demands were unreasonable were especially likely to experience such interruptions as burdensome. One described the early years of caring for a mother who suffered from Alzheimer's disease this way:

> I was working very close by, right around the corner from where she lived, and so she would call and say she was locked out of the house, or she didn't know who it was, but someone was in the backyard. Things like that. I would have to leave and go down the street to see what was going on, and I'd see that she was sitting in the living room saying, "Oh, hi! How nice to see you. I haven't seen you in four days. How nice of you to come and visit me." She wouldn't have remembered the phone call at all. I would have come running in with my hair flying and everything. I was having a difficult time with my anger at that point.

A woman whose mother lacked the excuse of mental impairment was even more enraged by being summoned at work:

> She'll call me whenever she wants. Sometimes it's because she
> doesn't have a postage stamp and wants me to mail something. She
> says I need to drive her to the doctor's. She refuses to take taxis de-
> spite the special coupons. I like to be at work if I possibly can. If I
> don't feel well, I'll be at work, I'll do my job. But I am called away for
> a lot of unnecessary reasons. When she goes to the hospital, of
> course, that goes without saying, that's different.

But interruptions also could have serious repercussions on wom-
en's ability to continue to work. Although two women sought employment that would let them control the pace and rhythm of work, a
woman who was self-employed as a writer commented:

> The first couple of years my parents were here, I would work in fits
> and starts, because the interruptions were very, very difficult for me.
> It would be very hard for me to switch gears and try to cope with ca-
> lamities, to determine what really was a calamity. These tearful calls
> from my mother are often over nothing, but sometimes, they're about
> something. I had started working on a project, but there kept being
> ongoing demands on my time. I guess I stopped working, or I let it
> drag, but I never acknowledged it. I kept saying, "I've got to get back
> and get to work," and I'd go back and I'd do a page, and then I
> wouldn't do it for another week, and I kept fooling myself. I needed
> the crutch of saying, "I'm working," I guess, to be able to give them
> an idea that I do something else. But at the end of six months time, I
> noticed I hadn't done anything. And if I'd been working every day
> the way I thought I was, I would. I'd been fooling myself. I didn't
> have anything to show for the time.

She interpreted her inability to resume writing after calls from her
parents as evidence of her own deficiencies:

> I can't go back and sit down at my typewriter and go to work after
> they call me in an emergency. I would love to know from people who
> have written all their lives, people who have better training and a bet-
> ter sense of how to operate. I've never studied to be a writer, and
> there are people who have spent many years learning the craft.
> Maybe there's a skill to it that I'm just not privy to. Maybe there's a
> way that you can go back right to your typewriter and start working.
> But I don't have that. I cannot seem to develop that skill where I can
> close out my parents. They still reach me on some level that I have no
> blocks to put up, no barricades.

Caregivers who work in offices rather than at home tend to be less
vulnerable to such intrusions. But two women lost pay several times
when they took time off during the work week. Three others worried

that their absences would negatively affect upcoming reviews. Responding to parents' demands also violated women's sense of workplace norms. An office manager described her response to phone calls from her mother, a victim of Alzheimer's disease:

> Before I had anyone to take care of her, she would call me fifteen times before lunch about the same thing. Sometimes I would be in the middle of a meeting with my bosses or whatever. It was very unnerving, and people were around me. They didn't say, "You can't have her calling," it was that I thought it was improper and I didn't want to be disturbed and so got very upset by things like that.

A secretary remarked: "People haven't gotten angry when my mother calls, but there are things that need to be done in a timely manner. I feel responsible." Although these two women suffered no sanctions from their employers, they had wanted to appear unconstrained by family demands.

It clearly is important to investigate not just whether care for elderly parents affects workforce participation but also whether paid employment affects caregiving. Because the sample was limited to women who had assumed caregiving responsibilities, it could not tell us whether waged work prevents women from becoming caregivers. Nevertheless, the study did help to illuminate how the allocation of caregiving responsibilities is influenced by women's subordinate position in the labor force. One woman was caring for both her husband's parents as well as her own mother. Because her husband earned the higher income and was the status-bearer of the family, her job was considered more dispensable. Although she continued to work, she bore the major share of caregiving responsibilities and was the only one summoned when crises arose during working hours. Another woman noted that her brother justified his lesser involvement in their mother's care by asserting that he had to support a family. She, too, worked full time, but her earnings were not considered essential to her family's well-being.

The women I interviewed were far more worried about the impact of caregiving on their ability to work full time than about the impact of paid employment on either the quantity or the quality of the care their parents received. A teacher, however, feared that the demands of her job prevented her from adequately evaluating and supervising aides and attendants and thus compromised her father's care. Two other women stated that they would have liked to be able to take their parents out more during the day.

A growing number of studies report that waged work has positive benefits for women (see Baruch, Biener, and Barnett, 1985). If most women I interviewed were unconcerned about the consequences of their work for their parents' care, they agreed that paid employment was good for themselves. It muted the emotional consequences of caregiving and provided them with an alternative source of personal identity and social rewards. Many, like the secretary quoted below, said that their jobs also helped them impose necessary limits on caregiving responsibilities: "Right now my job is saving my life. It's a good cop-out. It's a legitimate excuse my mother recognizes. If I wasn't working, it would be a total disaster. But she knows that work is important and that you have a responsibility to it." Even a woman who regretted her inability to go more places with her mother acknowledged that it also was helpful to have an excuse not to spend all day caring for her. And, although some women complained that they brought the strains of caregiving to work, others stated that their jobs protected them from becoming engulfed by caregiving obligations and helped them to gain emotional distance. For one woman who managed a physician's office, work was a welcome change from the burdens of care:

> How does caring affect me? I seem to be very preoccupied with my mother, looking after her needs. So how does it affect my life? It's depressing, it's aggravating, it kind of saps my energy. And it's made me appreciate my job more, that I could go and lose myself there. I work for a doctor, and it's kind of a one-person office. I've been with him for fifteen years, and it's a responsible job. I do everything; he has a terrible time without me. I enjoy it, I like my work, I like feeling responsible.

Women also relied on the information and skills they had acquired at work (see Matthews, Werkner, and Delaney, 1989). Both a nurse and a physician's office manager asserted that their familiarity with medical procedures served them in good stead as caregivers to chronically-ill parents. Two social workers were proud of their inside knowledge of nursing homes. Other women made professional contacts which helped them find community resources for their parents.

Part-Time Workers

Six respondents were employed part time. Although none reported that caregiving responsibilities interfered with her employment, two claimed that they would work more hours were they not constrained by the need to care for their parents. One was a writer. Like the full-time writer quoted above, she blamed herself for allowing her caregiving obligations to reduce her productivity. The other woman who wished to work more found it difficult to manage on her salary but hesitated to move into full-time work until she could make adequate arrangements for the care of her father, with whom she lived. He attended a day care center only ten hours a week, and she was reluctant to leave him alone for long periods at other times.

Students

Four women were enrolled in school full time. Although these women are included in other categories depending on their work status, they also can be discussed as a separate group. All were close to completing graduate degrees. They insisted that they had been able to integrate caregiving into their lives without sacrificing their school work. But two stated that the need to provide parental care severely restricted their range of employment. Although they faced tight job markets in their fields, they planned to limit their searches to the cities where they and their parents currently lived. In addition, one woman who lived with her mother intended to consider only positions that would permit her to remain home until 10:30 A.M. and return by 4 P.M.

Unemployed Caregivers

Finally, twenty-four of the respondents were unemployed at the time of their interviews. Eighteen stated that their work status was not related to their caregiving responsibilities. One, for example, had left her job before her father became ill in order to enroll in school full time. Three others had retired for reasons other than their caregiving obligations. (Two retirees, however, noted that they were glad they had withdrawn from the labor force before caregiving responsibilities became overwhelming because they could not have provided the same level of care had they continued to work full time.) Fifteen either never had worked for pay or had done so only before their children were born, many years earlier. These women had long-lasting marriages to men whose incomes were sufficient to support them.

But eight (one-third) of the unemployed caregivers had left the work force partly because of caregiving obligations. Two had relinquished part-time jobs, and six had left full-time positions. Studies based on structured interviews frequently assume that caregiving either determines women's decisions to depart the labor force or is irrelevant to those decisions (Brody et al., 1987; Stephens and Christianson, 1986; Stone, Cafferata, and Sangl, 1987; cf. Steuve and O'Donnell, 1984). But the impact of caregiving responsibilities on decisions to leave the work force rarely is unambiguous. The two women who gave up part-time employment had had only tenuous attachments to the labor force. Both had worked for their husbands and had not relied on their positions for either income or self-esteem.

Although most of the women who quit full-time jobs had been far more committed workers, various factors (in addition to parental responsibility) shaped their decisions to withdraw from the labor force. One, for example, had just been divorced when she decided to leave her job and move across the country to care for her mother. Three others withdrew from the labor force at least partly because their workplace opportunities seemed to be blocked. Yet another woman left her job as an elementary school teacher in part because she wanted more time for infertility tests.

But, if caring for elderly parents was not the only factor driving these women out of the work force, it significantly influenced their decision. The ex-teacher, for example, stated that the stress of caring for her father precipitated her departure from her job. Although she lived apart from him and was able to hire attendants around the clock, arrangements constantly came unraveled. She believed some attendants were incompetent, and others left abruptly. Moreover, her father lived an hour and a half away, and several days a week after school she drove that distance to visit him and supervise the helpers.

I have noted that five women in this study were unmarried and lived alone with severely impaired parents. Four of the women who left full-time jobs belonged to that group. The stories of two suggest that departure from the work force can have drastic consequences for women without husbands to support them.

Joan Hornstein* was a 57-year-old single woman who had managed an art gallery on the East Coast for many years when a new owner reduced her salary in 1979. She decided to return to Los Angeles and move into her parents' house because both were ailing and wanted her with them. Although she initially intended to transfer her skills to Los Angeles, she could not find a job that offered comparable pay or status. Moreover, her father became very ill almost immediately after she returned, and both parents strongly urged her not to work full time. She nursed her father for six years. When he died in

---

*Real names are not used in this study.

1985, it was apparent that her mother was suffering from Alzheimer's disease.

At the time of the interview, Joan's mother no longer could be left alone, and Joan had been caring for her for two years. Although Joan's mother qualified for assistance from a local agency, which provided an aide for a few hours a week, her mother had disliked the woman, and Joan decided to fire her. The agency was unable to find a replacement. Because Joan had not worked for ten years, she could not afford to hire aides independently. She was relieved of caregiving responsibilities only during the twelve hours a week her mother spent at a local day care center. Thus, although she had aspirations to work as a textile designer or become an art therapist, she had no time to pursue either goal. She refused to investigate nursing homes, believing that all institutional care was deficient. Joan believed that psychological difficulties also inhibited her return to the labor force. Because she had been living alone with her mother for several years, she felt that she had lost much of her initiative and sense of competence. She no longer viewed herself as someone who could function effectively in the work world. Although her mother's Social Security benefits and pension were adequate to cover the needs of both of them, fears about the future haunted her. At her mother's death, Joan would have no further income and would have spent many years without contributing to her own Social Security. Moreover, as she remarked, "I'll be older, and it will be harder to compete in the job market."

Marlene Epson, a former bookkeeper, was a 55-year-old single woman. She had been living with her mother, a victim of Alzheimer's disease, for three and one-half years prior to the interview. Marlene had lost her job in 1982 when a nursing home discharged her mother because she wandered. Marlene decided to bring her mother to her apartment while she continued to look for work. But searching for a job while caring for her mother proved to be more difficult than she had anticipated. Her mother was in day care only two days a week, between 10 A.M. and 3 P.M. Marlene and her mother lived on the latter's Social Security check and could not afford to hire attendants. Although Marlene tried to supplement this income by selling various merchandise over the phone, none of her ventures was successful. If Marlene had a job interview at a time when her mother was not in day care, she brought her mother with her. She considered temporary jobs, but most positions had erratic hours and would have required that she continually make new arrangements for her mother's care. Although she had investigated nursing homes that accepted Alzheimer's patients, she had found none that was even minimally accept-able.

Marlene stated that she desperately wanted a job. She was at her "wit's ends" from staying with her mother. When her mother died, moreover, Marlene's income would cease. Like Joan, she worried about a future without pensions or benefits: "I know I've got to get a job. I'm getting older myself, so I don't have much time left."

If the need to care for their parents helped to propel Joan and Marlene out of the labor force, caregiving also provided them with the means to do so—as long as they were living with their parents, they could rely on them for support. After relinquishing paid work, how-ever, they were unable to return to it. They lacked supportive services and could not afford to pay for aides and attendants. The few hours a week their mothers spent in day care were insufficient to permit them to explore career alternatives, train for new jobs, or work full time. Their reliance on their parents left them extremely vulnerable. Both were constantly aware that their incomes would cease as soon as their mothers died. These women thus experienced the economic depen-dence traditionally associated with wives. Because they believed their employability was waning, their futures looked bleak.

Leisure

Researchers consistently find that caregivers for the disabled el-derly routinely sacrifice vacations, social activities, and time alone (Cantor, 1983; George and Gwyther, 1986; Robinson and Thurnher, 1979; see Horowitz, 1985a). Most women I interviewed complained about their loss of leisure time. The following comment was typical: "There was a time when I really was doing. I went to classes, I went to dance class, I would go to the theater, which I love, I was really busy and doing things. I don't do any of that now."

These women gave several reasons why they engaged in few leisure activities. Time previously devoted to leisure pursuits, such as weekends or lunch hours, now was spent with parents or providing for their care. Although many women hired aides and attendants, few felt enough confidence in their arrangements to leave town for vaca-tions. The unpredictability of their parents' conditions made it difficult to plan ahead. And concerns about parents put a damper on activities the women did undertake. One woman discussed the effect of caregiv-ing this way:

My husband and I both love to go to baseball games. I love the out-
doors. We have a boat; we go fishing and sailing. I love to sew and
garden and cook. For a while I thought I could keep doing those
things, but I can't, it's not the same. If I had a good novel, I used to be
fine; I'd get lost in that novel. But I can't get lost in it. I read it, but
then I have to go back and read the page over again. I can't remember a darn thing I've read. I enjoy gardening when I'm doing it, but I
always know there's a limit to it. I'm never free.

Another commented:

We want to make my father back the way he was and make him
happy and doing things, but instead we watch the deterioration. It's
with you all the time. I may not physically be doing anything for him,
but it's always there mentally. If I go on a trip out of town, I wonder
what's going on. I'm not really enjoying myself when I think of him
sitting there and vegetating. It's a heavy feeling.

Because caregiving is a diffuse responsibility rather than a series of
discrete tasks, it never ends. Concerns about their parents' well-being
intruded whenever these women tried to demarcate a period for
reading, vacations, visits with friends, or hobbies.

Two groups of women found it particularly difficult to create time
for themselves. Many women who worked for pay expressed gratitude toward bosses who gave them special consideration or coworkers
who covered for them, but in fact these women frequently asked for
very little. Rather than seek concessions, they strove to compensate for
any costs their caregiving imposed on others. They assumed that their
primary goal should be to insulate their work lives from the intrusions
of caregiving responsibilities; thus, they worked late into the evening
to make up for time they took off during the day and used vacation
time when they had to be away from the office for hours at a stretch.
Asked whether caring for her mother interfered more with leisure or
work, one woman responded: "By cutting into the job, it cuts into the
leisure, because the things I have to do for her take place Monday
through Friday. So I take time off from the job to take care of her
needs, and then I have to give up my leisure to take care of the job. It's
a round robin."

If some caregivers had little opportunity for leisure because they
worked full time, the five unmarried women who shared households
with severely impaired parents had the opposite problem—because
they lacked paid employment, they had no way to set limits to the

demands of care and no money to pay for outside services. One woman described her days this way:

> I don't go to luncheons or anything. I don't go to any social functions at all. I don't even get to go to church. I can't go out. I have no social activity at all, it just stopped. I'd like very much to get up early in the morning and go to the post office and buy my stamps. I can't even do that. That's really difficult, not to get up early. If I get up very early, I still must stay in here to take care of my mother. I can't even go to a sale, a May Company sale! Sometimes if you come in at eight o'clock, they give you a certain discount on certain merchandise. No, my life is not like that.

Because her mother's needs were overwhelming, she had little relief from the daily grind. Asked how caregiving had affected her, a second woman responded simply, "My life has stopped." Deprived of even the smallest pleasures, these women led extremely narrow lives.

Conclusion

Informal care for the elderly frequently is heralded as an inexpensive alternative to government services. When family members shop for older people, drive them to the doctors, clean their houses, and help them walk, the government need not provide such services. A major goal of long-term care policies, therefore, is to prevent families from unloading these responsibilities on the state.

If informal care helps to control health care costs, however, it also inflicts a heavy toll on many women. The last chapter argued that some daughters find it difficult to cope with the emotional aspects of caring for dependent parents. This chapter demonstrates that caregiving also can disrupt women's lives in significant ways. The daughters I interviewed complained that their leisure was curtailed. Those who worked for pay felt that parent care interfered with their job commitments.

The women in this study who held paid jobs were more fortunate than many employed caregivers. None was mired in a blue collar position or in a low-level service sector job. Most had schedules that could be rearranged and leverage to demand special consideration. Nevertheless, eight quit their jobs, at least partly because of caregiving responsibilities. One woman forfeited her chance of a promotion, and three others sought less demanding jobs in order to accommodate their parents' needs. Caregiving impinged on the work lives of other women as well. They received phone calls from their parents during working hours and took time off their jobs to tend to their parents' needs. Women who suffered no sanctions from employers reported that responding to their parents often violated their own internalized work standards. A few found themselves adopting behavior they considered inappropriate to work settings. Women in professional and managerial occupations could not work at their customary level of intensity or perform as well as they wished.

If women in full-time employment wrestled with the antagonistic pulls of career and family, they also helped to illustrate the benefits of jobs. These women believed that their positions offered some protection from both emotional strains and parental demands.

Although most studies examining the impact of caregiving on employment have focused exclusively on women who already are working, this study suggests that caregiving may be an even more serious obstacle to women who wish to enter the labor force. Two women who had been unemployed for many years could not even conceive of carving out blocks of time, unimpeded by caregiving responsibilities, when they could work or attend school part time. Concern about care for her father prevented one part-time employee from taking a full-time position. The mobility of two women who were about to graduate and enter the job market was restricted by the need to remain close to dependent parents. Most seriously, some women who initially had viewed caregiving as a temporary alternative to work became trapped in that role and were unable to find a way back into the labor force.

If the women in this study differ significantly from caregivers employed in blue collar or low-level service sector jobs, they also may differ dramatically from future cohorts of caregivers. As noted, several women had followed traditional life paths, molding their lives around family needs. Many others had sought employment only after their children were grown. The rise in the numbers of women opting to remain childless, limiting their families to one child, or delaying childbearing until after they are established in careers suggests that women's attitudes toward childbearing have altered dramatically. Women who never have structured their lives around caring for children may respond very differently when their parents need help. Although some may welcome an excuse to take time off work, others may strongly resent the intrusion of caregiving responsibilities into their work lives.

Because care for elderly parents can demand substantial sacrifices from women, it is important to examine the type of assistance they obtain from others. The following two chapters discuss the extent to which caregivers receive material and emotional assistance from either formal service providers or their circles of family and friends.

8

Brokering Services

The enormous expansion of the health and social service system since the late nineteenth century has dramatically reduced the burdens of family care. Rather than disappearing, however, some caregiving responsibilities have changed form. Although outsiders now render a great deal of care for the sick and disabled, the job of mediating between dependent family members and formal service providers commands the attention of caregivers. Laura Balbo (1982:253–54) explains what this work entails:

> Women choose among alternatives, combine available resources from different sources—public and private—in terms of their understanding and assessment of their family needs, and correspondingly establish priorities. All this is *servicing*. Such complex patterns of family organization past societies have never known. Human, personal needs, because they differ from one person to another, from one stage in the individual life cycle to another, or even from one moment to the next, require constant interpreting, redefinition, and understanding. No amount of resources in quantitative terms is adequate to meet needs unless resources are transformed into services according to what an individual person requires. It is the work of women to mediate between the family's human needs and the external resources regulated by the logic of market profitability and state power.

This chapter examines three types of "servicing" work—deciding whether to place a relative in a nursing home, locating and arranging for services delivered by community agencies, and recruiting and supervising aides and attendants who are unaffiliated with formal organizations. Most researchers equate formal services with those furnished by bureaucratic agencies, ignoring the vast network of helpers recruited and reimbursed privately. The women in this study, however, relied disproportionately on unaffiliated providers. Because they devoted the most time and energy to the third type of servicing work, it will be discussed in the greatest detail.

Nursing Home Use

Policy analysts are deeply concerned to save money by preventing or delaying institutionalization. Emphasizing the need for "incentives" for informal caregivers, they imply that family members are overeager to exile elderly relatives to institutions. Although some families undoubtedly do forsake the disabled elderly, most of the women I interviewed perceived their situations very differently. Their primary goal was to ensure that their parents received good care, not to relieve their own stress; consequently, they were reluctant to consider nursing home placement. Seven women complained about and resisted pressure from physicians, friends, and relatives to institutionalize their parents. After listing the various people who had encouraged her to place her mother in a nursing home, one woman concluded: "There's a lot of prejudice toward having people go into rest homes." Three women had removed their parents from nursing homes because they could not accept the poor treatment their parents received. Even women who displayed the most hostility toward their parents and the greatest resentment at caregiving were adamantly opposed to nursing home placement.

When asked if they ever had considered the possibility of putting their parents in nursing homes, ten women stated that they realized that institutionalization was inevitable either because they would not be able to care for their parents at later stages or because their parents were exhausting the financial resources that made alternative arrangements possible. All of these women, however, had resolved to ward off nursing home entry as long as possible. The two women who had institutionalized their parents before the interviews had done so very reluctantly. One stated:

> I had hoped that I'd be able to keep her until she got to the point where she didn't know who I was. That's what I really wanted to do so badly. I didn't want to place her while she still knew me. . . . When you're a mother, when you have children, you always feel like you've done all you can do, but you never stop. You just don't. In a way, in taking care of mama, I felt like I was saying that I can't take care of this child anymore. Somebody else has to do it. It's like speaking Chi-

nese, it was so foreign to have to say that. That's why it'll take me time to get over the placing of her.

Many daughters asserted that they never would place their parents under any circumstances; some reported feeling trapped because their commitment to home care meant that caregiving would not end until their parents died.

Seven women explained their hostility to nursing homes by recounting horror stories about elderly residents who had been grossly mistreated. Eight had investigated nursing homes themselves and been stunned by the poor quality of care they discovered. Two had visited nursing homes in professional capacities and vowed never to put family members in such places. Five were convinced that their parents would die soon after entering nursing homes. Others feared that their parents would miss the personalized care that the daughters took pride in providing. A woman caring for a father with dementia remarked:

> I get a feeling with Alzheimer's people, that all they have left at the end is just that nice feeling of people caring for them and loving them and touching them. And that's what he wouldn't get enough of in a nursing home. I just think that's what would mean the most to him, just to be around people he knows at the end.

The daughters also were reluctant to take on the duty of visiting relatives in nursing homes. Although many observers contend that family caregiving ends with institutionalization, these women assumed that they would remain involved in their parents' care after admission to residential facilities. They preferred to give care at home, where they could exercise more control and avoid contact with other disabled persons.

Although these women were determined to postpone nursing home placement as long as possible, some women noted that access problems might make decisions about institutionalization moot. Four women caring for parents with dementia stated that almost all the facilities in their area refused admission to persons with that diagnosis. A woman whose mother was eligible for Medicaid noted that the only facility in her community certified to accept Medicaid beneficiaries had a long waiting list. A woman whose mother could pay privately complained about the size of the waiting list of the one desirable facility she had found. Others believed that their parents were priced out of nursing homes. The daughters did not want their parents to rely on Medicaid, but their parents' resources were insufficient for an extended stay.

Community and Home-based Services

Services delivered by formal organizations were notable by their absence in the lives of most caregivers. Because support groups affiliated with adult day care were an important source of recruitment for interviewees, it was not surprising that as many as thirteen women in the study had parents enrolled in day care programs. These women made relatively little use of services from other community agencies. Just four parents obtained any kind of transportation services, two relied on Meals on Wheels, two others obtained help from aides who were employed by agencies, and one received assistance from hospice volunteers. Although most of the parents of the women in the study lived close to senior citizen centers, none attended them.

Financial barriers prevented several women from making greater use of community and home-based services. Six women could choose only from publicly funded programs, but these tended to be extremely sparse. Three women noted that, although their parents were too affluent to qualify for subsidized services, they lacked the resources to pay privately.

Women gave several other reasons for failing to use formal services more extensively. Many services simply were unavailable. A woman living on the outskirts of a major city looked in vain for meals programs and transportation services before concluding that "it's like a desert here." Services that existed often failed to mesh with the specific needs of elderly parents. One woman reported that the only transportation service in her area limited its clientele to elderly persons confined to wheelchairs; although her mother had difficulty with mobility, the daughter feared that a wheelchair would prematurely label her impaired. A second woman found that a local senior citizen center did not exercise adequate supervision over persons with mental impairments. The one day her mother, an Alzheimer's disease victim, had attended a program at the center, she had walked out and spent several hours wandering alone in the neighborhood. More commonly, women complained that programs in their community were geared toward people who were more severely impaired than their parents. Attending a series of lectures for the elderly was a humiliating experience for this woman's mother:

I put her in a class at a center for two days a week, and that was a disaster. I did it with current events and gardening, because those are two things that she's very interested in. She knew more than both of the instructors. It's not that the instructors weren't good, it's just that she is also very well qualified in both of those areas. She went for her current events class, and she read the *Wall Street Journal*. She got up early to do this, before she went, and she read all of *Forbes Magazine*, so that she would be prepared. As you can imagine, she was just terribly disappointed. She was furious. She went three times, and then she just flat out refused.

Moreover, services frequently were fragmented. Two women who were employed full time failed to enroll their parents in day care programs because the centers provided no transportation, and the daughters could not leave work to drive their parents. A woman living alone with her mother did not bring her mother to a senior center for meals because she had no car and the round-trip taxi fare was $16. The low quality of services also deterred use. Two women had received the help of aides from a publicly funded program. Both were dissatisfied with the care provided by the workers, and they ultimately withdrew from the program.

When explaining why they did not make greater use of formal services, these women stressed their parents' opposition above all else. Many women identified what they considered adequate programs only to have their parents refuse to participate. Some women said that their parents did not want to be labeled elderly and were horrified by the suggestion that they receive services designed specifically for members of their age group. Other women commented that their parents viewed dependence as a sign of personal failure. One stated:

She didn't want help. Meals on Wheels, forget it. "I don't want anybody helping me." My mother had a real fetish about social workers and any kind of welfare. All the years she dealt with my retarded brother for any reason, she just never got any help. In her childhood, she spent a few years in an orphanage, and she kind of made a vow to herself: she would never ask anybody for anything.

Most women I interviewed did not consider formal services essential to either their own or their parents' well-being. Although they would have preferred that their parents participate in more programs, their parents' refusal was a relatively minor inconvenience. As the next section will discuss, over half the women in this study turned to private solutions, hiring aides and attendants who were not affiliated with formal organizations.

But the inability of women without ample resources to rely more extensively on formal services had serious repercussions. I have noted that five women had limited incomes and lived alone with severely disabled parents. One had no access to formal services of any kind. The services used by the other four women provided their only respite from care. A woman whose father had died three months before the interview described visits from hospice aides and volunteers:

> The only people we had coming in the last three months were hospice aides and volunteers. The aides would bathe him and shave him. I got so I couldn't wait for them to come, just to see somebody. . . . The hospice volunteers would say, "We want you to go out to a movie or see a friend." Well, that sounds very good, and had I not had cerebral palsy, possibly I would have done that. But usually when a volunteer came in for four hours, I went to bed, because I was exhausted.

Two other women, who brought their mothers to day care centers twice a week, just needed time alone:

> Sometimes all I do is come home and sit and read. Because otherwise I never have time to read.

> It feels wonderful to have the time. It's the only time I have for myself. Last week, I just went down to the beach and walked a little bit. Just the freedom of being alone for those four hours is very restorative.

The mother of the fourth woman attended a day care center twice before refusing to return. The daughter recalled: "The two days that she went, it was great. Because one morning, they picked her up around ten, they brought her back about six. I went to the museum that day, I had lunch out, all the things that I hadn't been able to do for a very long time." In describing what they gained from day care centers and visits from volunteers, these women revealed what they gave up as caregivers. Because few services were available to them, they led extremely circumscribed lives.

Whether they used services to gain a brief respite or to supplement other types of help, the daughters were the go-betweens, locating outside programs and making arrangements for their parents to participate. Several women had friends or relatives who were social workers or gerontologists and who could furnish the names of appropriate resources. One woman explained how she was able to find a place for her mother in the one day care center in her community with a good reputation: "One friend said, 'There's a very long line for [the day care center].' But she said, 'What are friends for, if not to push everybody else out of line?' And so she made some very necessary calls, and we got mother in, and it was wonderful because there was no place for her." Most were less fortunate. They were not connected to networks that furnished the information they needed, and they had no idea how to proceed. Some had made dozens of phone calls that seemed to lead nowhere.

Servicing work continued after initial arrangements were complete. When parents were enrolled in adult day care programs, the daughters tried to monitor their care by keeping in touch with the staff and participating in special activities for family members. Although none of the women I interviewed used her own money to pay agency fees, one made special donations to the center her mother attended. Some women also spent substantial amounts of time transporting their parents to community programs. Asked to describe a typical day caring for her mother, one woman responded:

> Three days she goes to the day care center. I'd drive her there, which is twenty-five miles, to bring her in, and twenty-five miles back, at nine thirty. Then I'd pick up her up at three, so I'd leave here at two, twenty-five miles in and twenty-five miles back. So there wasn't an awful lot that I could get done in between. On those three days, that was what my days consisted of, and I couldn't really plan much of anything else on those days.

Many observers worry that formal programs encourage informal caregivers to withdraw their services. This mother's participation in a day care center may have released the daughter from some practical tasks, but it also added new burdens to her day.

Aides and Attendants

Although the women as a group made relatively little use of services from bureaucratic agencies, they relied extensively on aides, attendants, and companions whom they hired through ad hoc, informal arrangements. These women lived in a city with a huge pool of immigrant domestic workers, and they depended on these workers for the delivery of care. Just fifteen used any service from a community agency, but twenty-eight hired helpers who were unaffiliated with formal agencies. Moreover, they received assistance from informal helpers for many more hours. Although three women employed aides and attendants just a few hours a week, nine employed them for forty hours each week, and sixteen had helpers who stayed with their parents around the clock.*

Deciding to Find Help

In some cases, a specific event triggered the use of aides and attendants. Three women stated that they first hired helpers when their parents were discharged from the hospital and could not manage on their own. More frequently, however, the daughters had to find some way of determining when such care was appropriate. This rarely was simply a technical matter. The stage at which these women solicited assistance was influenced as much by their relationship to their parents as by their assessment of their parents' functional status. The central issue, in fact, was not deciding that outside help was necessary but convincing their parents to accept it. Chapter 6 noted that hiring aides was one of the major events that required daughters to assert control over their parents' lives. The parents of most women in this study strongly resisted any suggestion that they required supervision. Although the daughters were willing to respect their parents' refusal to attend day care centers or participate in meals or transportation programs, they were less acquiescent when their parents insisted that they could manage on their own without aides or attendants. The daughters thus had to confront parents with their growing impairments. Some women felt they were undermining their parents' self image by pointing out disabilities and demanding that they get assistance.

Hiring outside help also was problematic because it meant declaring that there were limits to the care the daughters themselves would render. Although these women interpreted their parents' resistance to outside help in various ways, many claimed that their parents wanted any assistance to come from daughters, not paid helpers. One woman offered this explanation for her mother's hostility to the aides who tended her: "She would really like me over there a lot more. She

---

*Home attendants typically provide personal care services, while home health aides provide some medically oriented services. The women in this study, however, tended to use the terms interchangeably. Most of the workers they employed performed such household tasks as shopping, meal preparation, laundry, and cleaning and such personal care services as help with bathing, eating, and physical mobility. Although the boundary between personal care and health care often is indistinct, most of these workers did not change dressings or administer medications.

doesn't want these people in her house, she wants me." As already noted, many women felt strongly motivated to respond to their parents' requests for help, even when they considered them unreasonable.

In short, rather than relieving emotional strain, the process of hiring aides and attendants often exacerbated the two issues that were most difficult for caregivers—asserting control over their parents and resisting parental demands for increased help. Three women stated that this was the reason they waited longer to obtain such assistance than they later deemed appropriate. Three others stated that they would like to find outside help but had refrained from doing so in deference to their parents' wishes. Women who did manage to hire aides and attendants occasionally used ruses to gain their parents' acceptance. One woman, for example, initially sought to convince her mother that the home attendant who lived with her was simply a guest in her house.

But even after aides had begun to tend elderly parents, the latter often registered protests by finding fault with those caretakers. Some parents also refused to take advantage of the services of attendants, endangering themselves in order to preserve their independence. One woman complained that her mother allowed an aide to cook and clean for her but continued to bathe alone, despite a serious problem with balance. Daughters like this one engaged in an ongoing struggle to convince their parents to rely on outside assistance.

Recruitment

The women employed various methods of recruitment. Some followed medical and social service channels, asking physicians, nurses, and community service agencies for referrals. Others asked friends who had similar experiences. Most, however, located aides and attendants just as they found other types of domestic help—asking gardeners and housekeepers for the names of relatives and friends who needed work or advertising in the local Spanish-language newspaper. One woman arranged for her mother's housekeeper to double as an aide after the mother began to suffer memory loss. Some commentators draw a distinction between care for the needy and the personal services that the privileged routinely command (Waerness, 1984). The recruitment process suggests, however, that the boundary between these two types of services blurs when family members hire aides and attendants for disabled elderly persons.

Many women felt overwhelmed by the enormity of the task of

assessing personal characteristics and evaluating qualifications and references. Those whose parents lived alone, were very disabled, or suffered from some form of dementia were well aware of the great potential for abuse. Several women recited the old refrain about the difficulty of finding "decent help." They had heard stories about companions who stole from or abused their vulnerable clients and who performed their duties erratically. Three women subsequently discovered that the aides they hired lacked the experience or credentials they had claimed during interviews. The racial prejudices of parents further complicated the recruitment process. Although this study was conducted in a city where the overwhelming majority of low-paid workers are African-American, Hispanic, and Asian, some women looked only for white attendants in deference to their parents' wishes. One woman remarked: "A couple of the individuals I interviewed were Black, and I knew my dad would not relate well. Or maybe he would relate well, but what if he should get angry and insult someone on the basis of their race. I couldn't deal with that. I felt let's just not push it." Because arrangements often came unraveled, many women repeatedly had to recruit replacements. When workers quit abruptly or asked for sudden schedule changes, daughters had to find emergency substitutes.

Because few guidelines governed the relations between these workers and their elderly clients, all working conditions were subject to individual negotiation. Many women had no prior experience in this area. One had to decide whether an attendant could use her father's home as a site for conducting a private sewing business, doing her family's laundry, and entertaining friends. Daughters also were responsible for setting rates. Although wages varied greatly, most women paid between $5 and $5.50 an hour and between $50 and $60 for a twenty-four-hour shift. The majority did not pay benefits, whether Social Security, Workers' Compensation, or Unemployment Compensation.

Just four of the daughters who hired aides and attendants made any financial contribution to the cost. The remainder paid aides and attendants entirely from their parents' funds. A few women stated that their parents easily could absorb this expense; either their parents had ample resources, or they employed attendants and aides just a few hours a week. Most women, however, stated that their parents' funds were rapidly being exhausted and were terrified that the parents would outlive their ability to pay for this care.

Supervision

Because the workers hired by women in the study were unaffiliated with formal agencies, the daughters assumed responsibility for training and supervision. Most spent a day with new workers to orient them to the household, demonstrate how specific tasks should be performed, and tell them about the unique qualities of their elderly clients. Women whose parents suffered from dementia tended to be particularly scrupulous about monitoring the helpers they hired. One woman left her severely impaired mother alone with an attendant only when her mother was asleep; at all other times this women stayed with her mother and participated in her care. Although other women were more willing to entrust their parents to caretakers, they left precise instructions, visited at unpredictable times, and checked in regularly by phone. A woman who employed a staff of helpers to provide round-the-clock care for her bedridden father described herself as being "constantly on surveillance."

But these women were aware that strict control could be counter productive. Several asserted that aides would deliver better care if they were granted some autonomy and encouraged to exercise their own judgment and take pride in their work. Some daughters also tried to cultivate good relationships with attendants by performing special favors for them. Many aides and attendants had serious problems themselves. Some had recently arrived in the United States and worried about their immigration status. Many had concerns about their own family members. Some women I interviewed assumed the additional obligation of trying to assist the workers they hired. Two lent them money. Others brought special food, fixed up their parents' houses in accordance with the attendants' wishes, or gave them extra hours off.

Nevertheless, these women acknowledged that the favors they performed were not simply acts of generosity. Because the search for helpers was long and arduous, many women felt very dependent on the workers they hired; they were well aware that their arrangements were unstable. Catering to the needs of helpers was a way of ensuring their loyalty. One woman explained:

> This one person that I've hired to help me is a lovely person, very nice, very nice. But I don't know how long she'll be with us, because you never know what someone else's life will be. You're really dealing from weakness, so you just have to kind of do what you can to please

them. You tend to bend over backwards for the help because it's so hard to find, this kind of help, and I'm very particular. I'm not a person that's just going to call an agency and say, "Send somebody over."

The daughters also displayed concern for workers in order to obtain their good will and motivate them to provide decent care: "Sometimes you feel you're bending over backwards, but it's for my dad. You want everything for his well-being. I don't want people to take out their anger at me on my dad." Some women resented their obligation to respond to the needs of the helpers. A daughter who employed four different women to tend her bedridden father complained, "This is so traumatic for me—this constant contact with people out there, with their problems, their complaints, and it becomes as stressful as the actual worry and involvement with my father."

The attempts of these women to accommodate the wishes of paid helpers were fundamentally limited. Although the women wanted aides and attendants to recognize the unique worth of their parents, the women themselves often failed to acknowledge the humanity of their employees (see Dill, 1988). I noted that some women complained that their parents' prejudices complicated the process of recruitment; several daughters also revealed their own racial bias. Asked what country her mother's aide came from, one woman responded, "I forgot the name of the place, but she had this funny way of talking English. Where are black people from that talk this funny English?" Many referred to women they hired as "girls." Sociologist Judith Rollins (1985:159) observes that "this type of nomenclature, suggesting domestics are not adults, has been a tradition not only in this country but in all parts of the world." Just as caregiving frequently is seen as a natural female attribute (Rose, 1986; Ungerson, 1983), so many women in this study viewed the ability to care for elderly persons as an inherent trait of ethnic and racial minorities. The following comment was typical: "The woman I hired is from the Philippines. I don't want to make a generalization, but I think they have a certain feeling about the elderly, and they're very patient." Shellee Colen (1986:54) comments:

> "Naturalizing" the work implies that it is unskilled and not really worth wages, trivializing it. Devalued when passed from men to women in the society at large and within the same households, the work is further devalued when passed from one woman who chooses not to do it and can pay for it, to another woman who performs it in someone else's household for the wages she needs to maintain her own household.

Although many women complained about the financial burden on their parents, only one questioned whether the wages were sufficient to permit aides and attendants to maintain a decent standard of living. One woman justified the wages she paid this way: "Thirty-five dollars a day is good money because when they first come over from many Central American countries you can get them for practically nothing, because they have no language skill." Nor did any daughters acknowledge such other undesirable features of the work as monotony, isolation, social degradation, and the constant need to confront aging, illness, and death—although they were acutely aware of these problems when they themselves delivered care.

Quality of Care

Three women reported incidents of abuse. One found her mother tied to a chair; the second accused an attendant of touching her father's genitals inappropriately; and a third claimed that an aide had emotionally "tyrannized" her father. Although most other women expressed satisfaction with worker performance, a few had minimal expectations about household chores and their parents' basic physical needs. It would be impossible, these daughters insisted, to pay strangers to lavish the same attention or display the same empathy as family members. They were satisfied when workers simply arrived on time, prevented their elderly clients from harming themselves, or prepared adequate meals.

Most women, however, expected aides and attendants to provide the personalized care that the daughters considered critical. To such women, it was not enough for attendants to perform instrumental tasks proficiently; they also had to complete these tasks in ways that bolstered the elderly person's dignity and sense of self. Some women believed that differences in culture and values prevented aides and attendants from rendering such individualized care. Although all the women I interviewed were white, most of the helpers they employed were African-American or Hispanic. Several women complained that aides knew nothing about their parents' culture and could not share their interests. In a few cases, language differences made communication difficult, if not impossible. One woman commented that, as her mother's memory dimmed, she reverted increasingly to German, her first language; the attendant who cared for her was a Filipino immigrant with only rudimentary English skills.

But some women—especially those whose parents had severe memory problems—looked for more subtle forms of protective care.

Several daughters spoke with gratitude about workers who, despite barriers of race and ethnicity, recognized their parents' unique qualities and responded to their individual needs. For example, although one woman's father had suffered from dementia for several years, his daughter continued to view him as a proud man. She described the way an aide (one of the two males employed by the women in this study) respected her father's individuality and protected his self-image.

> This man makes an effort to be sensitive, and he is very careful. Like my father drinks apple juice all the time, and he doesn't want to give up the apple juice glass, and so Steve has now figured out that when he shows him the glass and that it is empty, Steve says "I see that glass is empty, and I am going to get you some more apple juice," but he doesn't do it condescendingly. It is as though that were part of the conversation. He makes sure that my father understands everything that he is going to do, and that helps tremendously.

A second woman spoke in similar terms about both her father and the care he received:

> Father had a lot of pride. He was a professional man, and he always ran everyone else's life and especially his own and had a very strong personality. . . . It takes ten minutes for him to get in and out of cars now because he has trouble moving his lower limbs and he's so stubborn. The aide just stands there and watches him. It's important to let him do as much as he can for himself, and it doesn't pay to have a fight. If anyone lost patience, he would have a total fit, and it would hurt his ego. He needs some help, and the aide seems to know how to handle it.

Some women claimed that aides were able to render good care because of the relationship they developed with the elderly. One woman discussed the bond between her mother, an Alzheimer's disease victim, and an attendant who sought to conceal the help she rendered:

> Marsha is absolutely marvelous, and there is such a bond and such a loving and caring and just everything. She treats her like a whole person. She does not, every time mother does something, she is not there like the woman is infirm. She treats her like she can do it herself, and when she sees that she can't do it herself or needs help, she gives her the help. There is not an issue made, and there is not a hovering, and there is a comradery. There is laughing. I think Marsha has a feel for older people. Mother is in a day care program that is not geared to-

wards dementia. If there is someone like mother with dementia, an aide has to go with them. The first day that we went there, I watched Marsha. When she was just watching the women exercising, Marsha was just smiling. It tickled her. When they got up to dance, she and mother were dancing, and she was looking down at Mother, and I saw pleasure.

Still another woman emphasized the ability of an attendant to render her work invisible and thus shield her client from having to confront her growing frailty:

Joan has these extra skills of observation and supervision, which she does so subtly that my mother thinks she's not doing anything. That's the biggest gift of all. I don't know if you can train somebody to do that, and do it as well as this woman does it. She just has a natural gift for it, to always make my mother feel as though she's making every decision and doing everything on her own, when really Joan is right there helping.

These women also argued that formal service providers could deliver good care precisely because they were less emotionally involved than kin. Policy analysts frequently assert that relatives render superior care because they are bound to the elderly by strong emotional attachments. But some women stated that the intensity of the daughter-parent relationship created an overcharged atmosphere and hindered the delivery of good care. Aides and attendants who had not spent a lifetime with their parents often could deal with them more effectively. Several women remarked that paid helpers accomplished tasks they had found impossible, such as training their parents to dress themselves and convincing them to engage in outside activities.

Aides and attendants also helped to transform the relationship between daughters and parents by creating emotional distance. Several women asserted that these workers enabled them to achieve the detachment that permitted them to remain involved in caregiving. One woman explained why she hired an aide to care for her father: "Unless I maintain a certain amount of distance, he tries to turn my relationship with him into his old relationship with my mother. As long as I have some distance, we can have a really good working relationship. But if I'm too close, he'll start picking fights." By hiring outside helpers, women also could avoid the most intimate aspects of personal care (which were especially troubling when the disabled parents were fathers). Finally, aides and attendants insulated women from the pain of witnessing the deterioration of their parents. A woman who stated that "the depressing part of caring for parents is to watch the decline" also noted that she was glad she was able to hire an aide to care for her father "because it would be terrible to face it so vividly." A woman whose mother had both physical and mental-health problems remarked: "It upsets me very much to see her the way she is. I don't think I could care for her on a one-to-one basis. It would be too hard on me emotionally because not only would I have to watch the decline, I put myself in her shoes and start thinking, maybe I'm going to be this way." Many women were convinced that distance was equally important to their parents. As one remarked, "I think that it's probably very hard for my mother to rely on me, and that she tries to protect me and keep me from knowing about things." A second woman explained that it was essential to her father's well-being that an aide rather than a family member help him to dress and use the toilet: "This way he can keep his dignity with us, because that's the way it's always been. There's no way he would have wanted us to help him. It's much better to have someone else."

Conclusion

Most studies of the intersection of formal and informal services focus exclusively on the allocation of tasks between family caregivers and formal providers (Edelman and Hughes, 1990; Greene, 1983; Litwak, 1985; Noelker and Bass, 1989; cf. Hasselkus, 1988). Because family members do not conceptualize caregiving solely in terms of discrete tasks, however, we would expect them to view formal services more broadly. I have noted that a primary concern of the women in this study was to preserve their parents' dignity. This concern inhibited some women from hiring aides and attendants but encouraged others to rely extensively on this type of assistance. Aides and attendants had complex and sometimes contradictory effects on the relationships between daughters and their parents. Before they could recruit helpers, the daughters had to set limits to the care they would render, assert authority over their parents, and confront them with their growing disabilities. These tended to be the most emotionally fraught aspects of parent care. Nevertheless, many women viewed their reliance on aides and attendants as a way of diminishing the intensity of their own relationships with their parents.

By obtaining services from aides and attendants who were unaffiliated with formal organizations, the women in this study avoided some of the difficulties of dealing with bureaucracies. They also may have received more personalized care than would have been available from employees of community agencies. Nevertheless, when established agencies were not involved, "servicing work" became exceedingly onerous. The daughters I interviewed were responsible for recruiting and supervising workers and for establishing wages and working conditions. Because the turnover of aides and attendants was high, these burdens rarely ended.

I did not interview paid helpers and therefore have no direct evidence of how they experienced their work. It is difficult to imagine, however, that they considered their wages to be adequate. Family caregivers who watched their parents' savings dwindling away may have felt unable to pay more. But a fee that seemed high to the daughters in this study frequently was too meager to constitute a living wage to the women they hired. As long as care for the elderly remains a private matter, family members will skimp on wages and benefits.* In some cases, racial prejudice may have further blinded caregivers to the economic needs of the workers they hired.

The highly personalized relationship between family caregivers and paid helpers may, paradoxically, be resented by the latter. I have argued that, because no outside organizations monitored worker performance or supplied replacements, the daughters felt very dependent on the aides they trusted. Many believed that they could retain these helpers and ensure that they provided decent care only by establishing good personal relationships with them. Some daughters complained that the need to cater to the desires of workers constituted yet another caregiving burden they shouldered. Studies of domestic servants in a variety of contexts, however, find that the workers often dislike receiving favors from employers. They recognize special treatment for what it is—a form of manipulation, intended to keep them working longer than they want and to obligate them to provide extra services (Glenn, 1986; Rollins, 1985; Romero, 1988).

The interests of family caregivers and paid helpers may have clashed in other ways as well. A few daughters expected aides and attendants to perform only practical chores, but most wanted the workers to provide emotional care, which the daughters considered necessary to their parents' well-being. Although some daughters failed to respect the helpers' human worth, most expected the workers to establish relationships with the elderly, respond to them as individ-

---

*Partly because funding for home care services is very limited, agencies also save money by relying on a cadre of marginal workers and by keeping wages low.

uals, and bolster their sense of dignity. It is possible that the bonds they established with the recipients of their care provided the workers with a measure of personal fulfillment. Studies of paid providers in a variety of fields report that they are drawn to their jobs primarily by the desire to deliver a service and that they derive job satisfaction from their emotional attachment to their clients (Lundgren and Browner, 1990; Sexton, 1982; Withorn, 1984). But Mary Romero argues that demands for empathetic care are a way of extracting "emotional labor" from domestic servants. The Chicana servants Romero interviewed tried to restrict their jobs to housecleaning chores and to avoid such highly personalized activities as child care, which they considered especially degrading (Romero, 1988).

Because this society defines care for the elderly as a private responsibility, it is not surprising that daughters caring for disabled parents rely heavily on individual solutions. In the absence of universal, publicly funded, high quality services, they turn to the large pool of marginal workers who cannot secure better employment. Desperate to find adequate help for their parents, they establish relationships with aides and attendants that contain many exploitative elements.

9

The Ambiguities of Social Support

At a time when pressures to find inexpensive alternatives to public services are overwhelming, many policymakers extol informal sources of support. If we can convince more people to look after their own, the argument goes, the demand for publicly funded services will diminish. We have seen that recent policies seek to further this goal. As the cost of caring for the burgeoning frail elderly population rises, family responsibility for aging persons increasingly is encouraged. This chapter explores the extent to which family caregivers, in turn, can rely on members of their social networks for help. Chapter 3 noted that, because bonds of kinship and community have gradually been attenuated in our society, women no longer view caregiving as a collective activity. But to what extent do they still receive important assistance from their circle of relatives and friends?

Although researchers have directed relatively little attention to this issue, the prodigious literature on social support provides a useful framework within which to examine it. Some researchers argue that social ties buffer individuals against stress (Antonovsky, 1974; 1979; Caplan, 1974; Cassel, 1976; Cobb, 1976). Others, however, caution us against viewing social relationships as an unambiguous good. Although social support does appear to increase well-being, the extent to which it protects individuals against the harmful effects of stress is by no means clear (see Thoits, 1982). Moreover, social networks are not converted automatically into social support. It hardly bears repeating that members of social networks can themselves be a source of stress (Rook and Dooley, 1985). When individuals close to us are in trouble, we often experience a "contagion of stress" (Wilkins, 1974). In addition, close relationships harbor a range of feelings, including anger and bitterness as well as love and affection. The term "social support" glosses over the complexity of human attachments. It implies that individuals are ensconced in relationships that invariably are warm and harmonious and ignores elements of power and conflict. As statistics about the rising divorce rate and the pervasiveness of family violence remind us, however, intimate relationships can foster tensions and abuse as well as warmth and solicitude.

Then too, even when friends and family act in ways intended to be supportive, they often fail to help. Words of comfort expressed to people who have suffered losses, for example, frequently are misguided. Unemployed women resent family and friends who seek to console them by trivializing their commitment to the workforce (Ratcliff and Bogdan, 1988). Parents mourning the death of an infant are offended by well-meaning comments that they are fortunate to have lost the child before they had a chance to grow more attached (Helmrath and Steinitz, 1978).

Finally, although we know little about the processes whereby individuals seek help, a variety of objective and subjective barriers constrain people from mobilizing whatever support might be available to them. Potential supporters may live far away or be overburdened with other problems (Eckenrode and Gore, 1981). Cancer patients hesitate to call upon potential supporters because they want to shield close relations from the intensity of their feelings (Dunkel-Schetter and Wortman, 1982).

Two schools of feminist writing would lead us to expect that support between men and women would be asymmetrical. Some feminist scholars assert that, as members of subordinate groups, women frequently operate from a desire to please people who have power over them; because they tend to submerge their own interests in relationships with men, they might well refrain from asking for the support they need (Hare-Mustin and Marecek, 1986). Feminist psychoanalytic theorists argue that women experience themselves as more strongly connected to others than do men (Chodorow, 1978). They thus furnish support not only from a sense of obligation and compulsion but also to achieve personal fulfillment.

Although research on gender differences in social support is scanty (Belle, 1987), what does exist suggests that social support is unevenly allocated between men and women. Various researchers have found that women seek more help than men throughout the life course, but they also give more support to others than they get in return (e.g., Belle, 1982; Belle, 1987). Studies of marriage report that men are more likely than women to confide in their spouses, suggesting an imbalance in the amount of emotional sustenance wives and husbands render (see Belle, 1987:264). Women also are called upon to deliver support to a broader array of individuals than are men. Children, for example, are more likely to turn to their mothers than their fathers in difficult times (Belle, 1987). Not only are women more likely to be donors than recipients of support, but they also experience more contagion stress. Some research suggests that men have greater immunity to the problems besetting members of their social networks. When asked to report distressing events, women note more difficulties in the lives of others, and they are more vulnerable to these troubles (Kessler and McLeod, 1984). When women do obtain support, they often receive it from female friends. A range of studies conclude that women have a more extensive web of relationships than men and that their friendships are characterized by greater emotional intensity (see Belle, 1987; see Rubin, 1985).

A few studies have found that the level of support received by caregivers divides predictably along gender lines. Although daughters who provide care are more likely than sons to live with dependent parents and perform tasks associated with high levels of stress, they receive less assistance. Daughters-in-law remain an important source of informal care. Sons caring for elderly parents thus obtain more material help and emotional support from their wives than daughters can expect from their husbands (George and Gwyther, 1984; Horowitz, 1985a; cf. Kleban et al., 1986).

Defining Social Support

Although researchers have conceptualized social support in a myriad of ways, many agree that it has the following components: instrumental assistance, emotional sustenance, affirmation, and companionship (see House, 1981; see Wortman, 1984). It is important to note that the situation of caregivers differs from many others in which people appear to need support. We have seen that caregiving for elderly parents encroached on various aspects of the lives of the women in this study and produced serious emotional difficulties. But it also was a profound human experience and could not neatly be subsumed under the terms "stress" and "burden." The women I interviewed wanted members of their social networks to affirm the value of their endeavor, not just help them deal with the problems it provoked. They were enraged when people belittled their attachment to their parents, trivialized their involvement in caregiving, and failed to acknowledge their parents' unique worth and humanity.

Nevertheless, these women did want assistance with problematic aspects of caregiving. They expressed a need for advice about critical decisions, help in limiting their responsibilities, assistance with concrete chores, and information about available resources. We will see that the women did obtain some of this support from a range of different sources. But a variety of factors prevented them from receiving some of the help they wanted.

Husbands

Of the 34 married women, just three stated unequivocally that their husbands were unsupportive. Although many of the other women noted that their husbands resented the time and energy caregiving consumed and the extent to which it dominated their lives and thoughts, they still characterized their husbands as supportive. When asked how they defined this term, the most common response was that their husbands assumed responsibility for their parents' financial affairs. In addition, some women noted that their husbands sometimes accompanied them when they visited their parents, did assorted chores for their parents, and treated them with consideration. Three women noted that, because their husbands were unencumbered by the emotional baggage of lifelong relationships to their parents, the husbands could deal with the parents more effectively. Said one:

> It's very hard for me to tell [my mother] what to do. For years and years and years, doctors have been telling her she should take a daily walk, and she should drink water, and she should do this, but she doesn't do any of these things. It's frustrating. My husband finally spoke up to her the last time she came out of the hospital. He said, "How many more times do you think we can go through this?" He said, "Don't you think it's time for you to take some responsibility?" He said, "There's things you could be doing to help yourself, and we expect you to do them." Somehow, he got the courage to say all that. I have tried to say it, but it doesn't come out quite as well as when he says it. Somehow it comes out kinder, and she accepts it better from him.

But other women indicated that their husbands' participation was far more limited. Three women stated that when they spent joint savings, their husbands did not protest. When three others referred to the support their husbands had given, they meant that these men had "allowed" their wives to devote substantial time to caregiving. How can we explain why women labeled as supportive husbands who did little more than tolerate their own caregiving? One explanation may lie in the fact that women typically hold themselves responsible for their marital relationships (Cancian, 1987). The women I interviewed may have felt that any expression of dissatisfaction with their husbands would reflect badly on themselves. An equally compelling explanation is that these women had low expectations about the assistance their husbands would render. Many women insisted that their husbands did not share the responsibility and that they had to be careful not to burden them with requests for aid and comfort. Such women believed that they had an obligation to shield their husbands from the consequences of caregiving. Their first duty, they stressed, was to support their husbands. Because they believed that the care they provided their parents detracted from what they would give their husbands, they felt they should be grateful for the lack of opposition to their involvement in caregiving. Feeling torn between their responsibilities as wives and as daughters, they assumed that they should bear the costs of caregiving alone and thus refrained from asserting their own needs for support.

Children

Thirty-six women in the study were mothers. When these caregivers spoke about their children, they again emphasized their own obligations, not the support they could elicit. I have noted that few had children under the age of 18 at home, but many felt ongoing responsibilities to older children.

Although these women welcomed any concern their children demonstrated, they were not surprised when little practical assistance was forthcoming. A common refrain was that their children were young and had their own lives to lead. Many women also absolved their children from responsibility because of the quality of the relationships the children had with their grandparents. Some women stated that their children never had been close to their grandparents and therefore owed them nothing. Other women exonerated their children for the opposite reason—because they had enjoyed a special relationship with their grandparents; these women did not want caregiving to intrude on that relationship. A woman whose mother suffered from Alzheimer's disease explained why she did not put pressure on her teenage daughter to spend time with the grandmother:

> I was afraid Jessica was not going to remember all the really good times. She was 3 years old when we moved into this house, and my mother had the bedroom downstairs. Jessica had a real problem. Our bedroom's one flight up, and she was real far away. It was like her grandma was her security blanket. I mean, for a long time I didn't know that she'd go into grandma's room and sleep with her because she didn't want to be by herself down there. When my mother moved out of here, Jessica went through this real trauma. So I think to see this happening to her grandma has been hard on her.

A second woman whose mother had dementia excused her daughter from visiting the grandmother because of the relationship the two had enjoyed when the daughter was a young adult:

> Our daughter and my mother were very, very close. My mother was probably her very best friend. Our daughter is gay, and my mother was a champion of Joan for a long time and always used to tease us, saying, "Don't knock it till you've tried it." Always was on Joan's side. My mother realized it before she came out of the closet. It's very hard for my daughter to see her now, to be with my mother.

Just one woman believed that involvement in the care for an elderly grandparent could be an important life experience for children. Others asserted that their children were too young to have to confront serious illness and death. One woman thus sought to protect her children from distressing events by discouraging them from visiting their grandmother in the psychiatric unit of a hospital.

Siblings

Although the women in this study sharply circumscribed the caregiving responsibilites of their husbands and children, they were less willing to let their siblings off the hook. Some did state that their brothers and sisters had legitimate reasons for being less involved: they lived far away, had serious personal problems themselves, or had paid their dues by caring for their parents during an earlier period. But several women, like the ones quoted below, expressed rage at brothers and sisters who evaded the most onerous obligations:

> My sister and I have been having problems around this. We were always very close, and we're not now. I don't think she comes down often enough. She's free to come. She calls, big deal; that's very different from spending three to four hours a day. . . . She does not wheel my mother to the doctor, she does not carry her to the car, she does not oversee the help.

Another woman was distressed that caregiving responsibilities were gender-biased:

> My brother, in the eight years that he's got ahead of me, fell into al-
> most a different generation, and he has a different philosophy. I sup-
> pose that a lot of men think that women are the caregivers and men
> are not. Also, it's easy to take pot shots at me working at home. We're
> actually a little bit closer now than we had been before, and we are
> trying to do things for our parents together. We're tying to work on
> separating their assets now, with these complicated California laws.
> Both my brother and I seem to be able to share the work that's in-
> volved with it. But I think if something were to hit, he would expect
> me to get in there and find people to hire and all. During the years
> when we were having disagreements, his answers always were,
> "Well, I've got a family to support." But are my earnings frivolous? I
> think he thinks that [caregiving] is something women do primarily.

Even if siblings would not share caregiving responsibilities equita-
bly, they could participate in various ways. Above all, the women in
this study wanted their sisters and brothers involved in major decisions because they had an equal stake in the outcome. Those without
siblings felt their absence keenly when critical decisions arose. Also,
because siblings shared a common family history, they could help to
interpret parental behavior and understand the emotional responses
of the caregivers. Several women remarked that they found it helpful
to recount disturbing incidents to brothers and sisters.

But the participation of siblings, even on a limited basis, could
bring additional problems. In many cases, this represented the first
intimate contact between them in many years. Although two women
said that the shared enterprise of caregiving brought them closer to
their sisters, most noted that renewed interaction reawakened old
feelings of competition and jealousy. Some were painfully aware that
their parents reacted more positively to their brothers or sisters. Two
women who had given months of sustained care noted bitterly that
siblings who made only fleeting appearances elicited more favorable
responses from their parents. In a few cases, the women I spoke to felt
embarrassed by the greater affection lavished on them. One woman
tried to correct the imbalance:

> I have to say I was my father's favorite. He always adored me more
> than anybody else, and I guess I realized that, and it was special that
> way, and it still is. He'll always give me credit for everything that's
> being done for him, even when my brothers will be sitting there. My
> brother will cook a wonderful meal for my father, and my father will

thank me for it. He always thinks in terms of me. I'm the one that's doing everything good. And I feel bad. I keep telling him, "Dad, you know, Jim fixed that wonderful meal," because my older brother was very rejected by my father, so I feel really bad about it, and I try really hard even at this late date to keep reminding my father my brother's doing a huge amount for him.

Moreover, siblings often disagreed about their parents' needs and favored different courses of action. One woman, for example, fought her sister's proposal to place their mother in a nursing home. Another clashed with her sister about more subtle aspects of care. While the latter wanted to encourage their bedridden father to learn to paint by numbers, my informant was convinced that he would consider such an activity demeaning.

And, although some women were buoyed and sustained by siblings who praised the care they provided, many resented unrealistic expectations about what they could accomplish. One woman's sisters repeatedly complained to her about the problems with their mother's housing, implying that she should be able to find a better option. Another woman felt that her brother was saying that she could halt the course of their mother's deterioration. Criticisms from siblings were particularly difficult for women who were struggling with their own feelings of inadequacy as caregivers.

Friends

The women in this study also looked to friends for various kinds of assistance. Several relied on a network of friends for emotional intimacy and assumed as a matter of course that they would discuss feelings about caregiving with them. Friends also relieved the tensions of caregiving by taking women out and diverting them from their troubles at home. In some instances, friends were an important source of advice. One woman, caring for a father with Alzheimer's disease, felt overwhelmed by the need to take control of her father's life. She explained how she was able to do so:

I would just call my friends up and talk to everybody. I would end up talking about how hard things are for me to everybody, and I'd get a lot of ideas and suggestions and support. And people just kept telling me over and over, my best friends would say, "Look, you have to do this, he's not capable at this point, and to do that, you are taking care of him." And that would give me the support to go ahead and be a little stronger. . . . I felt real guilty about putting his money into a trust. I thought, "Oh, Susan, you are doing this for yourself, so when he dies, you'll have an inheritance." And they just kept telling me, "No, you are doing it to help him." They pointed out he may need the money in the future for a nursing home and that it wasn't for me, and they were real, real supportive. If I didn't have their feedback, it would have been really bad.

Because the friends of several women in the study were professionals in the fields of gerontology or social welfare, they were able to connect the caregivers to community resources. Several women learned the names of nursing homes and home health aides from friends.

If most of the women acknowledged the critical help of friends, however, these relationships hardly constituted a bulwark against the stresses of providing care. In fact, the constant demands of caregiving made it difficult, if not impossible, for some women to sustain ongoing friendships. One of the five women living alone with severely impaired parents was interviewed shortly after her father's death. She commented: "I was so busy I didn't have time for anyone. You get terribly lonely, which is tough. You just have so much to do that I would look at my friends that I owed telephone calls to, and I would say, 'I can never do it.'" Because these women were compelled to renounce virtually all social activities, they often lost touch with friends.

Caregiving fractured friendships for other reasons as well. A few caregivers were hesitant about revealing family problems. A woman who tended a mother with Alzheimer's disease said:

> I'm embarrassed sometimes, because when people hear sometimes about some of the things my mother has done, they say, "Oh, my God." As much as I would like to be able to have someone say, "Oh, that's awful, you poor thing," and to ask me to tell them about it, on the other hand, there's a side of me that's very mistrustful, that if people find out how crazy my mother is that they'll reject me.

Another woman had brought her mother, also suffering from Alzheimer's disease, into her home. She explained her reluctance to invite friends to the house this way:

> I have to say when dealing with someone with Alzheimer's, no one really understands what you are living through, they really don't. An Alzheimer's person is an oddity. Friends would come and my mom would be sitting in the living room with us and she will say things that just really don't make sense and it causes an embarrassment. People are not as sympathetic to someone who has brain damage as

to someone who has cancer or a heart ailment. . . . When friends come, some of the time I would ask my mom to come and sit with us. It is embarrassing. I don't want her to be the focus, to be looked at like a freak, and I don't trust that friends understand, so I avoid having people over.

In addition, some women who prided themselves on being the more sympathetic and compassionate member of any relationship withdrew from friendships rather than continue to incur additional responsibilities. Asked whether she turned to her friends for support, one woman said: "I was always a better listener. I always used to be the one everybody came and told their problems to. When my mother arrived, I pretty much cut that out. I didn't have any room for any more problems."

When friendships persisted, caregivers exercised considerable caution about approaching their friends for help. The few women who asked friends to visit their parents did so only in emergencies or during the rare occasions when they left town. Clinging to an ideology of self-reliance, two women believed that it was inappropriate to turn to others for help with their troubles. Others perceived their friends as unsupportive. When these women first assumed caregiving responsibilities, friends failed to understand that they no longer could accept spur-of-the-minute invitations: "I haven't seen much of my friends. One friend, when she heard what was happening, her response was to call up and say, 'We're going out to dinner, do you want to come too?' Now how can I do that?" Nor could they linger over restaurant meals: "We were just saying today that one of our closest friends is alienated from us. He does not understand that I just don't have the energy anymore to spend three hours dining while he drinks two bottles of wine, and I'm falling asleep in my plate." Some friends who initially rallied around these women lost interest as caregiving continued to absorb their attention over a period of months and even years:

> Friends don't really want to hear too much about your problems. You can tell them from time to time the status report, but it's not a subject they really want to talk about. They might ask from time to time how my mom is doing and if I tell them that she's in the hospital, they say, "Isn't there some medication they could find that would fix that?" There's a lot of impatience with these chronic things. Nobody wants to deal with chronic anything.

Another woman reported that the occasional assistance she received from friends was insufficient to sustain her over the long haul; as a result, she found caregiving a very lonely experience. Asked whether her friends provided support, she responded:

> A couple have come and visited my mother with me, which is very helpful, and the mother of a friend of mine works as a social worker, and she helped me sort through places, which is very helpful. And others are just helpful in having someone to talk to. But it's interesting, when you ask that question, my immediate reaction was no, it's a lonely and isolating sort of thing to go through, because it seems endless, it just keeps on going. The supporters go home, and you're stuck with the situation.

Some friends who sought to be helpful undermined the caregivers by betraying a lack of sympathy for their undertaking. One woman was offended by a friend's suggestion that she get rid of her mother by putting her on a Greyhound bus. Another said that a friend urged her to get a full-time job so that she would have an excuse for limiting her involvement in her mother's care. And three complained about friends who counseled them to relinquish responsibility by institutionalizing their mothers. One contrasted the attitudes of her friends, all of whom were white, with the response of co-workers, who were members of diverse ethnic and racial groups:

> One of my closest friends really would like me to put my mother in a rest home. She just really thinks that it's too much to ask of anyone. She just sees it as sacrificing your life for someone else. And she's been pretty clear in saying she was really sorry I decided to do it. She'll still call me up and say, "Oh, I saw something on PBS about how older people really are much happier in a rest home, they're entertained, and they have activities for them." I'm trying to think if there's anyone that's really wholeheartedly behind me. Just a few people at work. I know one woman at work said, "Well, you've got to do it, she's your mother!" It was like there's no choice here, obviously that's the thing you're going to do. And it's interesting, some of my friends at work are from other cultures, and they tell me, "You're not like other Americans, you're going to do the right thing, you're going to care of your mom."

When friends belittled their investment in caregiving, women refrained from revealing their own ambivalent feelings.

Finally, although women in their fifties and sixties said that shared concerns about parents occasionally brought them closer to friends, younger women stated that caregiving responsibilities tended to isolate them. If they were the first members of their group to have to deal with aging parents, they felt out of step with their contemporaries.

Support Groups

Because I located many women through support groups, it was not surprising that almost half (twenty-four) of the caregivers in this study participated in them at least sporadically. Some women who considered it inappropriate to burden friends and family members with their troubles viewed caregiving groups as a place to discuss them. But some women claimed that they attended support groups in order to impart wisdom, not to gain it themselves; in the support group, as elsewhere, they obtained satisfaction from giving rather than getting help. Many women also were happy to discover that they were not singled out for misfortune. As Leonard I. Pearlin and Carol S. Aneshensel (1986:423) comment, "Misery doesn't just love company, misery is in active search of company and is often assuaged by it." Several women took comfort in finding that others were even worse off than themselves—they had less help, more needy parents, or were responsible for other relatives as well.

Support group members also exchanged information about local resources. Women caring for parents with Alzheimer's disease and related dementias frequently attended groups restricted to caregivers of relatives with similar afflictions. Such women traded information about the course of diseases and advice about dealing with their parents.

Most women I spoke to valued the exchange of experiential knowledge more than the acquisition of objective information. Support group members disclosed the rage, guilt, and self-doubt that periodically assailed them. Several women described their enormous relief at finding others who empathized with their plight. As they watched other participants mirror their feelings, their sense of isolation waned. The following comment was typical: "To go to those meetings and to hear everybody else talk just like me and think just like me and feel like me, it really was just marvelous." In the light of others' experiences, some women were able to reinterpret their parents' behavior so as to render it less painful. A woman whose father had dementia and continually betrayed his mistrust in her actions remarked: "The caregivers' group relieved me of a lot of anxiety and guilt that I was carrying. Just showing me that it's not my unique problem, that everybody has basically the same problems. And when I get upset about something, they told me that my father doesn't mean any harm to me. He just doesn't know what he's doing, just that's something that he can't help." The realization that others faced similar problems helped to alleviate her overriding sense of personal failure.

If some women asserted that they attended support groups to listen to others and respond to their concerns, others acknowledged that listening could be self-serving as well as altruistic. As they heard others narrate personal experiences, they drew comparisons with their own situation and acquired knowledge about themselves. A woman whose mother suffered from recurrent bouts of depression described how she gained critical distance by listening to members of her group and relating their accounts to her own life:

> This caregiver group is the one place that I feel I could go and I could tell whatever was happening and people would really understand. I don't think, unless you're going through it yourself, that you can understand it. So I would say that's my biggest resource, to be able to go every week to that meeting, and even if I don't talk very much about what's going on with me, I'll listen to the other people and I can identify so much with what they're going through, and that helps me.

She explained why much of her earlier rage gradually dissipated:

> I think in the beginning I was totally frustrated and very angry with the medical profession and with my mother for not taking better care of herself and with my father for leaving the scene so soon and not being there for all of us, and there was a lot of that built up anger and resentment. At the group, through each of us just listening to one another and sharing what we want to share about what we're going through, I think I've become more peaceful and calmer with the whole problem. I think that I was a lot more angry and a lot more resentful a year ago, and the group has helped me to work through a lot of that.

She attributed her growing acceptance of her mother's illness to the insights she gained from the other group members:

> They helped me in terms of understanding that I need to be letting go, and that I can't control my mother's death. I've just come to realize that whatever will be with my mother is not something that I can really decide. She's not my child. Most of the things that have affected her happened before I could have intervened and done anything. . . . What was most helpful was watching other people in the group struggling with these same issues. There are several people in earlier stages of discovery of this than I am, and there are others who are further along and who have graduated from the group and don't come anymore because they have recognized their limitations, and they don't need to keep coming and asking, "Well, am I doing enough?" or "Do you think this is OK?" . . . They don't need permission from the group anymore. They seem to know that whatever they're doing is the best they can do. And I think that I haven't com-

pletely finished that yet, that I'm still needing to know that I'm doing the best I can, and that the group is validating that for me. Whenever I listen to their struggle, then I think, oh, I'm going through that same struggle. And somehow that helps.

Other women similarly reported that support groups helped them to place appropriate limits on their obligations: to hire aides and attendants when the burdens began to seem intolerable, to refuse to bring their parents to live with them, to ignore requests for help that they considered unreasonable, and to readjust their expectations about what they could accomplish. One woman, for example, explained how she was able to contemplate institutionalizing her mother: "They really brought me to the point that I realized I had to do something. They really opened my eyes up to realize that I wasn't a bad person, I wasn't evil because I wasn't dumping my mother." She managed "Just by listening to them, and the way they felt and what they were going through, and what they were doing, and I thought, 'Well, gee, I've done that,' and it just really opened up everything for me to realize that I'd done all I could do. I couldn't do anymore." When she announced to the group that she finally had resolved to find a nursing home for her mother, the other members bolstered her decision:

> They were just wonderful, they really were. They were just wonderful. There were only six of us, you get very close when there's just six. . . . We were all individual, you know, but we were all under the same stresses and I just realized that I really had done all that I could. And they could see it in me. At some of the meetings right towards the end, before I actually said this is it and I'm going to do it, they could see that I wasn't really there, that I wasn't able to give anything, contribute anything. I felt like I'd said everything there is to say, and I'd done everything there was to do, and I was just under stress. I was, deep down inside, torn with the idea that I had to place her, and I didn't know how they would take it either, it was like going to confession. But they were wonderful, they were just wonderful.

Because all the members shared her experiences, she invested them with authority and attached enormous significance to their judgment.

This study was biased toward support group participants. Caregivers who were uncomfortable disclosing personal information to strangers or lacked the time to meet regularly thus were underrepresented. Nevertheless, two women had attended caregiving groups just once or twice before concluding that this activity was not for them. Even some who remained members over a substantial period had serious reservations about their usefulness. A few women found fault with the particular groups they attended. One complained that her group was too large to allow each member to speak at every meeting; she often found herself overlooked and thus left feeling even lonelier than before. Two women disapproved of the way other participants treated their relatives; because support groups depend on a basic level of trust, women who judged other members harshly could derive little from the exchange. Others resented spending their few spare hours discussing their parents and learning how to cope better. And two women criticized the entire enterprise. As one exclaimed, "The bottom line is that nobody can help you except yourself." She had joined the group at the behest of her physician but remained a reluctant participant. She felt demeaned by asking others for support and had little faith in their ability to either understand or alleviate her burdens.

Conclusion

Many women in this study received essential help from others. We have seen that they obtained advice about decisions, information that permitted them to plan ahead, assistance with concrete chores, linkages to community resources, companionship, and emotional support. But members of their social networks could not solve many of the most serious problems these caregivers encountered. In some cases, family and friends exacerbated distress as well as alleviated it. Some husbands resented the time women devoted to caregiving and their emotional investment in it. Children were an important source of "contagion stress." Renewed contact with brothers and sisters frequently reignited sibling rivalries. Friends who denied the significance of caregiving and siblings who criticized the type of care that was rendered also undermined the women I interviewed.

In addition, a variety of factors inhibited the daughters from seeking greater help: they believed it was improper to rely on others, they thought their friendships were too fragile to withstand repeated requests for assistance, and they lacked the time to visit with friends or attend support groups regularly. Above all, concern for the well-being of others compelled the caregivers to submerge their own needs. Some sought to insulate their children from exposure to illness and death. Women whose parents suffered from severe dementia also tried to preserve their parents' dignity. They wanted their children to remember their grandparents fondly, and they wished to protect ailing parents from the scrutiny of unsympathetic outsiders. And some women viewed care for parents as a privilege their husbands permitted them rather than a responsibility that entitled them to make demands for special consideration. Just as they tried not to impose on either co-workers or bosses, so they renounced spousal support and attempted to absorb the costs of caregiving themselves. The same responsiveness to others that may have encouraged these women to care for their parents impelled them to shield members of their networks from the consequences.

10

An Agenda for Change

Despite the rise of a vast system of health care and social services in the United States, care for the disabled elderly still is predominantly a private responsibility. Relatives deliver approximately three-fourths of all long-term care, and many do so without any assistance. Few publicly funded community and home-based services are available. Although the government finances a significant portion of nursing home care, reports of substandard conditions deter many family members from considering institutional placement.

The shortage of public resources devoted to long-term care services reflects two governmental concerns. The first is an ideological commitment to privatization. Idealizing the nineteenth-century world of caregiving, many policymakers view the household as the "natural" locus for caregiving and argue that, by returning care to the home, we reinforce traditional values and strengthen family bonds. But the rhetoric of family love and responsibility does not extend to the very wealthy, who can afford to purchase the supportive services policymakers would deny to others. We have seen, moreover, that the intensity of familial relationships can impede as well as facilitate the delivery of care. In this study, some daughters caring for disabled parents felt overwhelmed by the emotions that the experience provoked and believed they could continue to offer care only if they gained greater distance.

The second governmental concern is the fear that families will unload responsibilities on the state, astronomically increasing its financial burden. Many policymakers want to ensure that publicly funded community care does not replace services now provided "free" by family members. But caregiving is not costless to women. Although many daughters I interviewed pointed to gratifications they derived from caregiving, some became submerged in their daily responsibilities. Caregiving also disrupted women's lives. The great majority sacrificed vacations, social activities, and time alone. Like generations of women before them, some quit paid jobs, at least partly in response to the demands of care. Others forfeited promotions and took time off without pay. The Institute for Women's Policy Research estimates that adult children caring for disabled elderly parents lose an annual total of $4.8 billion in earnings (Spalter-Roth and Hartmann, 1988:7).

This book suggests that, even if we drastically reoriented public policies, we could do little to remedy some of the problems caregivers encounter. In delivering care, daughters must foster their parents' dignity while asserting authority over them. Although caregivers want appreciation, their definition of good care compels them to conceal their best efforts. Caregivers also must confront human experiences that typically are considered taboo in our society—old age, progressive chronic disease, disability, and death. And they must acknowledge their own limits. They cannot halt their parents' deterioration; often they cannot even enhance their emotional well-being. Caregivers frequently measure success in terms of their ability to affirm their parents' basic humanity, but some are tending parents who suffer from cognitive impairments that threaten to destroy their sense of self.

Nevertheless, policy reforms could affect many features of the caregiving experience. Although most women in this study were intensely concerned with providing the best possible care for their parents, they lacked the preconditions for good caring—an ability to relinquish obligations they found too burdensome, access to publicly funded services, and sufficient resources to purchase additional help. Without adequate assistance, some could not achieve the detachment they considered essential. Drawing on the personal reports of the women I interviewed, as well as other recent caregiving research, this chapter first examines three major policy recommendations and then explains why a broader agenda for change is necessary.

Financial Compensation

One of the most widely touted proposals to address the issues confronting caregivers is to provide financial compensation to them. Although allowances for caregivers are common throughout western Europe (Gibson, 1984; Moroney, 1986), financial support for family members in the United States is sparse. The limited economic assistance that exists takes three forms.

First, elderly veterans who receive a subsidy from the Veterans

Administration Aid and Attendance Allowance program may use it to pay relatives caring for them. Second, the federal Dependent Care Tax Credit allows families to claim a credit against federal tax liabilities for expenses incurred in caregiving. Because this credit is not refundable, it is valueless to the very poor, who owe no taxes. Also, families are eligible only if all taxpayers in the household are gainfully employed. The large proportion of caregivers who hold no paid jobs or who have dropped out of the labor force to look after relatives thus receive no benefits. An additional stipulation requires that the care recipient spend at least eight hours a day in the taxpayer's home. Studies have found, however, that both adult children and aging parents prefer to live apart (Harris and Associates, 1986; Horowitz and Dobrof, 1982). Using data from the 1982 Long-Term Care Survey, one researcher has calculated that only a small fraction of caregivers are eligible for the tax credit (Subcommittee on Human Services, 1987).

Third, a number of state programs reimburse family members for the long-term care services they render. According to a recent report, a majority of states have instituted arrangements for paying relatives of the elderly and disabled (Linsk et al., 1988). The major program is California's In-Home Supportive Services. Only recipients of Supplemental Security Income (ssi) or State Supplemental Payments (ssp) and persons who spend down to the ssi/ssp level are eligible. In 1984, 29,000 family members received a total of approximately $90 million for rendering care (Burwell, 1986). Most state programs limit payments to caregivers whose relatives are deemed to be most vulnerable to institutionalization. Stringent eligibility criteria often exclude spouses, children over the age of 18, families who live apart from the care receivers, and families with incomes over a certain level. Reimbursement levels tend to be low (Burwell, 1986).*

Many proponents of financial relief for caregivers view cash grants and tax allowances as cost-effective alternatives to institutionalization. Monetary relief, they contend, can provide an incentive to family members either to assume caregiving responsibilities or to delay nursing home placement (see Hendrickson, 1988). This argument rests on the economists' model of the rational, calculating person and ignores the complexity of forces affecting decisions about caregiving. People's

---

*In Los Angeles County, In-Home Supportive Services pays family members at a rate of just $4.25 an hour; family members receive no reimbursement for the great bulk of services they provide (Interview with Julia N. Takeda, Welfare Administrator, Department of Public Social Services, Los Angeles County, April 1990).

willingness to bestow care is shaped by a variety of determinants, including the nature of their attachment to the workforce, the texture of their bonds to the care recipient, and the strength of their adherence to such values as family love and filial responsibility. It is highly unlikely that most family members will respond in mechanistic ways to the inducements this group of policy analysts would offer them. On the other hand, should financial incentives succeed in encouraging family members either to assume caregiving responsibilities or to continue providing care after they otherwise might have considered nursing home placement, caregiving patterns may be distorted in two ways. First, family members who are emotionally ill-equipped to provide care might begin to do so (Kane, 1986). Second, because the goal of such a program would be to save money, benefit levels would be too low to induce any but the poorest paid workers to quit their jobs to care for relatives. Thus, the class and gender biases of caregiving would be reinforced.

It is possible, of course, to view financial compensation in a very different light. Instead of seeking to regulate the behavior of caregivers, we might try to alleviate their financial burdens and accord recognition to the work they perform. Some analysts note, however, that schemes to provide financial compensation leave untouched the most oppressive aspects of care for the elderly. As we have seen, the primary complaints of caregivers are the emotional difficulties of interacting with the care recipients and the incursions caregiving makes in their lives, not the financial costs. Commentators also fear that, when a financial reward is attached to the work of nurturance and caretaking, such work is transformed from a human service into a commodity (Arling and McAuley, 1983; Schorr, 1980). One study suggests that a significant portion of caregivers share this concern. When family members providing care were asked if they wished to receive financial support, several responded negatively. The following comments were typical: "It puts a price on your relative," and "I never thought in terms of getting paid, because it's a relative." Respondents with the lowest incomes tended to be most hostile to such proposals (Horowitz and Shindelman, 1983; see also Tennstedt and McKinlay, 1989).

But, if some caregivers spurn financial assistance, others desperately need it. When relatives with limited financial resources are severely impaired, the costs of special diets, equipment, and home modifications can mount up quickly. Two researchers report that 45 percent of nonspousal caregivers to highly impaired elderly persons provide regular financial assistance to them. For three-quarters of these caregivers, the contributions constitute one-tenth of their total incomes; for one-third of the caregivers, the contributions represent a fifth of their incomes (Stephens and Christianson, 1986). Caregiving also can create financial problems for family members who relinquish paid employment. We no longer need to be reminded that women work primarily as a result of economic need. Many women I interviewed who quit their jobs experienced serious economic hardships.

By demanding that caretaking be divorced from the cash nexus, we sentimentalize women's unpaid labor on behalf of their families. Women provide care not only out of love and concern but also out of a sense of obligation. As Chapter 2 argued, the deficiencies of the long-term care system compel some women to assume more caregiving responsibilities than they want. Moreover, payment does not prevent some members of such "caring" professions as social workers and nurses from becoming emotionally attached to their clients and providing high quality services. We know too little about the conditions that facilitate good caring to insist that remuneration would be detrimental (Waerness, 1983).

Unfortunately, it is not easy to design a model program of financial reimbursement for caregivers. One difficulty is deciding whether the purpose should be to seek to offset the expenses incurred in caring for the elderly, enable family members to purchase outside help, or compensate caregivers for the services they render. A strong case could be made for concentrating on the third objective. Because the out-of-pocket expenditures of caregivers tend to be far less onerous than the in-kind services they provide (Doty, 1986), programs that cover only the former would be grossly inadequate. Allocating a stipend to caregivers to purchase their own help would share the disadvantages of all other voucher schemes for social services, leaving clients with the responsibility for assessing and monitoring quality. Other countries that have attempted to provide income supplements to caregivers in lieu of directly furnishing supportive services have found that the private sector does not provide adequate services (Nusberg, 1984). The aim of providing concrete assistance to caregivers is better served by expanding publicly funded home and community-based services.

If payment mechanisms seek to reimburse family members for their care, however, some method must be found to assign a value to their services. One possibility is to pay family members the equivalent of a "shadow wage." Benefit levels would be based on the wages or salaries caregivers could command in the labor force. This approach would reinforce divisions among caregivers, rewarding the better educated more than the less educated, whites more than members of racial and ethnic minorities, and men more than women. It also would be prohibitively expensive as well as extremely cumbersome to establish. A more politically acceptable and economically feasible strategy would be to reimburse all caregivers at either minimum wage rates or at the levels of home health aides and attendants. But pay scales then would be uniformly low (see Brown, 1982; see Ferree, 1983).

An equally difficult problem is deciding whether financial compensation should take the form of tax allowances or cash subsidies. As one group of policy analysts notes, the advantages of relying on the tax system as a mechanism for subsidizing caregiving include "largely universal coverage, efficient and generally accepted mechanisms of transferring money, the absence of a welfare stigma, a relatively uniform system of administration, [and] the use of an existing structure" (Eustis et al., 1984). But many tax allowances have regressive effects. Tax deductions provide the greatest benefits to the wealthy, many of whom can easily afford the financial costs of caregiving. Tax credits do assist low income people more than others; however, unless the credits are refundable, they are not beneficial to the very poor, who have no tax liabilities.

If programs provide cash stipends to caregivers, a distributive principle still is required. Implementing some form of means test would target payments to those with the most limited economic resources. But benefits allocated on the basis of financial need stigmatize recipients, and they tend to be cut first during periods of retrenchment. Using disability as a condition of eligibility involves the problem of determining functional need. And, no matter how we allocate stipends, we need gatekeepers and mechanisms to monitor fraud.

In short, framing an agenda for compensating caregivers raises a number of thorny issues. But to delineate the difficulties is not to argue that the project should be abandoned. Because a significant fraction of caregivers need economic relief, some method of rewarding their efforts should be found.

Supportive Services

Although most policy initiatives focus on financial compensation, caregivers express a preference for supportive services, including transportation, home maintenance and chore services, personal care services, and adult day care (Horowitz and Shindelman, 1983). A critical demand of many caregivers is respite services, which can provide temporary relief from the burdens of care (Montgomery, 1988; Wallace, 1990).* Respite programs are widespread throughout western Europe, but they are extremely rare in the United States (Gibson, 1984; Nusberg, 1984; Stone, 1985).

Although this study did not systematically evaluate the impact of home and community-based services on caregivers, it helps to illuminate their benefits. Hiring aides and attendants permitted many women to retain paid employment and engage in at least some leisure activities. Some women insisted that paid helpers improved the quality of their own relationships with their parents and promoted the dignity of the elderly. The study also suggests that the absence of universally accessible services sharpens the divide between rich and poor. Five women living alone with severely impaired parents could not afford to pay for outside assistance. As a result, their experience of caregiving was very different from that of most of the other women I interviewed. Without paid help, these caregivers could not work for pay or even undertake job searches. While other women in the study gave up vacations, these women abandoned even the simplest pleasures. Walking on the beach and reading novels no longer were routine parts of their lives; instead, they became privileges to be enjoyed only on rare occasions. Because these women interacted constantly with their parents, they had more trouble than others achieving the emotional detachment that makes long-term caregiving bearable. Sequestered with severely disabled parents, some found it difficult to leave even to buy basic necessities.

During the mid-1970s, policy analysts frequently argued that home and community care could serve as a cheap substitute for nursing homes. A decade of research, however, has cast doubt on that claim. A series of studies have found that whatever cost savings can be achieved by keeping people out of nursing homes fail to offset the expense of providing community services (Kemper, 1988; see Kane and Kane, 1987). Moreover, home- and community-based care frequently serves as an "add on" rather than an alternative to existing services. The majority of clients of community programs are not potential clients of institutions; as a result, the expansion of these programs does not forestall the need for nursing home care (Weissert, 1985).

---

*Respite programs take the form of either homemaker and home health services in the home or adult day care and foster care homes in the community.

Most of these studies evaluated programs that were intended to provide cheap alternatives to nursing homes and therefore operated under strict funding caps. Were planners able to focus directly on the needs of caregivers, the cost of community and home care services might well soar. Programs shaped to meet caregivers' needs would offer a broader range and quantity of services than currently are available from most publicly funded programs. Rather than seeking to elicit greater family involvement, they would encourage relatives to relinquish the tasks they find most burdensome. The timing of service utilization also would be different. We saw in this study that women who have sufficient resources to pay privately for outside help tend to hire aides and attendants long before they begin to contemplate institutionalization. But most community programs funded by the government are compelled to direct their services at elderly persons who are on the verge of entering nursing homes. As a result, family members receive no assistance during most of the time they deliver care. Programs designed around the needs of family members would offer them help at an earlier stage in the caregiving process.

If planners sought to promote the interests of paid as well as unpaid caregivers, the cost of community and home care services would become still greater. Community agencies frequently attempt to make ends meet by keeping wages low. A recent survey of home care workers in New York City found that 99 percent are women, 70 percent are African-American, 26 percent are Hispanic, and almost half (46 percent) are immigrants. A very high proportion are single mothers with three or four children. They typically earn less than $5,000 a year. Eight percent cannot afford adequate housing, and 35 percent often cannot buy enough food for their families (Donovan, 1989). Not surprisingly, home care workers have extremely high turnover rates; over 60 percent leave their jobs each year (Holt, 1986–87).

In short, providing high quality care for the disabled elderly while promoting the well-being of those who tend them in both paid and unpaid capacities may well require an enormous outlay of government funds. Nevertheless, the costs are not unlimited. I have noted that frail elderly persons often are reluctant to take advantage of whatever services are available. A major component of the "servicing work" of adult daughters is overcoming the resistance of their parents to outside assistance. Many elderly people share with most other Americans the belief that dependence on any social service demonstrates personal inadequacy (Hooyman and Lustbader, 1986; Kane and Kane, 1985; Moen, 1978; see also Qureshi and Walker, 1989).

Having internalized a value system that glorifies self sufficiency, they often are unable to rely on others even when they are desperately needy. The same ideology that retards the expansion of home care programs thus inhibits the utilization of those that exist. Some elderly people also may cling to housekeeping chores as a way of separating themselves from their more severely impaired counterparts. An ability to manage routine tasks may serve as a source of self-esteem, especially for those who have suffered numerous other losses. Moreover, many Americans fear the intrusion of public services into their homes because they are unaccustomed to receiving them. Low income people and members of ethnic and racial minorities may be especially prone to view community agencies as alien and antagonistic.

Nor are family members eager to transfer caregiving to the state. We have seen that the women in this study defined responsibility for their parents very broadly. Other studies report that relatives who contact service agencies make more modest requests than professionals deem appropriate (Montgomery, 1988; see Horowitz, 1985a; see Moroney, 1986; see Sager, 1983). Although policymakers fear that the availability of formal services will encourage family members to withdraw, relatives are not anxious to surrender caregiving obligations.

Educational Programs, Counseling Services, and Support Groups

If supportive services and financial compensation for caregivers are surrounded by controversy, educational programs, counseling services, and support groups enjoy enthusiastic support.* Their attractions stem from a number of factors. Unlike either financial compensation or supportive services, they are relatively inexpensive; it is far cheaper to establish a ten-week course of lectures for caregivers than to provide them with the services of homemakers and home health aides over a period of months or even years. Self-interest also dictates that certain groups of professionals promote these programs. Counselors and health educators, for example, seek to expand their role in

---

*The lines between educational programs, counseling services, and support groups often are blurred. Counselors frequently dispense practical information about the course of diseases and the availability of community resources. Many support groups are led by counselors, and they invite educators to address them. Educational programs often seek to engender a sense of mutual support among the participants. Nevertheless, in what follows, these programs will be discussed separately.

an aging society by advocating the delivery of counseling and educational services to caregivers. Robert Moroney (1986:156–57) adds: "If professionals spend years preparing themselves to function as therapists using the most sophisticated therapeutic methods, personal satisfaction and a feeling of worth are associated with providing these services. The more concrete services are viewed as important, but their delivery is not necessarily a professional function."

Although educational programs, support groups, and counseling services have not been thoroughly evaluated, some evidence suggests that they can help caregivers develop capacities to cope with the problems they encounter (Clark and Rakowski, 1983; Gallagher, 1985; Greene and Monahan, 1989; Hartford and Parsons, 1982; Lazarus et al, 1981; Toseland, Rossiter and Labrecque, 1989). Many women I spoke to asserted that various programs provided important assistance. Educational programs that dispensed information about disease processes increased caregivers' confidence. Women caring for parents with dementia were especially prone to feel that they were negotiating new turf with few familiar signposts to guide them. Some believed that they could more easily tolerate troubling and even frightening behaviors if they understood the genesis of these behaviors and learned techniques for dealing with them. Information about disease processes also helped the women to gain emotional detachment from their parents. Moreover, by invoking medical authority (at least in their own minds), the caregivers were better able to make decisions that may have benefitted their parents but ran counter to the parents' wishes. A few women also found it helpful to attend lectures that discussed legal and financial affairs, community resources, and the psycho-social dimensions of caregiving. Nine consulted therapists to learn to disentangle unresolved emotional issues from the process of providing care. In addition, twenty-four participated in support groups, which helped to relieve the isolation surrounding caregiving. Many women asserted that they gained solace and strength by talking openly about their experiences and sharing information.

If educational programs, counseling services, and support groups have many positive aspects, however, a few programs also include potentially troubling features. Most counseling programs and support groups emphasize the need to change individual attitudes and behaviors; as a result, they may divert attention from underlying social structures. Rather than enhancing caregivers' sense of competence, educational programs may undermine their faith in their capacity to solve problems on their own. And some professional advice may have limited usefulness. For example, two researchers advocate teaching caregivers skills in time management (Clark and Rakowski, 1983). It is unclear what benefits will ensue from bringing the values of the factory to the home. As Nancy Hooyman and Rosemary Ryan (1985) remark, "Economizing on the amount of time required to change an incontinent person's bedding does not substantially minimize the stress of performing this task several times a night. Nor do models of efficiency offer solutions to the constant vigilance required by a cognitively impaired person's wandering." We have seen that many women caring for parents with dementia find it reassuring to acquire information about disease processes and are anxious to learn methods of dealing with their parents and managing their behavior. Others, however, remain skeptical about the value of perfecting techniques based on standardized knowledge.

Although most support groups promote personal adjustment rather than social reform, this emphasis is not inevitable. Sylvia Law (1986) proposes that support groups adopt the techniques of consciousness raising, encouraging members both to explore the common roots of their personal problems and to mobilize to demand change. A first step might be to help women understand the societal factors that compel them to assume caregiving responsibilities and make this burden so overwhelming. Many counselors attribute women's overinvolvement in caregiving to their personality structures or family relationships. Consciousness-raising groups could draw attention to cultural norms about women's responsibilities for care, the demands and expectations of other family members, and the absence of alternative sources of esteem for many women in our society. These groups also could discuss how the failure of this society to recognize caregiving as socially valuable work and to provide appropriate services threatens the well being of caregivers and thwarts their ability to render good care. Finally, consciousness-raising groups may encourage caregivers to seek common solutions to problems they previously viewed as individual.

Women Who Care, a support group for women caring for disabled husbands, offers a model for others. Organized in Marin County, California, in 1977, the group originally restricted its focus to providing mutual support and encouragement. As the women exchanged stories about the dearth of supportive services, however, they recognized the need to take collective action on their own behalf. With the help of a local agency, the group successfully established a program of respite care in their community. Joining forces with the Older Women's League, an advocacy group for aging women, members launched a national campaign to increase public awareness of the concerns of caregivers and to work for programs addressing their needs (Sommers and Shields, 1987).

Structural Changes

Although financial compensation for caregivers, supportive services, training and counseling programs, and support groups are the most common proposals to help family members caring for the disabled elderly, they remain inadequate solutions. Feminists repeatedly have demanded that we seek to eradicate the gender division of domestic labor. When we recognize that the work of caring is not confined to child rearing but extends throughout the life course, this concern becomes particularly pressing. As noted in the introduction, adult daughters provide more assistance than adult sons to elderly parents, and they receive less help from their husbands than sons obtain from their wives. If men took more responsibility for ensuring the physical and emotional well-being of family members, the burdens on women would be alleviated.

The feminist goal of restructuring the world of work also assumes greater urgency when we consider the entire life cycle of caring. The workplace makes little accommodation to the place of caregiving in the lives of employees. A survey of seventy corporations in New York in 1985 found that just 15 percent had programs to help employees caring for frail elderly relatives (Warshaw et al., 1986). The great majority of these programs provided only information and referral services (Subcommittee on Human Services, 1987:61; see Scharlach and Boyd, 1989). Alternative work arrangements, such as job sharing and flexible work hours, are essential for many relatives who seek to combine paid employment and caregiving responsibilities. Women who interrupt their work lives to care for the elderly need guarantees that their jobs will await them when they return and that they can continue to accrue pension credits (Spalter-Roth and Hartmann, 1988; Taub, 1984–85). Of the twenty-eight state legislatures that introduced bills for family leaves in 1987, however, just four included care for elderly parents as a component of the leave package (Wisensale and Allison, 1988). Leaves that focus solely on care for small children ignore the changing reality of women's caregiving obligations.

The restricted hours of physicians' offices and service agencies exacerbate the difficulties of integrating caregiving and work force participation. Many caregivers take time away from their jobs not because they must deliver care but because they can make appointments with physicians and other service providers only during working hours (Matthews, Werkner, and Delaney, 1989). Some offices thus should extend their hours to weekends and evenings.

Broad-scale reform of the nursing home industry would enable family members to consider residential placement a viable option when the pressures of care become overwhelming. This study suggests that many caregivers staunchly resist the suggestion that they place severely disabled relatives in nursing homes. Because we often assume that institutional care must be dehumanizing and depersonalizing, we compel family members to continue providing care long after they might reasonably be expected to stop.

Although noninstitutional services have received less scrutiny than nursing homes, equally grave scandals may be lurking there as well. As the Homecare Quality Assurance Act of 1986 declares, home care quality is "a black box—a virtual unknown" (*Black Box*, 1986). Because the work of home health care providers is invisible and often unsupervised, and because they tend very vulnerable patients, there are ample opportunities for abuse. Governmental monitoring systems should accompany the expansion of the home-based services caregivers desperately need (see Grant and Harrington, 1989; see Scanlon, 1988:12).

In addition, we should give greater consideration to the very high proportion of disabled elderly people without relatives to provide care. Approximately 10 percent of the elderly receiving long-term care lack any kin, and approximately 20 percent are childless (Soldo, 1985). By emphasizing familial obligations, policymakers privilege those older persons who obtain services from relatives. The needs of the elderly who have survived all their relatives, whose children are estranged, who remained childless, or who have lived their lives outside families are slighted. A very high proportion of the elderly in future decades will not have children to care for them. A fall in the fertility rate has coincided with the growth of the elderly population; because the baby boom generation is just beginning to reach the age at which most children start providing assistance to parents, the pool of caregivers soon will increase. But after 2020, when the baby boomers become aged themselves, the ratio of offspring to elderly persons will decline dramatically (Burwell, 1986). The same housekeeping, personal care, and transportation services that alleviate the burden on caregivers can permit some disabled elderly people to manage the activities of daily life without assistance from family and friends. Alternative living arrangements such as congregate or shared housing can enable older people to create supportive communities among themselves.

Finally, we should accord greater recognition to the work of caring. Although family assistance to the sick and disabled has been romanticized since the mid-nineteenth century, we live in a society that extols the virtues of independence, seeks to distance itself from basic life events, and trivializes the domestic activities of women. The refusal of the government to devote adequate resources to domestic caring reflects the low value placed on this work. The coping strategies of many women in this study suggest that they too accept the social devaluation of caregiving. Although virtually all the women I interviewed agreed that caregiving created difficulties for them, few believed that they were entitled to special consideration. Rather than pressing their demands for support, they expressed gratitude that others tolerated their involvement in care and sought to shield bosses, coworkers, and other family members from the consequences. Some women also revealed their lack of respect for caregiving when they skimped on the wages of paid helpers or denied the real skills these workers brought to their jobs.

But caregiving is an essential human activity. The social fabric relies on our collective ability to sustain life, nurture the weak, and respond to the needs of intimates. To improve the lot of women who care, we must create a society where this endeavor is both rewarded and esteemed rather than demanding enormous personal sacrifice.

Appendix

I located interviewees in various ways. A geriatrician at a major hospital in Los Angeles provided a list of the names, addresses, and phone numbers of patients whose daughters were caring for them. All the daughters I contacted from this list agreed to be interviewed. In addition, I attended caregiver support groups in five different parts of the city; I explained the purpose of my research and asked for volunteers. These groups included spouses and siblings as well as adult children; because I did not know how many of the members were daughters caring for disabled elderly parents, I also had no way of determining what proportion of the caregivers who fit my criteria agreed to participate in the study.

Some women were initially reluctant to volunteer for the study because they did not define themselves as "caregivers." Although they had joined support groups, they insisted that this term did not apply to them either because they did not live with their parents or because they had hired aides and attendants to deliver direct care. I explained that I wished to interview women who had major responsibility for elderly parents, regardless of their living arrangements or access to outside help.

When I phoned women to make arrangements for the interviews, I asked them where they would like to meet. One woman chose a coffee house, four others preferred their offices. I interviewed the rest in their homes. Privacy was very important to virtually all of the women. Although one wanted her husband present during the interview, the others tried to ensure that family members, including their parents, did not wander into the rooms where we were talking.

I was aware that, by recruiting many respondents from support groups, I would not be able to obtain a representative sample. Numerous researchers point out that family members who seek help dif-

TABLE 1
Characteristics of Caregivers (percent)

	Daughters in Informal Caregivers Survey	Study Sample
Age in Years		
14–44	24	18
45–64	63	78
65–74	13	4
Marital Status		
Married	56	67
Unmarried	44	33
Race		
White	78	94
Other	22	6
Number of Children Less than 18 Years of Age in Household		
None	76	96
1	11	2
2	9	2
3 or more	5	0
Living Arrangement		
Lives with parent	61	25
Lives separately	39	75
Employment Status		
Working	44	53
Quit work to become caregiver	12	16
Not working for other reasons	45	31
Length of Caregiving		
Less than 1 year	20	6
1–4 years	45	49
5 years or more	19	39
No longer giving care	14	6
Caregiver Tasks (multiple responses permitted)		
Personal care		
Hygiene	69	37
Mobility	44	20
Administration of medication	57	37
Household tasks	87	69
Shopping and/or transportation	91	94
Handling finance	59	86

Source: Stone, Cafferata, and Sangl, 1987.

Note: Percentages may not add up to 100 because of rounding.

TABLE 2
LEVEL OF IMPAIRMENT OF PARENTS ASSISTED BY DAUGHTERS
IN NATIONAL SAMPLE

	Percentage of Parents
ADL Score[a]	
0	19
1–2	41
3–4	21
5–6	20
IADL Score[b]	
0–3	22
4–5	22
6–7	31
8–9	26

Source: Stone, Cafferata, and Sangl, 1987.

Note: Percentages do not add up to 100 because of rounding.

[a]The number of activities of daily living (ADL)—such as eating, bathing, dressing, using the toilet, getting in and out of bed, and walking—in which assistance was needed.

[b]The number of instrumental activities of daily living (IADL)—such as taking medications; bandaging; preparing meals; managing finances; making telephone calls; doing laundry, housework, and shopping; getting around outside; and using transportation—in which assistance was needed.

fer from other caregivers (Barer and Johnson, 1990; Gwyther and George, 1986; Raveis, Siegel, and Sudit, 1988–89). I assumed, however, that women who joined support groups would have more contact than others with formal providers. Because I was interested in the interaction of caregivers with the formal service system, this was an important consideration.

Table 1 provides demographic information about the women in the study and compares them to the profile of daughters caring for elderly parents derived from the Informal Caregivers Survey (ICS), a component of the 1982 Health Care Financing Administration Long-Term Care Survey (Stone, Cafferata, and Sangl, 1987). The study sample differs from the national profile of caregivers in several important ways. First, a smaller proportion of my sample were members of racial minorities (6 versus 22 percent). Second, the caregivers I interviewed were far less likely to be living with their parents (25 versus 61 percent). And third, a smaller proportion of my respondents performed personal care and household tasks. Tables 2 and 3 suggest that

TABLE 3

LEVEL OF IMPAIRMENT OF PARENTS ASSISTED BY DAUGHTERS
IN STUDY SAMPLE

	Percentage of Parents[b]
ADL Score[a]	
0	17
1–2	17
3–4	28
5–6	25
7	14
IADL Score[c]	
0–3	11
4–5	33
6–7	56

Notes: Lists of activities included among the ADLS and IADLS come from Horowitz and Dobrof (1982:100). Percentages may not add up to 100 because of rounding.

[a]The number of activities of daily living (ADLS)—such as feeding, dressing and undressing, caring for appearance, getting around the house, getting up and down stairs, bathing and showering, and having control over bowel and bladder—in which assistance was needed.

[b]When the daughters were responsible for both parents, I only assessed the functional limitations of the more impaired parent.

[c]The number of instrumental activities of daily living (IADLS)—such as using the telephone, shopping for groceries, getting to places beyond walking distance, preparing meals, doing light housework, taking medication, and handling money—in which assistance was needed.

this discrepancy cannot be explained by differences in the levels of functional impairment of the two groups of care recipients. Gerontologists typically assess the level of functional impairment by asking whether elderly persons have limitations that prevent them from performing "activities of daily living" (ADL) and "instrumental activities of daily living" (IADL). Because the indicators of ADL and IADL that I used differed somewhat from those of the ICS, the figures in the two tables are not equivalent. Nevertheless, it can be seen that similar proportions of the care recipients in both surveys had no ADL limitations.

I believe that the women I interviewed were responsible for fewer tasks because they received a substantial amount of assistance from formal service providers. The parents of fifteen women in my sample used at least one service from a community agency; in addition, twenty-eight women hired aides, attendants, and companions who were not affiliated with service agencies. These women lived in a city with a large pool of immigrant domestic workers, and they relied on these workers for help with parent care. Just 10 percent of caregivers nationally receive any paid assistance (Stone, Cafferata, and Sangl, 1987).

I collected basic demographic information about both the caregivers and the parents they were tending. All the other questions in the interviews were designed to elicit open-ended responses. Because I wanted to understand how the women interpreted their own experiences, I began the interviews by asking them to tell me whom they were caring for, how long they had been providing care, and what seemed most significant to them about this activity. Although some women responded in a few short sentences, many embarked on lengthy descriptions of their experiences and their attitudes toward caregiving. The interview schedule also contained a series of questions about the women's caregiving responsibilities, their labor force participation, leisure activities, and reliance on formal service providers, the types of assistance they received from members of their social networks, and the nature of their relationships with their parents. All the interviews covered each of these topics, although not necessarily in the same order.

The interviewees were asked to discuss subjects that often were painful to them, and some spoke more freely than others. Yet, almost all the women said they were glad to have had an opportunity to discuss their experiences.

The interviews lasted an average of ninety minutes and were tape recorded, transcribed, and coded for content analysis. Early in the data collection period, provisional coding categories were established. As data collection proceeded, new coding categories were added and some earlier ones collapsed or refined. Although I approached the interviews with tentative hypotheses, the primary purpose was to generate hypotheses that could be useful for further study, not to test preexisting ones. Thus, most of the generalizations recorded in the study emerged from the interviews themselves.

Although this study explores a range of issues previous researchers have ignored, other types of studies also are needed. As several researchers have noted, because caregiving is a dynamic process, we need longitudinal studies, which examine how the experience of caregiving changes over time (Chenoweth and Spencer, 1986; Horowitz and Dobrof, 1982; Ory et al., 1985; Raveis, Siegel, and Sudit, 1988–89). We also should develop research methods that permit us to examine the relationships between caregivers and recipients. I argue in Chapter 4 that we cannot divorce the tasks of caregiving from the personal relationships within which they are embedded, but most research strategies use the individual as the unit of analysis. We therefore need methods that enable us to explore the caregiving dyad as well as broader social networks.

To understand the impact of gender on caregiving, we need in-depth studies of sons. To what extent do they have difficulties asserting authority over disabled parents? What types of relationships do they establish with the parents they tend? To what extent do they allow caregiving responsibilities to intrude on their work lives? Are they more scrupulous than daughters about safeguarding leisure time from the encroachments of care? Do they seek more assistance from paid providers and members of their social networks?

The most urgent need is for studies that examine the impact of class and race on caregiving. This study compares a small group of caregivers with very limited incomes to those with more adequate financial resources. However, we need far more information about caregivers who lack the ability to pay for outside help. We also need to learn more about how cultural variations affect the caregiving experience.

Bibliography

Abel, E. K. 1987. *Love Is Not Enough: Family Care of the Frail Elderly.* Washington, D.C.: American Public Health Association.

Abel, E. K., and M. K. Nelson. 1990. *"Circles of Care: An Introductory Essay."* In *Circles of Care: Work and Identity in Women's Lives,* ed. E. K. Abel and M. K. Nelson. pp. 4–34. Albany: State University of New York Press.

Addams, J. 1910. *Twenty Years at Hull House.* New York: Macmillan.

———. 1972. "Filial Relations." In *The Oven Birds: American Women on Womanhood, 1820–1920,* ed. G. F. Parker, pp. 305–14. New York: Doubleday.

Alderson, N. T., and H. H. Smith. 1942. *A Bride Goes West.* New York: Farrar & Rinehart.

Allen, E. 1946. *Canvas Caravans, Based on the Journal of Esther Belle McMillan Hanna.* Portland, Oreg.: Binfords & Mort.

Antler, J. 1987. *Lucy Sprague Mitchell: The Making of a Modern Woman.* New Haven: Yale University Press.

Antonovsky, A. 1974. "Conceptual and Methodological Problems in the Study of Resistance Resources and Stressful Life Events." In *Stressful Life Events: Their Nature and Effects,* ed. B. S. Dohrenwend and B. P. Dohrenwend, pp. 245–58. New York: Wiley.

———. 1979. *Health, Stress and Coping.* San Francisco: Jossey-Bass.

Apple, R. D. 1987. *Mothers and Medicine: A Social History of Infant Feeding, 1890–1950.* Madison: University of Wisconsin Press.

Arcana, J. 1979. *Our Mothers' Daughters.* Berkeley, Calif.: Shameless Hussy Press.

Archbold, P. G. 1983. "An Impact of Parent-Caring on Women." *Family Relations* 32 (January):39–45.

Arling, G., and W. J. McAuley. 1983. "The Feasibility of Public Payments for Family Caregiving." *The Gerontologist* 23(3):300–306.

Arpad, S. S., ed. 1984. *Sam Curd's Diary: The Diary of a True Woman.* Athens: Ohio University Press.

Auerbach, J., L. Blum, V. Smith, and C. Williams. 1985. "Commentary on Gilligan's *In a Different Voice." Feminist Studies* 11(1):149–62.

185

Ayer, S. C. 1910. *Diary of Sarah Connell Ayer 1805–1835*. Portland, Maine: Lefavor-Tower.

Bailey, M. S. 1980. "A Journal of Mary Stuart Bailey, Wife of Dr. Fred Bailey, from Ohio to California, April–October 1852." In *Ho for California! Women's Overland Diaries from the Huntington Library*, ed. S. L. Myres. San Marino, Calif.: Huntington Library.

Baker, S. J. 1980. *Fighting for Life*. Huntington, N.Y.: Robert E. Kreiger.

Balbo, L. 1982. "The Servicing Work of Women and the Capitalist State." *Political Power and Social Theory* 3:251–70.

Barer, B. M., and C. L. Johnson. 1990. "A Critique of the Caregiving Literature." *The Gerontologist* 30(1):26–29.

Baruch, G. K., L. Biener, and R. C. Barnett. 1985. *Women and Gender in Research on Stress*. Wellesley, Mass.: Wellesley College Center for Research on Women.

Bayer, R. 1986–87. "Ethical Challenges." *Generations* 2:44–47.

Beecher, C. 1977. *A Treatise on Domestic Economy*. New York: Schocken Books.

Belle, D. 1982. "Social Ties and Social Support." In *Lives in Stress*, ed. D. Belle, pp. 133–43. Newbury Park, Calif.: Sage.

———. 1987. "Gender Differences in the Social Moderators of Stress." In *Gender and Stress*, ed. R. C. Barnett, L. Biener and G. K. Baruch, pp. 257–77. New York: Free Press.

Berk, S. F. 1988. "Women's Unpaid Labor: Home and Community." In *Women Working*, 2d ed., ed. A. H. Stromberg and S. Harkess. Mountain View, Calif.: Mayfield.

Bertghold, L. 1987. "The Impact of Public Policy on Home Health Services for the Elderly." *Pride Institute Journal of Long Term Home Health Care* 6:12–21.

Bianchi, S. M., and D. Spain. 1986. *American Women in Transition*. New York: Russell Sage Foundation.

Bishop, C. E. 1986. "Living Arrangement Choices of Elderly Singles: Effects of Income and Disability." *Health Care Financing Review* 7(3):65–73.

Black Box of Home Care Quality, Hearing Before the Select Committee on Aging, House of Representatives. 1986. 99th Cong. 2d sess. (July 29). Comm. pub. no. 96–606. Washington, D.C.: Government Printing Office.

Blake, J. B. 1977. "From Buchanan to Fishbein: The Literature of Domestic Medicine." In *Medicine without Doctors*, ed. G. B. Risse, R. L. Numbers, and J. W. Leavitt, pp. 11–30. New York: Science History Publications.

Blau, P. 1964. *Exchange in Social Life*. New York: John Wiley.

Blenkner, M. 1965. "Social Work and Family Relationships in Later Life." In *Social Structure and the Family: Generational Relations*, ed. E. Shanas and G. F. Streib. Englewood Cliffs, N.J.: Prentice-Hall.

Bolsteri, M. J., ed. 1982. *Vinegar Pie and Chicken Bread: A Woman's Diary of Life in the Rural South, 1890–1891*. Fayetteville: University of Arkansas Press.

Boulton, M. G. 1983. *On Being a Mother: A Study of Women with Pre-School Children.* London: Tavistock Publications.

Bowers, B. 1990. "Family Perceptions of Care in a Nursing Home." In *Circles of Care: Work and Identity in Women's Lives,* ed. E. K. Abel and M. K. Nelson, pp. 278–89. Albany: State University of New York Press.

Braithwaite, V. 1990. *Bound to Care.* Sydney: Allen and Unwin.

Breault, J. C. 1976. *The World of Emily Howland: Odyssey of a Humanitarian.* Millbrae, Calif.: Les Femmes.

Brody, E. M. 1981. "'Women in the Middle' and Family Help to Older People." *The Gerontologist* 21(5):471–80.

———. 1985. "Parent Care as a Normative Family Stress." *The Gerontologist* 25(1):19–28.

Brody, E. M., M. H. Kleban, P. T. Johnsen, and C. Hoffman. 1987. "Work Status and Parent Care: A Comparison of Four Groups of Women." *The Gerontologist* 27(2):201–8.

Brody, E. M., and C. B. Schoonover. 1986. "Patterns of Parent Care When Adult Daughters Work and When They Do Not." *The Gerontologist* 26(4):372–81.

Brown, C. V. 1982. "Home Production for Use in a Market Economy." In *Rethinking the Family: Some Feminist Questions,* ed. B. Thorne with M. Yalom, pp. 151–67. New York: Longman.

Brown, E. R. 1979. *Rockefeller Medicine Men: Medicine and Capitalism in America.* Berkeley: University of California Press.

Brown, H. C. 1929. *Grandmother Brown's Hundred Years, 1827–1927.* New York: Blue Ribbon Books.

Brubaker, T. 1985. *Later Life Families.* Beverly Hills, Calif.: Sage.

Bulmer, M. 1987. *The Social Basis of Community Care.* London: Allen & Unwin.

Burdz, M. P., W. O. Eaton, and J. B. Bond, Jr. 1988. "Effects of Respite Care on Dementia and Nondementia Patients and Their Caregivers." *Psychology and Aging* 3:38–42.

Burke, T. R. 1988. "Long-term Care: The Public Role and Private Initiatives." *Health Care Financing Review,* Annual Supplement, pp. 1–5.

Burwell, B. O. 1986. *Shared Obligations: Public Policy Influences on Family Care for the Elderly.* Medicaid Program Evaluation Working Paper 2.1. Washington, D.C.: Health Care Financing Administration, Department of Health and Human Services.

Callahan, J. J., Jr. 1989. "Play It Again Sam—There Is No Impact." *The Gerontologist* 29(1):5–6.

Callahan, J. J., Jr., et al. 1980. "Responsibility of Families for Their Severely Disabled Relatives." *Health Care Financing Review* 1:40, 41.

Cancian, F. M. 1987. *Love in America: Gender and Self Development.* Cambridge: Cambridge University Press.

Cantor, M. H. 1983. "Strain among Caregivers: A Study of Experience in the United States." *The Gerontologist* 23(6):597–603.

Caplan, G. 1974. *Support Systems and Community Mental Health.* New York: Behavioral Publications.

Caro, F. G., and A. E. Blank. 1987. *Caring for the Elderly at Home: A Policy Perspective on Consumer Experiences with Publicly-Funded Home Care Programs in New York City.* New York: Community Service Society of New York.

Carpenter, H. 1980. "A Trip Across the Plains in an Oxen Wagon, 1857." In *Ho for California! Women's Overland Diaries from the Huntington Library,* ed. S. L. Myres. San Marino, Calif.: Huntington Library.

Cassedy, J. H. 1977. "Why Self-Help? Americans Alone with Their Diseases, 1800–1850." In *Medicine Without Doctors,* ed. G. B. Risse, R. L. Numbers, and J. W. Leavitt, pp. 31–48. New York: Science History Publications.

Cassel, J. 1976. "The Contribution of the Social Environment to Host Resistance." *American Journal of Epidemiology* 104:107–22.

Cayleff, S. E. 1987. *Wash and Be Healed: The Water-Cure Movement and Women's Health.* Philadelphia: Temple University Press.

Chambers-Schiller, L. V. 1984. *Liberty, A Better Husband: Single Women in America: The Generations of 1780–1840.* New Haven: Yale University Press.

Chenowith, B., and B. Spencer. 1986. "Dementia: The Experience of Family Caregivers." *The Gerontologist* 26(3):267–72.

Cherlin, A. J., and F. F. Furstenberg. 1986. *The New American Grandparent: A Place in the Family.* New York: Basic Books.

Chodorow, N. 1974. "Family Structures and Feminine Personality." In *Woman, Culture and Society,* ed. M. Z. Rosaldo and L. Lamphere, pp. 43–66. Stanford: Stanford University Press.

————. 1978. *The Reproduction of Mothering: Psychoanalysis and the Sociology of Gender.* Berkeley: University of California Press.

Chodorow, N., and S. Contratto. 1982. "The Fantasy of the Perfect Mother." In *Rethinking the Family: Some Feminist Questions,* ed. B. Thorne with M. Yalom, pp. 54–75. New York: Longman.

Clark, N. M., and W. Rakowski. 1983. "Family Caregivers of Older Adults: Improving Helping Skills." *The Gerontologist* 23(6):637–42.

Cobb, S. 1976. "Social Support as a Moderator of Life Stress." *Psychosomatic Medicine* 38:300–14.

Cohen, R. 1918. *Out of the Shadow.* New York: George H. Doran.

Colen, S. 1986. " 'With Respect and Feelings': Voices of West Indian Child Care and Domestic Workers in New York City." In *All American Women: Lines that Divide, Ties that Bind,* ed. J. B. Cole, pp. 46–70. New York: Free Press.

Committee on Nursing Home Regulation, Institute of Medicine. 1986. *Improving the Quality of Care in Nursing Homes.* Washington, D.C.: National Academy Press.

Community Council of Greater New York. 1978. *Dependency in the Elderly of New York.* New York: Community Council of Greater New York.

Comptroller General of the United States. 1977. *The Well-Being of Older People in Cleveland, Ohio.* Washington, D.C.: General Accounting Office.

Congressional Budget Office, Congress of the United States. 1988. *Changes in the Living Arrangements of the Elderly: 1960–2030.* Washington, D.C.: Government Printing Office.

Cornell, W. S. 1912. *Health and Medical Inspection of School Children.* Philadelphia: F. A. Davis.

Cott, N. F. 1983. *The Bonds of Womanhood: Woman's Sphere in New England, 1780–1835.* New Haven: Yale University Press.

Cotterill, P. G. 1983. "Provider Incentives under Alternative Reimbursement Systems." In *Long Term Care: Perspectives from Research and Demonstrations,* ed. R. J. Vogel and H. C. Palmer. Washington, D.C.: Health Care Financing Administration.

Cowan, R. S. 1983. *More Work for Mother: The Ironies of Household Technology from the Open Hearth to the Microwave.* New York: Basic Books.

———. 1987. "Women's Work, Housework, and History: The Historical Roots of Inequality in Work-Force Participation." In *Families and Work,* ed. N. Gerstel and H. E. Gross, pp. 164–77. Philadelphia: Temple University Press.

Coward, R. T., and E. Rathbone-McCuan. 1985. "Illuminating the Relative Role of Adult Sons and Daughters in the Long-term Care of Their Parents." Paper presented at the professional symposium of the National Association of Social Workers, Chicago, November.

Crystal, S. 1982. *America's Old Age Crisis: Public Policy and the Two Worlds of Aging.* New York: Basic Books.

Daniels, N. 1988. *Am I My Parents' Keeper: An Essay on Justice between the Young and the Old.* New York: Oxford University Press.

Davis, A. F. 1973. *American Heroine, The Life and Legend of Jane Addams.* New York: Oxford University Press.

Day, A. R. 1985. *Who Cares? Demographic Trends Challenge Family Care for the Elderly.* Washington, D.C.: Population Reference Bureau.

Dill, B. T. 1988. " 'Making Your Job Good Yourself': Domestic Service and the Construction of Personal Dignity." In *Women and the Politics of Empowerment,* ed. S. Morgen and A. Bookman, pp. 33–52. Philadelphia: Temple University Press.

Dinnerstein, D. 1976. *The Mermaid and the Minotaur: Sexual Arrangements and Human Malaise.* New York: Harper.

Dodge, H. A., ed. 1901. *Gail Hamilton's Life in Letters.* Vol. 1. Boston: Lee and Shepard.

Donnell, C. T. 1896. "The Oregon Pilgrimage—Its Genesis and the Exodus." In *Crossing the Plains,* ed. O. Thomson, pp. 9–14. Fairfield, Wash.: Ye Galleon Press.

Donnell, E. H., ed. 1982. "Rowe Creek, 1890–91: Mary L. Fitzmaurice Diary." *Oregon Historical Quarterly* 83(2):171–94; (3):288–10.

Donovan, R. 1989. " 'We Care for the Most Important People in Your Life': Home Care Workers in New York City." *Women's Studies Quarterly* 17(1–2):56–65.

Doty, P. 1986. "Family Care of the Elderly: The Role of Public Policy." *The Milbank Memorial Fund Quarterly/Health and Society* 64(1):34–75.

Douglas, A. 1988. *The Feminization of American Culture*. New York: Doubleday.

Dunkel-Schetter, C., and C. B. Wortman. 1982. "The Interpersonal Dynamics of Cancer: Problems in Social Relationships and Their Impact on the Patient." In *Interpersonal Issues in Health Care*, ed. H. S. Friedman and M. R. DiMatteo, pp. 69–100. New York: Academic Press.

Dyer, T. 1982. *To Raise Myself A Little: The Diaries and Letters of Jennie, A Georgia Teacher, 1841–1886*. Athens: University of Georgia Press.

Eckenrode, J., and S. Gore. 1981. "Stressful Events and Social Supports: The Significance of Context." In *Social Networks and Social Support*, ed. B. H. Gottlieb, pp. 43–68. Newbury Park, Calif.: Sage.

Eddy, F. M. 1981. "An American Spinster." In *Victorian Women: A Documentary Account of Women's Lives in Nineteenth-Century England, France, and the United States*, ed. E. O. Hellerstein, L. P. Hume, and K. M. Offen, pp. 155–57. Stanford: Stanford University Press.

Edelman, P., and S. Hughes. 1990. "The Impact of Community Care on Provision of Informal Care to Homebound Elderly Persons." *Journal of Gerontology* 45(2):74–84.

Edwards, M. 1981. "Letters to Sabrina Bennett." In *Farm to Factory: Women's Letters, 1830–1860*, ed. T. Dublin, pp. 82–87. New York: Columbia University Press.

Ehrenreich, B., and D. English. 1978. *For Her Own Good: 150 Years of the Experts' Advice to Women*. Garden City, N.Y.: Anchor Press/Doubleday.

Ellis, A. 1929. *The Life of an Ordinary Woman*. Boston: Houghton Mifflin.

England, P., and L. McCreary. 1987. "Gender Inequality and Paid Employment." In *Analyzing Gender*, eds. B. B. Hess and M. M. Ferree, pp. 286–321. Newbury Park, Calif.: Sage.

Estes, C. L., and T. Arendell. 1986. "The Unsettled Future: Women and the Economics of Aging." Paper presented at conference, "Who Cares for the Elderly? Caregiving in Women's Lives," University of California, Los Angeles, April 19.

Estes, C. L., and E. A. Binney. 1989. "The Biomedicalization of Aging: Dangers and Dilemmas." *The Gerontologist* 29(5):587–96.

Estes, C. L., and J. B. Wood. 1985. "The Non-Profit Sector and Community-Based Care for the Elderly in the U.S.: A Disappearing Resource?" Unpublished paper, Institute for Health and Aging, University of California, San Francisco.

Eustis, N., J. Greenberg, and S. Patten. 1984. *Long-Term Care for Older Persons: A Policy Perspective*. Monterey, Calif.: Brooks/Cole.

Evandrou, M., S. Arber, A. Dales, and G. N. Gilbert. 1986. "Who Cares for the

Elderly? Family Care Provision and Receipt of Statutory Services." In *Dependency and Independence in Old Age: Theoretical Perspectives and Policy Alternatives*, ed. C. Phillipson, M. Bernard, and P. Straug (London: British Society of Gerontology).

Everett, J., and S. Everett. 1939. "Letters of John and Sarah Everett: Miami County Pioneers." *The Kansas Historical Quarterly* 8(1):3–34; (2):143–74; (3):279–310.

Everett, M. H. 1977. "Duty Commands You." In *The Female Experience: An American Documentary.* ed. G. Lerner, pp. 172–78. Indianapolis: Bobbs-Merrill.

Evers, H. 1985. "The Frail Elderly Woman: Emergent Questions in Ageing and Women's Health." In *Women, Health and Healing: Toward a New Perspective*, eds. E. Lewin and V. Olesen. London: Methuen.

Ewen, E. 1985. *Immigrant Women in the Land of Dollars: Life and Culture on the Lower East Side, 1890–1925.* New York: Monthly Review Press.

Faragher, J. M. 1979. *Women and Men on the Overland Trail.* New Haven: Yale University Press.

Faragher, J. M., and C. Stansell. 1979. "Women and Their Families on the Overland Trail to California and Oregon, 1842–1867." In *A Heritage of Their Own: Toward a New Social History of American Women*, eds. N. F. Cott and E. H. Pleck, pp. 246–67. New York: Simon and Schuster.

Fay, B. 1975. *Social Theory and Political Practice.* London: Allen and Unwin.

Feder, J., and W. Scanlon. 1980. "Regulating the Bed Supply in Nursing Homes." *Milbank Memorial Fund Quarterly/Health and Society* 58:54–88.

Feldblum, C. R. 1985. "Home Health Care for the Elderly: Programs, Problems, and Potentials." *Harvard Journal on Legislation* 22:193–254.

Ferree, M. M. 1983. "Housework: Rethinking the Costs and Benefits." In *Families, Politics, and Public Policy: A Feminist Dialogue on Women and the State*, ed. I. Diamond, pp. 148–67. New York: Longman.

Fields, A. 1970. *Life and Letters of Harriet Beecher Stowe.* Detroit: Gale Research Company.

Fiore, J., J. Becker, and D. B. Coppel. 1983. "Social Network Interactions: A Buffer or a Stress?" *American Journal of Community Psychology,* 11:423–39.

Fischer, L. R. 1986. *Linked Lives: Adult Daughters and Their Mothers.* New York: Harper & Row.

Fischer, L. R., and N. N. Eustis. 1988. "DRGs and Family Care for the Elderly: A Case Study." *The Gerontologist* 28(3):383–89.

Fitting, M., P. Rabins, M. J. Lucas, and J. Eastham. 1986. "Caregivers for Dementia Patients: A Comparison of Husbands and Wives." *The Gerontologist,* 26(3):248–52.

Flax, J. 1978. "The Conflict between Nurturance and Autonomy in Mother-Daughter Relationships and within Feminism." *Feminist Studies* 4(2):171–91.

Fox-Genovese, E. 1988. *Within the Plantation Household: Black and White Women of the Old South.* Chapel Hill: University of North Carolina Press.

Frink, M. A. 1897. *Journal of the Adventures of a Party of California Gold-seekers (Indiana to California, 1850).* Privately printed.

Gallagher, D. 1985. "Intervention Strategies to Assist Caregivers of Frail Elders: Current Research Status and Future Directions." *Annual Review of Gerontology and Geriatrics* 5:249–82.

Gallagher, D., A. Wrabetz, S. Lovett, S. DelMaestro, and J. Rose. 1989. "Depression and Other Negative Affects in Family Caregivers." In *Alzheimer's Disease Treatment and Family Stress: Directions for Research,* ed. E. Light and B. D. Lebowitz, pp. 218–44. Rockville, Md.: Department of Health and Human Services.

Gardiner, J. K. 1987. "Self Psychology as Feminist Theory." *Signs* 12(4):761–80.

George, L. K., and L. P. Gwyther. 1984. "The Dynamics of Caregiver Burden: Changes in Caregiver Well-Being over Time." Paper presented at the 34th Annual Scientific Meeting of the Gerontological Society of America, San Antonio, Tex., November.

———. 1986. "Caregiver Well-Being: A Multidimensional Examination of Family Caregivers of Demented Adults." *The Gerontologist* 26 (3):253–59.

Gerson, K. 1985. *Hard Choices: How Women Decide about Work, Career, and Motherhood.* Berkeley: University of California Press.

Gerson, M. J., J. L. Alpert, and M. S. Richardson. 1984. "Mothering: The View from Psychological Research." *Signs* 9(3):434–53.

Gerstel, N., and H. E. Gross. 1987. "Introduction and Overview." In *Families and Work,* ed. N. Gerstel and H. E. Gross, Philadelphia: Temple University Press.

Gibson, M. J. 1984. "Family Support Patterns, Policies and Programs." In *Innovative Aging Programs Abroad: Implications for the United States,* ed. C. Nusberg, pp. 159–95. Westport, Conn.: Greenwood.

Gilligan, C. 1982. *In a Different Voice: Psychological Theory and Women's Development.* Cambridge: Harvard University Press.

Glazer, N. Y. 1988. "Overlooked, Overworked: Women's Unpaid and Paid Work in the Health Services' Cost Crisis." *International Journal of Health Services* 18(1):119–37.

Glenn, E. N. 1986. *Issei, Nisei, Warbride: Three Generations of Japanese American Women in Domestic Service.* Philadelphia: Temple University Press.

———. 1987. "Gender and the Family." In *Analyzing Gender: A Handbook of Social Science Research,* ed. B. B. Hess and M. M. Ferree, pp. 348–80. Newbury Park, Calif.: Sage.

Goldman, H. H. 1982. "Mental Illness and Family Burden: A Public Health Perspective." *Hospital and Community Psychiatry* 33(7):557–60.

Graham, H. 1983. "Caring: A Labour of Love." In *A Labour of Love: Women,*

Work and Caring, eds. J. Finch and D. Groves, pp. 13–30. London: Routledge & Kegan Paul.

―――. 1985. "Providers, Negotiators, and Mediators: Women as the Hidden Carers." In *Women, Health and Healing: Toward a New Perspective,* ed. E. Lewin and V. Olesen, pp. 25–52. New York: Tavistock.

Grant, L. A., and C. Harrington. 1989. "Quality of Care in Licensed and Unlicensed Home Care Agencies: A California Case Study." *Home Health Care Services Quarterly* 10(1/2):115–38.

Greene, V. L. 1983. "Substitution between Formally and Informally Provided Care for the Impaired Elderly in the Community." *Medical Care* 21:609–19.

Greene, V. L., and D. J. Monahan. 1989. "The Effect of a Support and Education Program on Stress and Burden among Family Caregivers to Frail Elderly Persons." *The Gerontologist* 29(5):472–77.

Grob, G. N. 1971. "Mental Illness, Indigency, and Welfare: The Mental Hospital in Nineteenth-Century America." In *Anonymous Americans: Explorations in Nineteenth-Century Social History,* ed. T. K. Hareven, pp. 250–79. Englewood Cliffs, N.J.: Prentice-Hall.

Gubrium, J. F. 1988. "Family Responsibility and Caregiving in the Qualitative Analysis of the Alzheimer's Disease Experience." *Journal of Marriage and the Family* 50:197–207.

Gubrium, J. F., and R. J. Lynott. 1987. "Measurement and the Interpretation of Burden in the Alzheimer's Disease Experience." *Journal of Aging Studies* 1(3):265–85.

Gutman, H. G. 1976. *The Black Family in Slavery and Freedom, 1750–1925.* New York: Random House.

Gutmann, D. L. 1980. "Psychoanalysis and Aging: A Developmental View." In *The Course of Life,* vol. 2, ed. S. I. Greenspan and G. H. Pollock. Bethesda, Md.: National Institute of Mental Health.

Gwyther, L. P., and L. K. George. 1986. "Symposium: Caregivers for Dementia Patients: Introduction." *The Gerontologist* 26(3):245–47.

Habermas, J. 1971. *Knowledge and Human Interests.* Boston: Beacon Press.

Hagestad, G. O. 1986. "The Aging Society as a Context for Family Life." *Daedalus* 115 (1):119–40.

Haley, W. E., S. L. Brown, and E. G. Levine. 1987. "Experimental Evaluation of the Effectiveness of Group Intervention for Dementia Caregivers." *The Gerontologist* 27(3):376–82.

Haley, W. E., E. G. Levine, S. L. Brown, J. W. Berry, and G. H. Hughes. 1987. "Psychological, Social, and Health Consequences of Caring for a Relative with Senile Dementia." *Journal of the American Geriatrics Society* 35:405–11.

Hampsten, E. 1982. *Read This Only to Yourself: The Private Writings of Midwestern Women, 1880–1910.* Bloomington: Indiana University Press.

Hareven, T. K. 1987. "The Dynamics of Kin in an Industrial Community." In

Families and Work, ed. N. Gerstel and H. E. Gross, pp. 55–83. Philadelphia: Temple University Press.

Hare-Mustin, R. T., and Marecek, J. 1986. "Autonomy and Gender: Some Questions for Therapists." *Psychotherapy* 23:205–12.

Harrington, C., and J. H. Swan. 1985. "Institutional Long Term Care Services." In *Long Term Care of the Elderly: Public Policy Issues,* eds. C. Harrington, R. J. Newcomer, C. L. Estes, and Associates. pp. 153–75. Beverly Hills, Calif.: Sage.

Harris, L., and Associates, Inc. 1986. *Problems Facing Elderly Americans Living Alone.* Study no. 854010, New York.

Hartford, M. E., and R. Parsons. 1982. "Groups with Relatives of Dependent Older Adults." *The Gerontologist* 22(3):394–98.

Hartsock, N. C. M. 1983. *Money, Sex and Power: Toward a Feminist Historical Materialism.* Boston: Northeastern University Press.

Hasselkus, B. R. 1988. "Meaning in Family Caregiving: Perspectives on Caregiver/Professional Relationships." *The Gerontologist* 28(5):686–91.

Hatfield, A. B. 1987. "Families as Caregivers: A Historical Perspective." In *Families of the Mentally Ill: Coping and Adaptation,* ed. A. B. Hatfield and H. B. Lefley, pp. 3–29. New York: The Guilford Press.

Haun, C. 1982. "A Woman's Trip Across the Plains in 1849." In *Women's Diaries of the Westward Journey,* ed. L. Schlissel, pp. 165–86. New York: Schocken Books.

Hecox, M. M. 1966. *California Caravan: The 1846 Overland Trail Memoir of Margaret M. Hecox.* San Jose, Calif.: Harlan-Young Press.

Heiser, A. H. 1941. *Quaker Lady: The Story of Charity Lynch.* Oxford, Ohio: Mississippi Valley Press.

Helmrath, T. H., and E. M. Steinitz. 1978. "Death of an Infant: Parental Grieving and the Failure of Social Support." *Journal of Family Practice* 6:785–90.

Hendrickson, M. C. 1988. "State Tax Incentives for Persons Giving Informal Care to the Elderly." *Health Care Financing Review,* Annual Supplement, pp. 123–28.

Herndon, S. R. 1902. *Days on the Road: Crossing the Plains in 1865.* New York: Burr Printing House.

Hess, B. B., and B. J. Soldo. 1985. "Husband and Wife Networks." In *Social Support Networks and the Care of the Elderly: Theory, Research and Practice,* ed. W. J. Sauer and R. T. Coward, pp. 67–92. New York: Springer.

Hochschild, A. R. 1975. "The Sociology of Feeling and Emotion: Selected Possibilities." In *Another Voice: Feminist Perspectives on Social Life and Social Science,* ed. M. Millman and R. M. Kanter, pp. 280–307. Garden City, N.Y.: Anchor Press/Doubleday.

———. 1989. *The Second Shift: Working Parents and the Revolution at Home.* New York: Viking.

Holt, S. W. 1986–87. "The Role of Home Care in Long Term Care." *Generations* 11(2):9–12.

Hooyman, N. R., and W. Lustbader. 1986. *Taking Care: Supporting Older People and Their Families*. New York: Free Press.

Hooyman, N. R., and R. Ryan. 1985. "Women as Caregivers of the Elderly: Catch 22 Dilemmas." Unpublished paper.

Horowitz, A. 1985a. "Family Caregiving to the Frail Elderly." *Annual Review of Gerontology and Geriatrics* 5:194–246.

———. 1985b. "Sons and Daughters to Older Parents: Differences in Role Performance and Consequences." *The Gerontologist* 25(6):612–17.

Horowitz, A., and R. Dobrof. 1982. *The Role of Families in Providing Long-Term Care to the Frail and Chronically Ill Elderly Living in the Community*. Final report submitted to the Health Care Financing Administration, Department of Health and Human Services (grant no. 18-P-9754/2-02), Washington, D.C.

Horowitz, A., and L. W. Shindelman. 1983. "Social and Economic Incentives for Family Caregivers." *Health Care Financing Review* 5(2):25–33.

House, J. S. 1981. *Work, Stress, and Social Support*. Reading, Mass.: Addison-Wesley.

Iverson, L. H. 1986. *A Description and Analysis of State Preadmission Screening Programs*. Minneapolis: Inter-Study, Center on Aging and Long-Term Care.

Ivins, V. W. 1905. *Pen Pictures of Early Western Days*. Privately printed.

Jaggar, A. M. 1983. *Feminist Politics and Human Nature*. Totowa, N.J.: Rowman & Allanheld.

Jeffrey, J. R. 1979. *Frontier Women: The Trans-Mississippi West, 1840–1880*. New York: Hill and Wang.

Johnson, C. L. 1983. "Dyadic Family Relations and Social Support." *The Gerontologist* 23(4):377–83.

Johnson, C. L., and D. J. Catalano. 1983. "A Longitudinal Study of Family Supports to Impaired Elderly." *The Gerontologist* 23(6):612–18.

Johnson, M. M. 1988. *Strong Mothers, Weak Wives: The Search for Gender Equality*. Berkeley: University of California Press.

Jones, J. 1985. *Labor of Love, Labor of Sorrow: Black Women, Work and the Family from Slavery to the Present*. New York: Basic Books.

Joseph, G. I. 1981. "Black Mothers and Daughters: Their Roles and Functions in American Society." In *Common Differences: Conflicts in Black and White Feminist Perspectives*, ed. G. I. Joseph and J. Lewis, pp. 75–126. Garden City, N.Y.: Doubleday.

Kaiser, L. M., and P. Knuth, eds. 1961. "From Ithaca to Clatsop Plains: Miss Ketcham's Journal of Travel." *Oregon Historical Quarterly* 62(3)237–87; (4)337–402.

Kane, N. M. 1989. "The Home Care Crisis of the Nineties." *The Gerontologist* 29(1):24–31.

Kane, R. A. 1986. "A Family Caregiving Policy: Should We Have One?" *Generations* 10(1):33–36.

Kane, R. A., and R. L. Kane. 1987. *Long-Term Care: Principles, Programs, and Policies*. New York: Springer.

Kane, R. L., and R. A. Kane. 1985. *A Will and A Way: What the United States Can Learn from Canada about Caring for the Elderly.* New York: Columbia University Press.

Katz, M. B. 1986. *In The Shadow of the Poorhouse: A Social History of Welfare in America.* New York: Basic Books.

Kemper, P. 1988. "The Evaluation of the National Long Term Care Demonstration: Overview of the Findings." *HSR: Health Services Research* 23(1):161–75.

Kessler, R. C., and J. D. McLeod. 1984. "Sex Differences in Vulnerability to Undesirable Life Events." *American Sociological Review* 49:620–31.

Kessler-Harris, A. 1982. *Out to Work: A History of Wage-Earning Women in the United States.* New York: Oxford University Press.

Kleban, M. H., E. M. Brody, C. B. Schoonover, C. Hoffman. 1986. "Sons'-in-Law Perceptions of Parent Care." Paper presented at the 39th Annual Scientific Meeting of the Gerontological Society of America, Chicago, November.

Koin, D. 1989. "The Effects of Caregiver Stress on Physical Health Status." In *Alzheimer's Disease Treatment and Family Stress: Directions for Research,* ed. E. Light and B. D. Lebowitz, pp. 310–21. Rockville, Md.: Department of Health and Human Services.

Koren, M. J. 1986. "Home Care—Who Cares?" *New England Journal of Medicine.* 314(14):917–20.

Kovar, M. G., G. Hendershot, and E. Mathis. 1989. "Older People in the United States Who Receive Help with Basic Activities of Daily Living." *American Journal of Public Health* 79(6):778–79.

Land, H. 1978. "Who Cares for the Family?" *Journal of Social Policy* 7:257–84.

Land, H., and H. Rose. 1985. "Compulsory Altruism for Some or an Altruistic Society for All?" In *In Defence of Welfare,* ed. P. Bean et al., pp. 74–96. London: Tavistock.

Lang, A. M. and E. M. Brody. 1983. "Characteristics of Middle-Aged Daughters and Help to Their Elderly Mothers." *Journal of Marriage and the Family* 45:193–202.

Larson, M. S. 1977. *The Rise of Professionalism: A Sociological Analysis.* Berkeley: University of California Press.

Lasch, C. 1977. *Haven in a Heartless World.* New York: Basic Books.

Law, S. 1986. "Equality: The Power and the Limits of the Law." *Yale Law Journal* 95(8):1769–86.

Lawton, M. P., E. M. Brody, and A. R. Saperstein. 1989. "A Controlled Study of Respite Service for Caregivers of Alzheimer's Patients." *The Gerontologist* 29(1):8–16.

Lazarus, L. W., B. Stafford, K. Cooper, B. Cohler, and M. Dysken. 1981. "A Pilot Study of an Alzheimer Patients' Relatives Discussion Group." *The Gerontologist* 21(4):353–58.

Leavitt, J. W. 1982. *The Healthiest City: Milwaukee and the Politics of Health Reform.* Princeton: Princeton University Press.

————. 1986. *Brought to Bed: Child-Bearing in America, 1750–1950.* New York: Oxford University Press.

Leavitt, J. W., and R. L. Numbers. 1985. "Sickness and Health in America: An Overview." In *Sickness and Health in America: Readings in the History of Medicine and Public Health,* ed. J. W. Leavitt and R. L. Numbers. Madison: University of Wisconsin Press.

Lensink, J. N. 1989. *"A Secret to Be Burried": The Diary and Life of Emily Hawley Gillespie, 1858–1888.* Iowa City: University of Iowa Press.

Lerner, G. 1971. *The Grimke Sisters.* New York: Schocken.

————. 1977. *The Female Experience: An American Documentary.* Indianapolis: Bobbs-Merrill.

Leutz, W. 1986. "Long-Term Care for the Elderly: Public Dreams and Private Realities." *Inquiry* 23:134–40.

Lewin and Associates. 1987. *An Evaluation of the Medi-Cal Program's System for Establishing Reimbursement Rates for Nursing Homes.* Submitted to the Office of the Auditor General, State of California, Sacramento.

Lewis, J., and B. Meredith. 1988. *Daughters Who Care: Daughters Caring for Mothers at Home.* London: Routledge.

Lindeman, D., and J. Wood. 1985. *Home Health Care: Adaptations to the Federal and State Cost Containment Environment.* San Francisco: Institute for Health and Aging, University of California.

Linsk, N. L., S. M. Keigher, and S. E. Osterbusch. 1988. "States' Policies Regarding Paid Family Caregiving." *The Gerontologist* 28(2):204–12.

Liptzin, B., M. C. Grob, and S. V. Eisen. 1988. "Family Burden of Demented and Depressed Elderly Psychiatric Inpatients." *The Gerontologist* 28(3): 397–401.

Litwak, E. 1985. *Helping the Elderly: The Complementary Roles of Informal Networks and Formal Systems.* New York: Guilford Press.

Liu, K., K. G. Manton, and B. M. Liu. 1985. "Home Care Expenses for the Disabled Elderly." *Health Care Financing Review* 7:51–58.

Loines, E., ed. 1955. "Hard Cash; or a Salem Housewife in the Eighteen Twenties." *Essex Institute Historical Collections* 91(3):246–65.

Lundgren, R., and C. H. Browner. 1990. "Caring for the Institutionalized Mentally Retarded: Work Culture and Work-Based Social Support." In *Circles of Care: Work and Identity in Women's Lives,* ed. E. K. Abel and M. K. Nelson, pp. 150–72. Albany: State University of New York Press.

Lyman, K. A. 1988. "Infantilization of Elders: Day Care for Alzheimer's Disease Victims." *Research in the Sociology of Health Care* 7:71–103.

————. 1989. "Bringing the Social Back In: A Critique of the Biomedicalization of Dementia." *The Gerontologist,* 29(5):597–605.

Mace, N. L., and P. V. Rabins. 1981. *The 36-Hour Day: A Family Guide to Caring for Persons with Alzheimer's Disease, Related Dementing Illnesses, and Memory Loss in Later Life.* Baltimore: Johns Hopkins University Press.

Macken, C. L. 1986. "A Profile of Functionally Impaired Elderly Persons

Living in the Community." *Health Care Financing Review* 7(Summer): 33–49.

Manton, K. G., and B. J. Soldo. 1985. "Dynamics of Health Changes in the Oldest Old: New Perspectives and Evidence." *Milbank Memorial Fund Quarterly/Health and Society* 63:206–75.

Markides, K. S., and C. H. Mindel. 1987. *Aging and Ethnicity.* Newbury Park, Calif.: Sage.

Markson, E. W. 1980. "Institutionalization: Sin, Cure, or Sinecure for the Impaired Elderly." In *Public Policies for an Aging Population,* ed. E. W. Markson and G. R. Batra. Lexington, Mass.: D. C. Heath.

Matthews, S. H. 1979. *The Social World of Old Women.* Beverly Hills, Calif.: Sage.

Matthews, S. H., J. E. Werkner, and P. J. Delaney. 1989. "Relative Contributions of Help by Employed and Nonemployed Sisters to Their Elderly Parents." *Journal of Gerontology* 44(1):S36–44.

Melosh, B. 1982. *"The Physician's Hand": Work Culture and Conflict in American Nursing.* Philadelphia: Temple University Press.

Miller, B. 1989. "Adult Children's Perceptions of Caregiver Stress and Satisfaction." *Journal of Applied Gerontology* 8(3):275–93.

———. 1990. "Gender Differences in Spouse Management of the Caregiver Role." In *Circles of Care: Work and Identity in Women's Lives,* ed. E. K. Abel and M. K. Nelson, pp. 92–104. Albany: State University of New York Press.

Miller, J. B. 1976. *Toward a New Psychology of Women.* Boston: Beacon Press.

Minkler, M. 1987. "The Politics of Generational Equity." *Social Policy,* Winter, pp. 48–52.

Minkoff, K. 1978. "A Map of the Chronic Mental Patient." In *The Chronic Mental Patient,* ed. J. A. Talbott, pp. 11–37. Washington, D.C.: American Psychiatric Association.

Mintz, S., and S. Kellogg 1988. *Domestic Revolutions: A Social History of American Family Life.* New York: Free Press.

Mitchell, L. S. 1953. *Two Lives: The Story of Wesley Clair Mitchell and Myself.* New York: Simon and Schuster.

Moen, E. 1978. "The Reluctance of the Elderly to Accept Help." *Social Problems* 25:293–303.

Montgomery, R. J. V. 1988. "Respite Care: Lessons from a Controlled Design Study." *Health Care Financing Review,* Annual Supplement, pp. 133–38.

Montgomery, R. J. V., and E. F. Borgatta, 1985. *Family Support Project.* Final report to the Administration on Aging. Seattle: University of Washington, Institute on Aging/Long-Term Care Center.

———. 1989. "The Effects of Alternative Support Strategies on Family Caregiving." *The Gerontologist* 29 (4):457–64.

Montgomery, R. J. V., J. G. Gonyea, and N. R. Hooyman. 1983. "Caregiving and the Experience of Subjective and Objective Burden." *The Gerontologist* 23:377–83.

Montgomery, R. J. V., K. Kosloski, and E. Borgatta. 1988–89. "The Influence of Cognitive Impairment on Service Use and Caregiver Response." *Journal of Applied Social Sciences* 13(1):142–69.

Moore, M. L. 1977. "Nursing an Aging Mother." In *The Female Experience: An American Documentary,* ed. G. Lerner, pp. 172–78. Indianapolis: Bobbs-Merrill.

Morantz, R. M. 1984. "Making Women Modern: Middle-Class Women and Health Reform in Nineteenth-Century America." In *Women and Health in America,* ed. J. W. Leavitt, pp. 346–58. Madison: University of Wisconsin Press.

Morantz-Sanchez, R. M. 1985. *Sympathy and Science: Women Physicians in American Medicine.* New York: Oxford University Press.

Moroney, R. M. 1986. *Shared Responsibility: Families and Social Policy.* New York: Aldine.

Morycz, R. K. 1985. "Caregiver Strain and the Desire to Institutionalize Family Members with Alzheimer's Disease." *Research on Aging* 7(3): 329–61.

Motenko, A. K. 1989. "The Frustrations, Gratifications, and Well-Being of Dementia Caregivers." *The Gerontologist* 29(2):166–72.

Motz, M. F. 1983. *True Sisterhood: Michigan Women and Their Kin, 1890–1920.* Albany: State University of New York Press.

Myerson, J., and D. Shealy, eds. 1987. *The Selected Letters of Louisa May Alcott.* Boston: Little, Brown.

Myres, S. L. 1982. *Westering Women and the Frontier Experience, 1800–1915.* Albuquerque: University of New Mexico Press.

Nelson, H. F. 1977. *South of the Cottonwood Tree.* Broken Bow, Nebr.: Purcella.

Neugarten, B., and D. Gutmann. 1968. "Age-Sex Roles and Personality in Middle Age." In *Middle Age and Aging,* ed. B. Neugarten. Chicago: University of Chicago Press.

Newman, S. 1976. *Housing Adjustments of Older People: A Report from the Second Phase.* Ann Arbor, Mich.: Institute for Social Research.

Nightingale, F. 1860. *Notes on Nursing.* New York.

Noddings, N. 1984. *Caring: A Feminine Approach to Ethics and Moral Education.* Berkeley: University of California Press.

Noelker, L. S., and D. M. Bass. 1989. "Home Care for Elderly Persons: Linkages Between Formal and Informal Caregivers." *Journal of Gerontology* 44(2):S63–70.

Noelker, L. S., and A. L. Townsend. 1987. "Perceived Caregiving Effectiveness: The Impact of Parental Impairment, Community Resources, and Caregiver Characteristics." In *Aging, Health and Family: Long-Term Care,* ed. T. H. Brubaker, pp. 58–79. Newbury Park, Calif.: Sage.

Numbers, R. L. 1977. "Do-It-Yourself the Sectarian Way." In *Medicine without Doctors,* ed. G. B. Risse, R. L. Numbers, and J. W. Leavitt, pp. 49–52. New York: Science History Publications.

———. 1985. "The Rise and Fall of the American Medical Profession." In

Sickness and Health in America: Readings in the History of Medicine and Public Health, ed. J. W. Leavitt and R. L. Numbers, pp. 185–96. Madison: University of Wisconsin Press.

Nusberg, C. 1984. "Community Services, Community Care." In *Innovative Aging Programs Abroad: Implications for the United States,* pp. 115–35. Westport, Conn.: Greenwood.

Oliphant, J. O., ed. 1927. "Mrs. Lucy Ide's Diary." *Washington Historical Quarterly* 18:122–31, 191–98, 277–85.

Oren, L. 1974. "The Welfare of Women in Laboring Families: England, 1860–1950." In *Clio's Consciousness Raised: New Perspectives on the History of Women,* ed. M. S. Hartman and L. Banner, pp. 226–44. New York: Harper & Row.

Ory, M. G., T. F. Williams, M. Emr, B. Lebowitz, P. Rabins, J. Salloway, T. Sluss-Radbaugh, E. Wolff, and S. Zarit. 1985. "Families, Informal Supports, and Alzheimer's Disease: Current Research and Future Agendas." *Research on Aging* 7(4)623–44.

Palmer, P. 1988. "Household and Household Worker: Employee Relations in the Home, 1928–1941." In *Gender, Race and the Sexual Division of Labor in the United States, 1780–1980: Selected from the Sixth Conference on the History of Women,* ed. C. Groneman and M. B. Norton, pp. 179–95. Ithaca: Cornell University Press.

Paringer, L. 1983. *The Forgotten Costs of Long-Term Care.* Washington, D.C.: Urban Institute.

Parsons, T., and R. Fox. 1985. "Illness, Therapy, and the Modern American Family." *Journal of Social Issues* 8:31–44.

Pateman, C. 1988. "The Patriarchal Welfare State." In *Democracy and the Welfare State,* ed. A. Gutmann, pp. 231–60. Princeton: Princeton University Press.

Paul, M. 1981. "Letters." In *Farm to Factory: Women's Letters, 1830–1860,* ed. T. Dublin, pp. 97–132. New York: Columbia University Press.

Pearlin, L. I. 1989. "The Sociological Study of Stress." *Journal of Health and Social Behavior* 30:241–56.

Pearlin, L. I., and C. S. Aneshensel. 1986. "Coping and Social Supports: Their Functions and Applications." In *Applications of Social Sciences to Clinical Medicine and Health Policy,* ed. L. H. Aiken and D. Mechanic, pp. 417–38. New Brunswick, N.J.: Rutgers University Press.

Pearlin, L. I., H. Turner, and S. Semple. 1989. "Coping and the Mediation of Caregiver Stress." In *Alzheimer's Disease Treatment and Family Stress: Directions for Research,* ed. E. Light and B. D. Lebowitz, pp. 198–217. Rockville, Md.: Department of Health and Human Services.

Pollock, L. A. 1983. *Forgotten Children: Parent-Child Relations from 1500 to 1900.* Cambridge: Cambridge University Press.

Pratt, C., T. Nay, L. Ladd, and B. Heagerty. 1989. "A Model Legal-Financial Education Workshop for Families Caring for Neurologically Impaired Elders." *The Gerontologist* 29(2):258–62.

Preston, S. H. 1984. "Children and the Elderly: Divergent Paths for America's Dependents." *Demography* 21(4):435–57.

Qureshi, H., and A. Walker. 1989. *The Caring Relationship: Elderly People and Their Families.* Philadelphia: Temple University Press.

Rabin, D. L., and P. Stockton. 1987. *Long-Term Care for the Elderly: A Factbook.* New York: Oxford University Press.

Ratcliff, K. S., and J. Bogdan. 1988. "Unemployed Women: When 'Social Support' Is Not Supportive." *Social Problems* 35:54–63.

Raveis, V. H., K. Siegel and M. Sudit. 1988–89. "Psychological Impact of Caregiving on the Careprovider: A Critical Review of Extant Research." *Journal of Applied Social Sciences* 13(1):40–79.

Reese, W. J. 1986. *Power and the Promise of School Reform: Grass-Roots Movements during the Progressive Era.* Boston: Routledge & Kegan Paul.

Reid, A. J. 1936. *Letters of Long Ago.* Caldwell, Idaho: Caxton.

Reverby, S. M. 1987. *Ordered to Care: The Dilemma of American Nursing, 1850–1945.* New York: Cambridge University Press.

Ricardo-Campbell, Rita. 1988. "Aging and the Private Sector." *Generations,* Spring, 19–22.

Rich, A. 1976. *Of Woman Born: Motherhood as Experience and Institution.* New York: Norton.

Riessman, C. K. 1989. "Women and Medicalization: A New Perspective." In *Perspectives in Medical Sociology,* ed. P. Brown, pp. 190–220. Belmont, Calif.: Wadsworth.

Riley, G. 1982. " 'Not Gainfully Employed': Women on the Iowa Frontier, 1833–1870." In *Our American Sisters: Women in American Life and Thought,* ed. J. E. Friedman and W. G. Shade, pp. 267–90. Lexington, Mass.: D. C. Heath.

———. 1988. *The American Frontier: A Comparative View of Women on the Prairie and the Plains.* Lawrence: University Press of Kansas.

Risse, G. B., R. L. Numbers, and J. W. Leavitt, eds. 1977. *Medicine without Doctors: Home Health Care in American History.* New York: Science History.

Rivlin, A. M., and J. M. Wiener. 1988. *Caring for the Disabled Elderly: Who Will Pay?* Washington, D.C.: Brookings Institute.

Rix, S. E. 1984. *Older Women: The Economics of Aging.* Washington, D.C.: Women's Research and Education Institute of the Congressional Caucus for Women's Issues.

Robinson, B., and M. Thurnher. 1979. "Taking Care of Aged Parents: A Family Cycle Transition." *The Gerontologist* 19(5):586–93.

Rollins, J. 1985. *Between Women: Domestics and Their Employers.* Philadelphia: Temple University Press.

Romero, M. 1988. "Sisterhood and Domestic Service: Race, Class and Gender in the Mistress-Maid Relationship." *Humanity & Society* 14(4):318–46.

Rook, K. S. 1984. "The Negative Side of Social Intervention: The Impact on Psychological Well-Being." *Journal of Personality and Social Psychology* 45(5):1097–1108.

Rook, K. S., and D. Dooley. 1985. "Applying Social Support Research: Theoretical Problems and Future Directions." *Journal of Social Issues* 41:5–28.

Rose, H. 1986. "Women's Work: Women's Knowledge." In *What Is Feminism? A Re-examination*, ed. J. Mitchell and A. Oakley, pp. 161–83. New York: Pantheon.

Rosenberg, C. E. 1974. "Social Class and Medical Care in 19th-Century America: The Rise and Fall of the Dispensary." *Journal of the History of Medicine and Allied Sciences* 29:32–54.

———. 1979. "Florence Nightingale on Contagion: The Hospital as Moral Universe." In *Healing and History: Essays for George Rosen*, ed. C. E. Rosenberg, pp. 116–36. Kent, England: William Dawson and Sons.

———. 1987. *The Care of Strangers: The Rise of America's Hospital System.* New York: Basic Books.

Rosenwaike, I. 1985. "A Demographic Portrait of the Oldest Old." *Milbank Memorial Fund Quarterly/Health and Society* 63(2):187–205.

Rosner, D. K. 1982. *A Once Charitable Enterprise: Hospitals and Health Care in Brooklyn and New York, 1885–1915.* New York: Cambridge University Press.

Rossi, A. S. 1985. "Gender and Parenthood." In *Gender and the Life Course*, ed. A. S. Rossi. New York: Aldine.

Rothman, S. M. 1978. *Woman's Proper Place: A History of Changing Ideas and Practices, 1870–Present.* New York: Basic Books.

Rubin, L. B. 1985. *Just Friends: The Role of Friendship in Our Lives.* New York: Harper & Row.

Rudd, L. A. 1982. "A Woman's Trip across the Plains in 1848." In *Women's Diaries of the Westward Journey*, ed. L. Schlissel, pp. 187–98. New York: Schocken Books.

Ruddick, S. 1982. "Maternal Thinking." In *Rethinking the Family: Some Feminist Questions*, ed. B. Thorne, pp. 76–94. New York: Longman.

———. 1983. "Preservative Love and Military Destruction: Some Reflections on Mothering and Peace." In *Mothering: Essays in Feminist Theory*, ed. J. Trebilcot, pp. 231–62. Totowa, N.J.: Rowman & Allanheld.

Ryan, M. P. 1975. *Womanhood in America, From Colonial Times to the Present.* New York: New Viewpoints.

———. 1982. *The Empire of the Mother: American Writing about Domesticity, 1830–1860.* New York: Institute for Research on History and the Haworth Press.

Sacks, K. B. 1990. "Does It Pay to Care?" In *Circles of Care: Work and Identity in Women's Lives*, ed. E. K. Abel and M. K. Nelson, pp. 182–206. Albany: State University of New York Press.

Sager, A. 1983. "A Proposal for Promoting More Adequate Long-Term Care for the Elderly." *The Gerontologist* 23(1):13–17.

Salmon, J. W., ed. 1990. *The Corporate Transformation of Health Care: Issues and Directions.* Amityville, N.Y.: Baywood.

Sankar, A., R. Newcomer, and J. Wood. 1986. "Prospective Payment: Systemic Effects on the Provision of Community Care for the Elderly." *Home Health Care Services Quarterly* 7(2):93–117.

Savitt, T. L. 1985. "Black Health on the Plantation: Masters, Slaves and Physicians." In *Sickness and Health in America: Readings in the History of Medicine and Public Health,* ed. J. W. Leavitt and R. L. Numbers, pp. 313–30. Madison: University of Wisconsin Press.

Saxton, M. 1978. *Louisa May: A Modern Biography of Louisa May Alcott.* New York: Avon Books.

Scanlon, W. J. 1980. "Nursing Home Utilization Patterns: Implications for Policy." *Journal of Health Policy, Politics and Law* 4:619–41.

———. 1988. "A Perspective on Long-Term Care for the Elderly." *Health Care Financing Review,* Annual Supplement, pp. 7–15.

Scharlach, A. E. 1987. "Role Strain in Mother-Daughter Relationships in Later Life." *The Gerontologist* 27(5):627–31.

Scharlach, A. E., and S. Boyd. 1989. "Caregiving and Employment: Results of an Employee Survey." *The Gerontologist* 29(3):382–87.

Scharlach, A. E., and C. Frenzel. 1986. "An Evaluation of Institution-Based Respite Care." *The Gerontologist* 26(1):77–82.

Schlissel, L. 1982. *Women's Diaries of the Westward Journey.* New York: Schocken.

———. 1989. "The Malick Family in Oregon Territory, 1848–1867." In *Far from Home: Families of the Westward Journey,* ed. L. Schlissel, B. Gibbens, and E. Hampsten, pp. 3–106. New York: Schocken Books.

Schorr, A. 1980. *Thy Father and Thy Mother.* Social Security publication no. 13-11953. Baltimore: Social Security Administration.

Schulz, R. 1990. "Theoretical Perspectives on Caregiving: Concepts, Variables, and Methods." In *Aging and Caregiving: Theory, Research and Policy,* ed. D. E. Biegel and A. Blum, pp. 27–52. Newbury Park, Calif.: Sage.

Sexton, P. C. 1982. *The New Nightingales: Hospital Workers, Unions, New Women's Issues.* New York: Enquiry Press.

Shanas, E. 1979a. "The Family as a Social Support System in Old Age." *The Gerontologist* 19:169–74.

———. 1979b. "Social Myth as Hypothesis: The Case of the Family Relations of Old People." *The Gerontologist* 19(1):3–9.

Siegel, J. S., and C. M. Taeuber. 1986. "Demographic Perspectives on the Long-Lived Society." *Daedalus* 115(1):77–118.

Silliman, R. Z., and J. Sternberg. 1988. "Family Caregiving: Impact of Patient Functioning and Underlying Causes of Dependency." *The Gerontologist* 28(3):377–82.

Simon, K. 1982. *Bronx Primitive: Portraits in a Childhood.* New York: Harper & Row.

Skocpol, T. 1988. "The Limits of the New Deal System and the Roots of Contemporary Welfare Dilemmas." In *The Politics of Social Policy in the*

United States, ed. M. Weir, A. S. Orloff, and T. Skocpol, pp. 293–312. Princeton: Princeton University Press.

Smith, D. S. 1974. "Family Limitation, Sexual Control, and Domestic Feminism in Victorian America." In *Clio's Consciousness Raised,* ed. M. S. Hartman and L. Banner, pp. 119–36. New York: Harper & Row.

———. 1986. "Accounting for Change in the Families of the Elderly in the United States, 1900–Present." In *Old Age in a Bureaucratic Society: The Elderly, The Experts and the State in American Society,* ed. P. Stearns and D. D. Van Tassel, pp. 87–109. Westport, Conn.: Greenwood.

Smith, J. 1984. "The Paradox of Women's Poverty: Wage-Earning Women and Economic Transformation." *Signs* 10:291–310.

Smith-Rosenberg, C. 1975. "The Female World of Love and Ritual: Relations between Women in Nineteenth-Century America." *Signs* 1(1):1–29.

Snell, J. W., ed. 1971. "Roughing It on Her Kansas Claim: The Diary of Abbie Bright." *Kansas Historical Quarterly* 37(3):233–68; (4):394–28.

Sokoloff, N. J. 1981. *Between Love and Money: The Dialectics of Women's Home and Market Work.* New York: Praeger.

Soldo, B. J. 1985. "In-Home Services for the Dependent Elderly." *Research on Aging* 7(2):281–304.

Soldo, B. J., E. M. Agree, and D. A. Wolf. 1989. "The Balance between Formal and Informal Care. In *Aging and Health Care,* ed. M. G. Ory and K. Bond, pp. 193–216. London: Routledge.

Soldo, B. J., and K. G. Manton. 1985. "Health Status and Service Needs of the Oldest Old: Current Patterns and Future Trends." *Milbank Memorial Fund Quarterly/Health and Society* 63:286–319.

Soldo, B. J., and J. Myllyluoma. 1983. "Caregivers Who Live with Dependent Elderly." *The Gerontologist* 23(6):605–11.

Sommers, T., and L. Shields, 1987. *Women Take Care: The Consequences of Caregiving in Today's Society.* Gainesville, Fla.: Triad.

Spalter-Roth, R. M., and H. I. Hartmann. 1988. *Unnecessary Losses: Costs to Americans of the Lack of Family and Medical Leave, Executive Summary.* Washington, D.C.: Institute for Women's Policy Research.

Special Committee on Aging, United States Senate. 1987a. *Developments in Aging: 1987,* vol. 1. Washington, D.C.: Government Printing Office.

———. 1987b. *Developments in Aging: 1987,* vol. 3. Washington, D.C.: Government Printing Office.

———. 1988. *Home Health Care at the Crossroads: An Information Paper.* Washington, D.C.: Government Printing Office.

———. 1989. *Developments in Aging: 1989,* vol. 1. Washington, D.C.: Government Printing Office.

Springer, M., and H. Springer, eds. 1986. *Plains Woman: The Diary of Martha Farnsworth, 1882–1922.* Bloomington: Indiana University Press.

Stacey, J., and B. Thorne. 1985. "The Missing Feminist Revolution in Sociology." *Social Problems* 32 (4):301–16.

Stack, C. 1974. *All Our Kin.* New York: Harper Colophon.

Stage, S. 1984. "The Woman behind the Trademark." In *Women and Health in America,* ed. J. W. Leavitt, pp. 255–69. Madison: University of Wisconsin Press.

Starr, P. 1982. *The Social Transformation of American Medicine: The Rise of a Sovereign Profession and the Making of a Vast Industry.* New York: Basic Books.

Stephens, S. A., and J. B. Christianson. 1986. *Informal Care of the Elderly.* Lexington, Mass.: Lexington Books.

Steuve, A., and L. O'Donnell. 1984. "The Daughters of Aging Parents." In *Women in Midlife,* eds. G. Baruch and J. Brooks-Gunne. New York: Plenum.

Stevens, R. 1989. *In Sickness and In Wealth: American Hospitals in the Twentieth Century.* New York: Basic Books.

Stoller, E. P. 1983. "Parental Caregiving by Adult Children." *Journal of Marriage and the Family,* November, pp. 851–58.

———. 1990. "Males as Helpers: The Role of Sons, Relatives, and Friends." *The Gerontologist* 30(2):228–35.

Stone, R. I. 1985. *Recent Developments in Respite Care Services for Caregivers of the Impaired Elderly.* Administration on Aging grant no. 90AP003.

Stone, R. I., L. Cafferata, and J. Sangl. 1987. "Caregivers of the Frail Elderly: A National Profile." *The Gerontologist* 27(5):616–26.

Stone, R. I., and P. Kemper. 1989. "Spouses and Children of Disabled Elders: How Large a Constituency for Long-Term Care Reform. *Milbank Memorial Fund Quarterly* 67(3–4):485–506.

Strasser, S. 1982. *Never Done: A History of American Housework.* New York: Pantheon.

Stratton, J. L. 1981. *Pioneer Women: Voices from the Kansas Frontier.* New York: Simon and Schuster.

Subcommittee on Human Services, Select Committee on Aging, House of Representatives. 1987. *Exploding the Myths: Caregiving in America.* 100th Cong. 1st sess., Comm. pub. no. 99–611.

Swan, J. H., and C. Harrington. 1986. "Estimating Undersupply of Nursing Home Beds in States." *HSR: Health Services Research* 21(1):57–83.

Task Force on Long-Term Health Care Policies. 1987. *Report to Congress and the Secretary.* Washington, D.C.: Government Printing Office.

Taub, N. 1984–85. "From Parental Leaves to Nurturing Leaves." *Review of Law and Social Change* 13:381–405.

Tennstedt, S. L., and J. B. McKinlay. 1989. "Informal Care for Frail Older Persons." In *Aging and Health Care: Social Science and Policy Perspectives,* ed. M. G. Ory and K. Bond. London: Routledge.

Thoits, P. A. 1982. "Conceptual, Methodological, and Theoretical Problems in Studying Social Support as a Buffer against Life Stress." *Journal of Health and Social Behavior* 23:145–59.

Thorne, B. 1982. "Feminist Rethinking of the Family: An Overview." In *Rethinking the Family: Some Feminist Questions*, ed. B. Thorne with M. Yalom, pp. 1–24. New York: Longman.

Thorne, B., with M. Yalom, eds. 1982. *Rethinking the Family: Some Feminist Questions*. New York: Longman.

Tileston, M. W., ed. 1918. *Caleb and Mary Wilder Foote: Reminiscences and Letters*. Boston and New York: Houghton Mifflin.

Toseland, R. W., C. M. Rossiter, M. S. Labrecque. 1989. "The Effectiveness of Peer-Led and Professionally-Led Groups to Support Family Caregivers." *The Gerontologist* 29(4):465–71.

Travelers Companies. 1985. *The Travelers' Employee Caregiver Survey* Hartford, Conn.: Travelers Insurance Companies.

Trebilcot, J., ed. 1983. *Mothering: Essays in Feminist Theory*. Totowa, N.J.: Rowman and Allanheld.

Uhlenberg, P. 1980. "Death and the Family." *Journal of Family History*, 313–20.

Ulrich, L. T. 1987. "Housewife and Gadder: Themes of Self-Sufficiency and Community in Eighteenth-Century New England." In *"To Toil the Livelong Day": America's Women at Work, 1780–1980*, ed. C. Groneman and M. B. Norton, pp. 21–34. Ithaca: Cornell University Press.

———. 1990. *A Midwife's Tale: The Life of Martha Ballard Based on Her Diary, 1785–1812*. New York: Alfred A. Knopf.

Ungerson, C. 1983. "Women and Caring: Skills, Tasks and Taboos." In *The Public and the Private*, ed. E. Gamarnikow et al., pp. 62–77. London: Heinemann.

———. 1987. *Policy Is Personal: Sex, Gender, and Informal Care*. London: Tavistock.

Verbrugge, M. H. 1979. "The Social Meaning of Personal Health: The Ladies' Physiological Institute of Boston and Vicinity in the 1850s." In *Health Care in America: Essays in Social History*, ed. S. Reverby and D. Rosner, pp. 45–66. Philadelphia: Temple University Press.

Vine, P. 1982. *Families in Pain: Children, Siblings and Parents of the Mentally Ill Speak Out*. New York: Pantheon.

Vladeck, B. C. 1980. *Unloving Care: The Nursing Home Tragedy*. New York: Basic Books.

Vogel, M. J. 1980. *The Invention of the Modern Hospital: Boston, 1870–1930*. Chicago: University of Chicago Press.

Waerness, K. 1983. "On the Rationality of Caring." Paper presented at the International Conference on the Transformation of the Welfare State: Dangers and Potentialities for Women, Bellagio, Italy, August 23–27.

———. 1984. "Caring as Women's Work in the Welfare State." In *Patriarchy in a Welfare State*, ed. H. Holter. Oslo: Universitetsforlaget.

Wallace, S. P. 1990. "The No-Care Zone: Availability, Accessibility, and Acceptability in Community-Based Long-Term Care." *The Gerontologist* 30(2):254–61.

Warshaw, L. J., et al. 1986. *Employer Support for Employee Caregivers.* New York: New York Business Group on Health.

Weissert, W. G. 1985. "Seven Reasons Why It Is So Difficult to Make Community-Based Long-Term Care Cost-Effective." *HSR: Health Services Research* 20(4):423–33.

———. 1988. "The National Channeling Demonstration: What We Knew, Know Now, and Still Need to Know." *HSR: Health Services Research* 23(1):175–87.

Wilkins, W. 1974. "Social Stress and Illness in Industrial Society." In *Life Stress and Illness,* ed. E. Gunderson and R. Rahe. Springfield, Ill.: Charles C. Thomas.

Wilson, E. 1977. *Women and the Welfare State.* London: Tavistock.

Wisensale, S. K., and M. D. Allison. 1988. "An Analysis of 1987 State Family Leave Legislation: Implications for Caregivers of the Elderly." *The Gerontologist* 28(6):779–85.

Withorn, A. 1984. *Serving the People: Social Services and Social Change.* New York: Columbia University Press.

Wolf, D. A., and B. J. Soldo. 1986. "The Households of Older Unmarried Women: Micro-decision Models of Shared Living Arrangements." Paper presented at the Annual Meeting of the Population Association of America, San Francisco.

Wood, J. B., P. J. Fox, C. L. Estes, P. R. Lee, and C. W. Mahoney. 1986. *Public Policy, the Private Nonprofit Sector, and the Delivery of Community Based Long Term Care Services for the Elderly.* Final Report: Executive Summary. San Francisco: Institute for Health and Aging, University of California.

Wortman, C. B. 1984. "Social Support and the Cancer Patient: Conceptual and Methodological Issues." *Cancer* 53:2339–60.

Wright, F. 1983. "Single Carers: Employment, Housework, and Caring." In *A Labour of Love: Women, Work and Care,* ed. J. Finch and D. Groves, pp. 89–105. London: Routledge and Kegan Paul.

Yalom, M. 1981. Introduction to Part 4: "The Older Woman." In *Victorian Women,* ed. E. O. Hellerstein, L. P. Hume, and K. M. Offen. pp. 452–62. Stanford: Stanford University Press.

Young, A. 1980. "The Discourse on Stress and the Reproduction of Conventional Knowledge." *Social Science and Medicine,* 14B:133–46

Young, J. R. 1977. "Patent Medicines and the Self-Help Syndrome." In *Medicine without Doctors: Home Health Care in American History,* ed. G. B. Risse, R. L. Numbers, and J. W. Leavitt, pp. 95–116. New York: Science History Publications.

Yzenbaard, J. H., and J. Hoffmann, eds. 1974. " 'Between Hope and Fear': The Life of Lettie Teeple, 1829–1850." *Michigan History* 58(3):219–78.

Zaretsky, E. 1982. "The Place of the Family in the Origins of the Welfare State." In *Rethinking the Family: Some Feminist Questions,* ed. B. Thorne, pp. 188–224. New York: Longman.

Zarit, S. H., C. R. Anthony, and M. Boutsellis, 1987. "Interventions with

Caregivers of Dementia Patients: A Comparison of Two Approaches." *Psychology and Aging* 2:225–32.

Zarit, S. H., K. E. Reever, and J. Bach-Peterson. 1980. "Relatives of the Impaired Elderly: Correlates of Feelings of Burden." *The Gerontologist* 20:649–55.

Zarit, S. H., P. A. Todd, and J. M. Zarit. 1986. "Subjective Burden of Husbands and Wives of Caregivers: A Longitudinal Study." *The Gerontologist* 26:260–66.

Zola, I. K. 1988. "Policies and Programs Concerning Aging and Disability: Toward a Unifying Agenda." In *The Economics and Ethics of Long-Term Care,* ed. S. Sullivan and M. E. Levin, pp. 90–130. Washington, D.C.: American Enterprise Institute.

Index